INSIDE
THE MANI

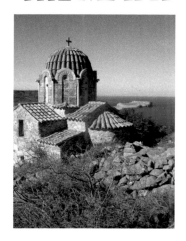

a guide

Inside Mani
Travel

Full On-Line Service

Accommodation in Southern Peloponnese
(from studios to villas)
~*~
Car Hire and Fly Drive Itineraries
~*~
Airport Transfers
~*~
Excursions
~*~

www.inside-mani-travel.com

INSIDE
THE MANI

www.insidemani.gr

Inside the Mani also publishes an annual magazine
and a walking guide with 10 walks local to
Kardamyli and Stoupa. All these publications are
now available on-line: www.insidemani.gr

Published by Matthew Dean 2006
Copyright Matthew Dean, Stoupa, Messinia 24024, Greece.

Printed in Athens
ISBN: 960-631-307-7
       978-960-631-307-3

Contents

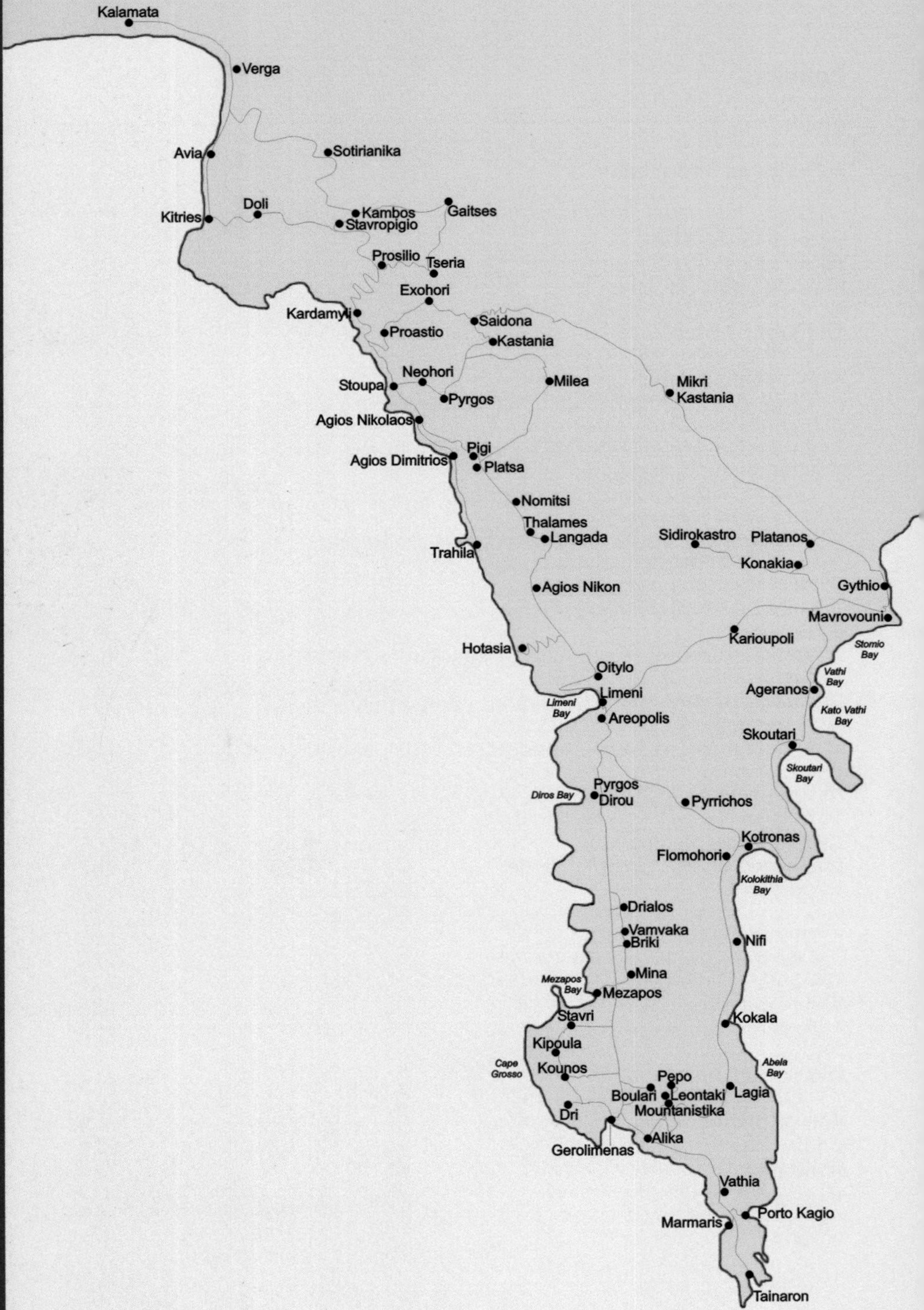

Kalamata

Verga

Avia

Sotirianika

Doli

Kitries

Kambos
Stavropigio
Gaitses

Prosilio
Tseria

Exohori

Kardamyli

Proastio
Saidona
Kastania

Stoupa
Neohori
Milea

Pyrgos
Mikri
Kastania

Agios Nikolaos

Pigi
Agios Dimitrios
Platsa

Nomitsi

Thalames
Langada

Sidirokastro
Platanos

Trahila
Konakia

Agios Nikon
Gythio

Mavrovouni

Hotasia
Karioupoli
Stomio
Bay

Oitylo
Vathi
Bay

Limeni
Ageranos

Limeni
Bay
Kato Vathi
Bay

Areopolis

Skoutari

Pyrgos
Dirou
Skoutari
Bay

Diros Bay
Pyrrichos

Flomohori
Kotronas

Kolokithia
Bay

Drialos

Vamvaka
Briki
Nifi

Mina

Mezapos
Bay
Mezapos

Stavri
Kokala

Kipoula

Cape
Grosso
Kounos

Pepo
Abela
Bay

Boulari
Leontaki
Lagia

Dri
Mountanistika

Gerolimenas
Alika

Vathia

Marmaris
Porto Kagio

Tainaron

About the book

Welcome to the Mani. This book was written with the aim of answering the question of "Where shall we go now we have hired a car for a couple of days?" By dividing the area into eight, colour-coded sections and by providing a detailed index at the back of the book, the intention is for the reader to be able to quickly decide on a satisfactory itinerary. A day out in the Mani can incorporate a range of differing experiences from swimming in secluded coves, enjoying a fish lunch in a sleepy taverna, walking along old mule paths (*kalderimi*), visiting 1000 year old churches or simply getting off the beaten track to explore less trodden routes to soak in the atmosphere of this unique part of Greece. We have tried, as far as possible, to summarise the nature of each section to help the decision process and have included a sufficient number of photographs to portray the character of each village/church/beach. The photographs included were taken throughout the year to illustrate how the area changes from season to season. In our opinion there is no one best time to come here. Spring is great for walking and for wild flowers, summer for swimming, autumn for both of the former and winter to experience life out of season.

The orientation of the book is unashamedly biased towards the west coast and in particular the established tourist resorts of Stoupa, Kardamyli and Agios Nikolaos as this is where most visitors to the area are now based. The accommodation section has been included on our recommendation for two reasons. Firstly to offer a suggestion for an overnight stay if required or, alternatively, to create a tailor-made itinerary for the independent visitor wishing to book in advance.

a secluded cove

'kalderimi' - a stone mule path

a 1000 year old church

spring cyclamen

Each section map is intended to give a rough guide to the network of roads that span the area and where each village is located on them. The roads are coloured according to condition – red for tarmac/asphalt, yellow for dirt (a state that is likely to change quite rapidly from the time of print). For updates, refer in advance to www.insidemani.gr. For more detailed maps we would recommend the generally excellent Anavasi series, widely available locally.

The walking section is based on one principle – that all the walks are circular. Therefore a walk can easily be combined in a day-out in a hired car. In Deep Mani, where there is generally more to see and do, the walks are deliberately shorter (most are around 2 hours) to allow time for other pursuits. We have also included longer walks for those who want to really get away from it all and are quite happy to use a hired car for a day or two to achieve this aim.

About the authors

Mat Dean first came to the Mani in 1989 and has lived here full time since 2000. During this time he has had a number of jobs including guiding walking groups down the whole peninsula and working as a travel rep in Kardamyli. He has now settled happily into publishing, producing the annual Inside the Mani magazine and a walking book based around Stoupa and Kardamyli.

Bob Barrow has had a very 'restless'

background. Born in Argentina of an English father and a Canadian mother, he lived in Ceylon before going to England. Expelled from school in England at 16, he was a soldier for ten years; a policeman for four years; a publican; a sales rep and then a marketing manager for a brewery and finally came to live and work in the Mani in 1995. Knowing nothing of ancient, Byzantine or Ottoman history, churches or frescoes, he became fascinated by Greece and the Mani and during the last eleven years has been on what he describes as a "an amazing learning curve that has stimulated me beyond anything I could have imagined".

Our Recommended 'Must Do's

Walking in the spring. I can't state my favourite as there are so many to choose from, but it is the time if year that is important. April/May is best as the flowers are out but the tourist season is not yet in full swing, which means you have the wonderful old stone paths (*kalderimia*) to yourself.

Driving over the mountains from Saidona/Exohori to Gythio in a 4x4. If you have spent a few days enjoying the beach, this experience comes as a sudden culture shock as you leave civilisation behind for a day. Not only is it fun to be in a jeep, but on a clear day, the views are stunning – from sea level it is not obvious just how extensive the mountains really are.

Sitting for a minimum of half an hour at the lighthouse at Cape Tainaron.

Mat – trying hard....

Bob in his fustanella

There is something very special about this place. The Aegean meets the Ionian Sea in a totally peaceful setting. The only signs of life are ships passing between the Mani and Crete, heading for other Mediterranean ports or beyond....

Lunch or an evening meal in a taverna in one of the villages above Stoupa/Kardamyli. Saidona, Kastania, Platsa, Pigi, Exohori and Proastio all have somewhere to eat. A different experience to dining on the coast.

Swimming on the east coast. There are some great places to stop and swim if you are out and about for the day or indeed if you just fancy a full day on a more secluded beach. The pebbly coves to the south will certainly offer this and the longer sandy bays nearer Gythio will also be relatively empty during the week as well as being conveniently en route to Gythio, Sparti and Mystras.

Mountanistika. The road up to the village is an adventure in itself – very narrow with vertiginous drops. I used to drive up in a mini-bus as part of a walking tour when the road was not even asphalt. Truly terrifying. But once up, it is a sensational place. Superb views combine with an eerie quality, as the village is barely inhabited now. And at 600m above sea-level, it is not unusual for clouds to suddenly come wafting through the deserted towers.

Churches. Even if churches and their frescoes are not usually your cup of tea, they are as intrinsic to the area as tower houses. Perhaps, like many of our friends have, you too may find that it is a case of 'the more put in the more get out' and in any case, so many of those referred to in the book are worth visiting just for their location.

walking in the Mani

the lighthouse at Cape Tainaron

Stomia Bay, near Gythio

Mountanistika

A note about the spelling of Greek words in the book. Basically, it is a nightmare deciding how to approach this issue. Spelling phonetically leaves some words looking offensively wrong – you can't spell Giorgios with a 'Y'. And other consonants do not translate easily – a 'c' is closest to the 'ch' sound in lo**ch** but again it does not look right and the risk is taken of forgetting this phoneme and instead using the 'ch' sound in **ch**urch. Neo-**ch**ori would therefore sound ridiculous. In the end we decided to have a mixed bag – phonetic where appropriate, keeping the Greek wherever possible: for example, this is why the adjective 'Maniat' is spelt with an 'a' and not an 'o' as it would be in English. Confused? So are we......

Acknowledgements

Many thanks to the following in providing much-needed help in putting the book together: John Chapman – lively debate and suggestions; Anna Butcher and Dave Rochelle – the accommodation section; the Martin family, Jacinthe Raymond and Stephanie Ambridge – the walking section; Melanie Wicks, Glenda Dean and Andy Bostock – proof reading; Kostas Dimitreas – layout and design; and finally, our sponsors, Greekscape.

Taxiarches church, Glezos

A Brief History of the Mani

The history of the Mani is as dramatic as its landscape. Its very remoteness made it an ideal refuge from which to resist foreign invaders, while its key position on early trade routes (from Italy to the east and from Greece to North Africa) made it attractive to ambitious Europeans wanting to control the seas. This will explain why an area on the fringe of mainstream Greece has a strong international dimension to its history: Sparta, Rome and Byzantium, the Franks, Venetians and Turks all played a significant role. What follows here is a summary of that history to provide a framework for what you will see on your travels.

dramatic landscape

Roman theatre, Gythio

Neolithic Age c. 4000–2000 B.C.

A period when, for once, war seems not to have been the driving force: people farmed, made pots and worshipped the Earth Goddess. The caves at Pirgos Dirou, only discovered in the last fifty years, provide an astonishing window into that world.

Mycenaean Period: 1600–1100 B.C.

An age of warrior kings and their heroic (and unheroic) deeds. They lived in fortified palaces, never very far from the sea, and competed with each other in trade and war; the famous Mycenaean gold is proof of just how wealthy and sophisticated were those who triumphed. This was the time of the Trojan War and the stories told by Homer in the Iliad and the Odyssey. On the Peloponnese Mycenae, Tiryns and Pylos are probably the best-known palaces but there were also many Mycenaean settlements in the Mani, mentioned by Homer as contributors to the Greek force which sailed to Troy – Kardamyli, Messe (Mezapos), Oitylo, Las (Passava), Enope (later Gerenia, now Kambos) and Kranai (the island off Gythio). And in the south-east of the peninsula near Lagia were the quarries of the purple antico

Neolithic caves, Pyrgos Dirou

Mycenean Tholos tomb, Kambos

rosso marble used to decorate the bee-hive tombs at Mycenae. Mycenaean tombs can be found at Kambos and Proastio.

Classical Age: the fifth century B.C.

After the collapse of the Mycenaean world Greece was plunged into its dark ages, only to emerge, centuries later, as a more brilliant version of its earlier self. The fifth century is known as its golden age, a time when the independent city-states, which had replaced the earlier kings, continued the tradition of competition and rivalry. The main players in this contest were Athens and Sparta and while Athens was the undisputed cultural victor, it was the military might of Sparta that triumphed in the long so-called Peloponnesian War between them and their respective "allies". During this period the Mani was totally dominated (even enslaved on the Messinian side of the Taygetos Mountains) by Sparta. Only Gythio, Sparta's vital access point to the sea, could claim any status in its own right.

The Fourth Century B.C.

A period when the focus of power in Greece shifted. The Spartan machine was finally defeated – by Thebes – and a new force emerged in the north of Greece: Macedon. King Philip, father of the more famous Alexander, brought his armies deep into the Mani and delivered a final blow to Sparta in 218 B.C. As a result, the Mani enjoyed a period of relative freedom and stability. New cities like Messene, near Kalamata, were founded in a mood of optimism and Gythio became head of a league of Free Laconians, later officially recognised by the emperor Augustus.

The Roman Period

Freedom is often, however, short-lived and it was Rome who provided the next threat. Seventy years of intermittent campaigning (215-146 B.C.) brought Greece into the expanding Roman Empire, although the Romans, impressed no doubt by the sophistication of its new subjects, allowed Greece a fair amount of independence. Greek remained the official language of the Eastern empire and the two cultures seem to have lived together in relative harmony for more than three centuries. Statue-bases found in Deep Mani honouring Roman political figures must suggest a level of acceptance.

Byzantium 330-1460 A.D.

When Rome fell to Alaric and the Goths in 410 A.D., the eastern part of the empire, formed some 80 years earlier at Constantinople, was able to develop into the Byzantine Empire, pursuing its interpretation of Christianity. There is some debate as to when Orthodox Christianity arrived in the Mani but it is probable that isolated pockets on the coastal areas were converted in the 6th century A.D. – basilicas on Tigani and at Kyparissos help to prove this. The area's population grew rapidly from people seeking refuge from the Slavic invasions of the Peloponnese from the 10th century onwards, one tribe of which, known as the Meligs or Melingi, penetrated the Mani and were a disruptive force, especially in the mountains until completely absorbed into the Greek population. The indigenous population had other foreign threats to contend with. In 1204 the Frank Geoffrey de Villehardouin made haste from Syria to join in the looting of Constantinople. Bad weather blew him west and this inauspicious event led to half a cen-

tury of Frankish domination of the southern Morea (Peloponnese) and the building
of a series of castles in the Mani. The
Venetians were also active in the area at
this time and when the Mani was returned
to Byzantium after the Frankish defeat at
the battle of Pelagonia in 1259, Methoni
and Koroni across the Messinian bay
remained in Venetian hands. The coastal
towns of the Southern Peloponnese,
including the Mani, were also attacked
from time to time by Normans, Franks,
Genoese, Catalans and Turks. This constant threat caused the Empire to reform
the Byzantine armed forces and gave land
grants to senior commanders. This created a feudal "aristocracy" of elite landown-
ers to whom the local peasantry owed
allegiance and for whom they had to fight
when called upon. In the Mani, the peas-
ants or *Achamnoteroi* (low born) became
even more dependent on the *Megaloyenitai* (high born). This social structure was
further intensified by the Turkish capture
of nearby Mystras (the Byzantine seat of
power on the Peloponnese) in 1460 as
more noble-blooded Byzantines fled
across the Taygetos Mountains to establish themselves in the Mani.

Post-Byzantine

The increase in population in the Mani
following the fall of Mystras, a population
dominated by the *Megaloyenitai* or
Niklianikoi families, shaped the area's late
medieval history. The need to control limited local resources gave rise to Tuscan-
like tower houses being built from which
the clans launched violent attacks on their
rivals (often neighbours). This intense
feuding was most prevalent in *Mesa*
(Inner) Mani. The ferocity of the Maniats
made it difficult for the Ottoman Turks to
gain control of the area. In the four centuries following the fall of Mystras the
area witnessed a violent and turbulent
history – a history of internal fighting, of
piracy and of constant conflict with the
Turks. For periods the Turks gained some
control after a number of bloody inva-

Messene, near Kalamata

inscribed statue base, Kiparissos

6th century basilica, Kiparissos

Venetian stronghold at Methoni

sions, usually characterised by the occupation of important strategic castles in the Mani – namely Kelefa, Passava and Zarnata. The Maniats often found themselves allied to the Venetians based in Crete but even they (the Venetians), at the very end of the 17th century, held political power in the area. Through these turbulent times, a system of local administration developed where power was held by leading Maniat families with the title of *Kapetanios:* they were responsible for the welfare and conduct of the Maniats within their *Kapetanato.* This system was further developed by the Turks at the end of the 18th century amidst the added chaos of Turko–Albanian forces operating in the area. In negotiations held in Gythio, the war-weary Maniats accepted the "Bey" system where one of the *Kapetanioi* would be selected to be overall leader of the area, though subject to the Sultan and responsible for collecting an amount of tax per year. The idea was that enough autonomy in other areas along with a military alliance when needed would both end feuding and improve relations between the Maniats and the Turks. This final attempt to make a Turkish presence in the Mani work inevitably failed as it became clear that not only was the Bey system doomed, but also that Turkish control over 'Greece' as a whole had limited time. The war for independence began in 1821.

the Mavromichalis Tower dominating Limeni

Post Revolution

In 1827, at the Battle of Navarino at Pylos, a combined fleet of French, English and Russian ships destroyed a Turkish–Egyptian fleet and effectively brought an end to the war – a seven year struggle instigated by the Maniat clans. However, the Maniat interpretation of independence did not encompass the whole of Greece but rather independence for themselves and their way of life. They did not take kindly to the idea of taxation and control by a central government of Greece – any more than they had accepted the same from the Ottomans – and consequently the family feuds and opposition to government interference continued for some time. This is most clearly expressed in the fact that the Mavromichalis clan murdered the first national president, Kapodistrias and foiled 3 attempts by Bavarian troops sent by their newly imposed King Otto to tear down their tower houses for refusing to give up their right to collect local taxes. The last great Maniat family feud was finally brought to an end in 1870, when a detachment of regular troops, supported by artillery, was sent to Kita and forced two families to stop fighting each other. From here on, the history of the Mani reflects that of modern Greece but the individual character of the peninsula, and its inhabitants, remains unchanged.

A More Detailed Chronology of Post-Byzantine Maniat History

1460 Mystras fell to the Ottoman Turks. The Sultan failed to get the support of the leading Maniat chieftain, Korkodilos Kladas.

1462 The first Turkish–Venetian war started and Kladas gave support to the Greeks of Arcadia and Sparta, themselves fighting on the side of Venice. The Turks won, causing even more refugees to flee into the Mani from Arcadia and Sparta as well as the withdrawl of the Venetians. Left to defend themselves alone, the Maniats initially conceded parts of the Mani to the Turks.

Turkish invasions – Mystras 1460

1480 Kladas led an army from Messinia and re-took the strategic points of Oitylo and Kastania.

1481 Two large Turkish armies attacked the Mani, capturing Pyrgos and Oitylo and in the east Mavrovouni and Passava. Villages in Mesa Mani, south of Areopolis also fell. Kladas himself was defeated at Porto Kayio but managed to escape to Epirus. The Maniats continued to attack from the safety of the mountains and forced the Turks to withdraw to fortifications at Mavrovouni. They never again occupied these villages on the plains south of Areopolis.

Mavrovouni 1481

1537 Another Turkish–Venetian war erupted also ending badly for the Mani with the Turks taking possession of Zarnata and Bardounia castles.

1571 Attempted uprising against the Turks led by the Melissinoi brothers. Don Juan, the leader of the Christian Alliance that pledged to free all Christian nations from Ottoman domination, promised support. The Turkish fleet was defeated at Lepanto but the Alliance fell apart soon after, once again leaving the Maniats to defend themselves and the uprising was crushed. This pattern of rebellion with foreign support continued for most of the 17th century.

Oitylo 1481

Zarnata 1537

1645 The Turks attacked the Venetians in Crete, laying siege to the capital Chandia.

1659 In response, the Venetian commander, Morosini, attacked Kalamata with Maniat support, landing first at Kitries, and capturing it from the Turks. He abandoned it and the Maniats however in 1660 and left them once again to face Turkish vengeance on their own.

1666 A large Ottoman fleet sailed up the coast to Kitries but a concerted effort by the Maniats prevented them from landing there and also further south in the area of Androuvitsa (Kardamyli).

1670 The Turks mounted their biggest attack on the Mani. A force of 6,000 men marched from the coast and captured Zarnata. They expanded Zarnata castle and used this as a strong base to move along the coast to Oitylo and across to Gythio. They built the castle at Kelefa, which overlooks Oitylo and the Bay of Limeni and also rebuilt a stronger fortification at Porto Kayio. The Turks put the captured Maniat pirate, Lyberakis Gerakaris, in charge of the Oitylo-Kelefa area where his dire threats against two prominent families (the Iatrani and Stephanopoli) resulted in a massive migration from Oitylo to Italy and Corsica respectively.

1684 Following the defeat of a massive Ottoman force which attacked Vienna, Russia and Venice declared war on the empire. Once again the Maniats were called upon for help to capture the Peloponnese. The Ottoman commander Ismail Pasha led 10,000 men against the Mani but was defeated by a combined Maniat and Venetian force and the castles of Passava, Porto Kayio, Zarnata and Kelefa were occupied by Maniats under the

command of Venetian officers.

Gerakaris now switched sides and attacked Turkish shipping. He was caught and imprisoned for the second time at Constantinople where he switched sides again. This time he would be proclaimed "His Highness, the Sovereign of Mani" if he helped the Turks recapture their lost ground. The Sultan agreed but in 1696, Gerakaris pulled another switch and joined forces with the Venetians!

1699 Treaty of Karlowitz formally ceded the Peloponnese to the Venetians who became the benign rulers of the Mani with a government centre at Kelefa Castle. The co-operation between the Venetians and the Maniats lasted for some 15 years until the Ottoman Empire struck back. A force of 100,000 troops and 100 ships, led by the Grand Vizier Ali Kumurji attacked the Peloponnese and within a few months had driven the Venetians out of the area.

1718 Although the Turks were eventually defeated when they turned against the Austrian Empire the Treaty of Passarowitz returned the Peloponnese to Ottoman rule. In the Mani, Turks again occupied the castles and fortresses but they still did not control the whole area, only the areas of the occupied castles.

1770 Catherine the Great of Russia, taking advantage of the weakened state of the Ottoman Empire, had been fighting a successful border war with the Turks. To further weaken the Ottoman position, a deputy was sent to Limeni to talk with the powerful Mavromichalis family. The offer of Russian aid was accepted with the proviso that they would not rebel until military support actually arrived to help them. They had learned the lesson after being so often left to bear the brunt of Turkish retaliation after previous abortive rebellions. In February 1770, the Orlov brothers, Alexis and Theodore, arrived in Limeni Bay with five ships and 1,000 men. A council was held in Dekoulou Monastery but the Maniats were reluctant to take any action because the Russians had sent such a small force. They eventually agreed to take action if the Russian force supported the Maniats in an attack on the Turkish held castle at Koroni, just across the mouth of the Bay of Messinia. In the end, a three-pronged strategy was agreed upon, attacking the Turks at Koroni, Kalamata and Passava. The Turkish garrisons put up a fierce defence and the allies quarrelled over their strategy. A meeting to discuss plans was held at Oitylo but when the Orlovs publicly insulted Ioannis Mavromichalis, he withdrew his force of 400 men and, acting independently from the alliance, attacked Messini. The rebellion had lost its initial impetus and the Turks began to organise a counter-offensive. They dis-patched a large force of Turks and Turko-Albanians from mainland Greece into the Peloponnese causing the retreat of the Allies from near Tripoli to Gythio and the Orlovs to abandon Koroni and Methoni. As so often before, the Maniats were left to their own devices and the retribution of an angry Ottoman Empire.

1776 The Ottomans soon discovered that they had a 'loose cannon' in their midst because the wild and ruthless Turko-Albanians also started to attack their own forces. Faced with the prospect of having to fight these renegades as well as the Maniats, the Sultan decided to try for a compromise with the latter. Negotiations were held at Gythio and the Maniats, rav-aged and depleted by years of endless war, readily accepted the generous terms offered by the Sultan. These were that one of the Kapetanioi would be selected to be "*Bey*" of the Mani – that is to say 'leader' of all the Maniats. The empire would acknowledge Maniat independence but at the same time pledge to protect the

modern-day Kitries

Kardamyli harbour – Turks repelled here in 1666

Kelefa Castle – Maniat, Turkish and Venetian in the 18th century
Dekoulou Monastery

Maniats from the Turko-Albanians. The Bey could call upon the Turks to fight the Turko-Albanians and he could also call for Turkish troops to suppress fighting among the Mani families or Kapetanioi. He was also responsible for collecting, on behalf of the Sultan, a tax that would be imposed in the sum of 15,000 '*grossia*' per year. For his own personal funds, he could collect two thirds of all the customs duties from the various ports in the Mani while the Kapetanios of each port kept the other third. The various subsequent Beys probably collected most of their share of the customs duties but the Sultan never got his grossia. The first Bey Zanetos Koutifaris of Zarnata (1776-1779) failed to stop the feuding and the Turko-Albanian raids. He was inveigled to board an Ottoman ship "for a conference", taken to Constantinople and beheaded.

1779 Michael Troupakis of Kardamyli (1779-1782) was then appointed Bey but his appointment ultimately failed because he could not control the Maniat clans. Proof of this is the Passava massacre by the Grigorakis clan and the incident at Mikri Kastania with Konstantinos Kolokotronis. As far as the Ottomans were concerned, Michael Troupakis had failed dismally to fulfil his obligations and he too was captured and beheaded.

1782 The third Bey, Zanetos Grigorakis of Gythio and Mavrovouni (1782-1798) - usually called Zanetbey - is one of the Mani's great heroes. He not only negotiated with the French - first with Louis XVI and then with Napoleon - for support against the Turks but also helped the escape of a notorious pirate, Lambros Katsonis, who had been attacking Turkish ships from his fortified base at Porto Kayio.

1798 The Turks deposed Zanetbey and Koumoundouros of Zarnata (1798-1803) was made Bey. To cause disruption among the Maniats and within the Grigorakis family, he was removed from office four years later and Zanetbey's nephew, Antonios Grigorakis of Ageranos (1803-1808) was made Bey. Koumoundouros would not accept this and, helped by Theodoros Kolokotronis, resisted a Turkish force which attacked his tower at Kambos. Koumoundouros was taken prisoner and sent to Constantinople where he died but Kolokotronis, although wounded, managed to escape.

1808 Antonbey was also deposed because the Turks thought he was helping the guerrilla efforts of his uncle, the former Zanetbey, and Pantelis Zervakos (1808-1810) was made Bey. He was pro-Turkish so the Maniats refused to accept him and drove him out of the Mani. He was killed by the Turks in Constantinople for his failure and replaced by Theodoros Grigorakis of Mavrovouni (1810-1815).

1815 This appointment of yet another member of this family caused great discontent in western Mani and so power was then transferred to Petros Mavromichalis of Limeni (1815-1821). He made contact with the *Philiki Etairia* - the secret society that was plotting a revolution against the Turks throughout Greece - despite the fact that his sons were held hostage in Constantinople. Petrobey then negotiated with the Kapetanioi of the leading Mani families and in 1821 he secured a '*treva*' or truce among the families and united them in the common cause of revolution.

1821 On 17th March, he led his forces out of Tsimova, which they renamed Areopolis, 'City of Ares' (the god of war) and marched up the Mani to Kardamyli where he joined forces with Kolokotronis, Mourtzinos and the Messinian Maniats. They attacked the Turks at Kalamata on 23rd March, securing the first victory in the war that finally liberated Greece after hundreds of years of foreign occupation but it was a long, hard struggle.

It was not a 'conventional' European war like those so recently fought against Napoleon with massed, disciplined armies, cavalry regiments and artillery batteries fighting 'set-piece' battles. The Turks had a standing, trained army with organised supplies, munitions and lines of communication between fortified positions. The Greeks had no army as such, just a nucleus of dedicated men like Kolokotronis, Mavromichalis, Mourtzinos, Pappa Phlessas, Ypsilantis and others who gathered 'armies' together, fought guerrilla actions, ambushes, sieges and the occasional pitched battle and then dispersed. Men had to be persuaded to fight and sometimes bribed, cajoled and threatened to leave their villages and take up arms. Kolokotronis explained the problem when he said,

"*In Europe, the commander-in-chief gave his orders to his generals, the generals to the colonels, and the colonels to the majors and so throughout. The general formed his plan of campaign and it was carried out. If Wellington had given me an army of forty thousand, I could have governed it; but if five hundred Greeks had been given to him to lead, he could not have governed them for an hour. Every Greek had his caprices and his hobby, and to get any service out of them, one had to be menaced and another to be cajoled, according to the nature of the man.*"

Bitter jealousy, rivalry and distrust between commanders and among emerging politicians who made up the Provisional Government, made organising and

Life in the Mani – walking the goat, Sotirianika

making olive soap, Kardamyli

preparing greens, Pyrgos

Epiphany, Gythio

training, let alone paying an army almost impossible. Supplies were always desperately short. No European nation openly supported the Greeks with munitions or weapons so they relied on what they captured from the Turks and the odd shipment obtained through private enterprise. Kolokotronis frequently mentions these shortages –

"Niketas the Turk eater" then marched into Argos and despoiled the mosques and minarets and sent us the lead which he took from them, for we were in want of lead and paper, and we therefore made use of the library of the monastery of Demitsana, and also those of other monasteries, in order to make cartridges".

1827 The Battle of Navarino saw a combined fleet of French, English and Russian ships destroy a Turkish-Egyptian Fleet and effectively brought an end to the war. The Protocol of St. Petersburg and the Treaty of London had established that the combined powers of France, England and Russia would 'mediate' in the conflict and the naval action at Pylos, often called the last great battle of the age of sail, was unplanned and started by accident.

Kita – scene of the last Maniat feud in 1870

1828 War again broke out between Russia and the Ottoman Empire and the severe setbacks experienced by the Turks effectively prevented them taking any more action in Greece.

1830 The first President of Greece, Ioannis Kapodistrias, angered the Mavromichalis clan, especially when he denied the Maniat kapetanioi the right to collect customs duties at their ports, and imposed a government tax on them. A revolt was fermenting in Limeni and rumours were circulating of a Maniat attack on Nafplio, the capital of Greece at that time. Petrobey was a virtual hostage at Nafplio and when he tried to leave, was captured and imprisoned. This action subdued the revolt and a delegation was sent to the Mani to negotiate peace with the clan and persuade the eastern Maniats, who were preparing for a war with the clan, to remain where they were and not to attack.

1831 The Mavromichalis clan were still not satisfied, especially as Petrobey was still being held prisoner. Giorgios and Konstantinos Mavromichalis, the son and brother of Petros, assassinated Kapodistrias at Nafplio in September. Konstantinos was killed the very same day by an angry mob. Giorgios was arrested, brought to trial and executed by firing squad. The following year, Petrobey was released from prison and played an active role in Greek politics. He was President of the Senate during the reign of King Otto.

1832 Greece remained highly volatile but was recognised as an independent kingdom under the protection of France, Russia and Great Britain. They gave Otto, the son of Louis I of Bavaria, the throne of Greece but, as he was only seventeen years old, regents were appointed until he came of age in 1835.

1833 The very soul of Maniat culture came under attack when it was decreed that the Mani towers would have to be pulled down. The situation was made worse by rumours that the Greek Orthodox Church was under threat from Bavarian Catholicism, and by the arrest of Kolokotronis on charges of treason. The first attempt to enforce this decree in 1834 resulted in a detachment of Bavarian troops being surrounded, forced to surrender, stripped naked and ransomed for a derisory price. A second attempt by a larger Bavarian force resulted in heavy losses and a forced withdrawal. A third attempt with 6,000 regular troops again failed to enforce the order and a negotiated settlement resulted in the order being rescinded and the towers were left intact. Many towers were built after this time but they tended to be wider and designed to live in as well as retaining their defensive character.

1839 The Earl of Carnarvon recorded the Maniat dissatisfaction with the new state.

"*Many even, in their disgust at the new civilization which had promised so much and done so little, which had destroyed political and feudal power, and which had given no compensation in the form of material prosperity for what it had taken away, were tempted to regret the days of Turkish rule, when a rude autonomy prevailed.*"

1870 The last great Maniat family feud was finally brought to an end when a detachment of regular troops, supported by artillery, was sent to Kita and forced two families to stop fighting each other.

Life in the Mani: olive picking

traffic jam

fishing, Stoupa

the 'kafenion', Pyrgos

Visitors to the Mani

The book frequently quotes the words written by people coming to the Mani over the years. Whether they came to travel, to research and record their experiences or were here for diplomatic and military reasons, it is worth noting when they came and for what reason.

A doctor from Greek Asia Minor, **Pausanias** must be the first to have visited Greece (in the 2nd century A.D) with the specific intention of writing a guide on her historical buildings, statues and tombs (as well as giving information on their mythological, historical and religious backgrounds). Kardamyli and Stoupa (Leuktra) get a brief mention– in those days the town of Kardamyli was *"a mile from the sea"*, set on a rocky acropolis which you can still scramble up to if you feel the need and of course he refers to Homer and the offer of Agamemnon to Achilles. As for Leuktra, he writes that *"on the acropolis is a sanctuary of Athene with a statue, and there are a shrine and a sacred wood of Love"*, the latter of which is now obviously long gone. He also refers to Homeric "Enope", the town that once stood around the hill of Zarnata by the modern day village of Cambos, which in Pausanias' time was known as Gerenia. He describes a bronze statue of Machaon (Asklepios's son), which explains the name of one of the coffee shops in Cambos. Like all serious travellers in the Mani he did not just explore the Outer Mani but ventured south through Thalames and Oitylo to get into Deep Mani, describing various statues and shrines along the way. He made it right to the end of the peninsula to Cape Tainaron., passing en route "Sandy Harbour" (now called Porto Kaiyo) and "Achilles Harbour" (Marmaris). At the cape itself he describes *" a shrine shaped like a cave with a statue of Poseidon in front of it"* as well as a bronze statue of Arion the musician, mounted on a dolphin. He also refers to a magic pool that gave a reflection of the future when looked into– that is until some ill-informed local woman took her washing there and therefore destroyed this special power.

Hundreds of years after Pausanias had written his guide to Greece, his book became a main reference to many of the Mani's visitors as Europe, woken from medieval times, became increasingly interested in the world of Ancient Greece. It would take a long time to list all of these visitors, so here is just a sample of what was written and recorded over the last five centuries:

One of the first to visit was a Calabrian merchant and antiquarian, **Ciriaco Anconitina**, who toured Italy, Greece, Asia Minor and Egypt. Through his acquaintance with the Palaiologo despots he was inspired to come to the Mani before the Turks sacked Mystras in 1460 and landed by ship at Marmaris in the south in 1447. He made extensive notes and drawings of the monuments and inscriptions he found here – all of his travels were written up in six huge volumes, only to be destroyed by fire in 1514. Fortunately some excerpts were copied before this disaster, including this drawing of an antique grave stele recycled into the walls of a thirteenth century church in the village of Keria. With the fall of neighbouring Mystras and the ensuing efforts of the Turks to gain control of the Mani, the remainder of the fifteenth century and the next two hundred years did not provide conducive conditions for exploration for the sake of exploration– instead foreigners who visited came for reasons associated with war. For example, one Fabiano Barbo came here in 1571 to sign a pact between the Maniat chiefs and the Venetians and twenty years later the Italian geographer Giuseppe Rosaccio visited to plot ports and staging posts in The the Mani to form part of his book that covered Venice to Constantinople. The seventeenth century saw a continuation of mainly foreign emissaries coming to the Mani as the conflict with Turkey intensified and placed the area in the middle of a battle between Western Europe and the Ottoman Empire. For example in 1618 envoys from the Duke of Nevers, a distant descendant of the Byzantine Palaiologos family, were sent in response to the Maniat pleas for military help. Although nothing came to fruition, the records made by the Duke's representatives provide an insight into life at that time. For example, the size of various villages were noted, according to how many families lived in them (and at that time a family could have consisted of up to ten or more members):

Oitylo– 400 families. The largest settlement in the Mani– this situation would change only 57 years later with the mass emigration of the Stephanopoli and Iatrani families to Corsica and Tuscany respectively (see Leigh Fermor, "the Mani",chapter 8).

Kelefa– 300 families
Kastania– 150 families
Androuvista– 80 families
Tseria– 40 families
Nomia– 30 families
Kita– 80 families
Lagia– 100 families

During this time of war it was not just westerners who recorded what they saw but the "enemy" as well. In the successful campaign of 1670,

sketch of grave stele by Ciriaco Anconitina and the actual sculpture

Tseria – 40 families

the Turkish army in the Mani carried with it a war historian by the name of **Evliya Celebi**. Naturally as the enemy and as a muslim he was not too complimentary in what he wrote about the Maniats. Constantly referring to them as the "infidel" who, due to excessive wine drinking, "sleep like pigs", he painted a very poor picture of life in Deep Mani. "The place is covered with stones—there is no soil at all". This particularly upset him as he saw no vines, fruit trees or gardens and he comments that the only water available was collected in cisterns. He also recorded the sizes of various villages but rather than counting by the number of families he used the number of houses as his measurement; as an example:

Doli– 300 "tiled-roof houses"
Proastio– 300
Androuvista–1000
Milea– 200
Platsa– 45
Oitylo– 1000
Tsimova (Areopolis)– 80

He also gives a description of a typical male from Deep Mani;

"they are dark-skinned, small in stature with large heads, round eyes with voices like sheep dogs, thick, black hair of shoulder length, slim trunk, slender legs, broad feet and they leap from crag to crag like fleas."

Moving into the eighteenth and early nineteenth centuries and the age of Enlightenment, the reasons for visiting Greece started to change from the diplomacies of war to a thirst for a comprehensive classification of human knowledge at the centre of which was ancient Greece. Although the Mani was not yet free from conflict with the Ottomans (and in fact her role in European political affairs increased due to her strategic position in the Mediteranean), the number of visitors coming here, some clutching Pausanias as a guide, steadily increased. A good example of how visiting Greece slowly became part of the "Grand Tour" (as opposed to just Italy) to wealthy western Europeans are the letters written home by **JBS Morritt**. At the age of 22, he set out from Yorkshire on a tour of Italy, Asia Minor and Greece. As he entered the Morea (Peloponnese) he was made aware of the potential dangers of getting as far south as Mani;

" It (Mani) is inhabited by Greeks, the real descendants of the Lacedemonians, and they have in this corner resisted all the efforts of the Turks, to whom they pay neither tribute nor obedience, and who dare not approach the country. They are all robbers, or rather pirates and infest the seas with small armed boats, which pillage all the small craft from port to port. In their country a total stranger is sure to be stripped of everything he has, though they seldom murder; but we understand that by applying at Kalamata, a town near them, we may get such protection as to be able to visit anything to be seen there in perfect safety."

Morritt took the risk of coming to Mani, largely lured by the belief that he was the first foreigner to go there. Having applied for security at Kalamata, he found things to be a little different from what he was expecting, as he wrote to his sister:

"If I see any danger of not getting out of it (Mani), it is not from banditti but from the hospitality and goodness of its inhabitants and we really have thoughts of domiciliating and staying in Maina"

Other than hospitality, perhaps there was another Maniat trait that was tempting him to stay. Whilst in Kardamyli he stayed with a man who had four daughters who "were beautiful beyond measure."

As 1821 approached, the year the war for freedom against the Ottomans began in Greece, so it was inevitable that the European powers would send an increasing number of envoys here to conduct diplomacy and record the strategic, geographical and military situations they found. In 1805 Lieutenant-colonel **William Martin Leake** was sent from Britain for this very reason and true to his cloth, recorded what he saw with military precision. As well as being fastidious on timings– *"...proceeding in a south-east direction, we arrive at 9.55 upon the summit of a ridge...."*– he also recorded specific facts and figures to do with the area. To quote a few;

Mani, "in abundant years", exported 8-10,000 barrels of olive oil, each barrel weighing 48 *okes* (a brass weight weighing 1.28kg)
At its peak, the area produced:
180,000 okes of cotton
2000 okes of silk was produced and sent mainly to Mystras
10,000 okes of honey
"Salted quails, put into lamb-skin, are carried to Constantinople"
"In abundant years, two ship-loads of small horse beans are exported to Italy"
"The Maniats reckon their population at 30,000 and their muskets at upwards of 10,000."
"The villages are reckoned at 117 in number; few of them are very small". Leake gives six as the average size of a family.
"The village of Kita has no less than 22 *pyrghi* (tower houses)....it contains 80-100 families." (the very same estimate made in 1618 by the envoy from the Duke of Nevers).3

But Leake was not only interested in statistics that may have been of use

an oka

8-10,000 barrels of olive oil

10,000 okes of honey

to his government: he too carried Pausanias and held an interest in the area's ancient heritage. For example, he surmised that the church of Asomati at Tainaron had a much older history. Having measured "*parts of the church walls formed of ancient wrought blocks*" he concluded, perhaps inaccurately, that "*the church, instead of facing to the east as Greek churches usually do, faces south-eastward, towards the head of the port, which is likely to have been the aspect of the temple. There can be little or no doubt that it was the celebrated temple of Tainarian Neptune.*"

Others visited not to classify the ancient remains to be found here but in the case of John Sibthorp, the flora of the area. In 1795 he collected plant specimens from the peaks of Taygetos. A few years later, the botanist Dimo Stephanopoli, himself a descendant from Oitylo came with his nephew, on the instruction of Napoleon, to gather information about the area. Likewise, in 1829, a team of enthusiastic geographers, surveyors, scholars, botanists and archaeologists formed the French Scientific Expedition in the Peloponnese and came down to Mani. By 1833, Greece had firmly established itself as an independent nation, free at last from Ottoman control, with the arrival of their new King, Otto of Bavaria. Conditions were now much easier for foreign visitors and a steady flow of archaeologists, historians, and sociologists came to Mani. The **3rd Earl of Carnarvon** is a good example of how the sphere of interest in the area widened from the earlier motives of international diplomacy or the study of ancient relics. He came in 1839 and stayed with the famous Mavromichalis family in Limeni. He wrote on a wide variety of aspects of Maniat life, from administrative organisation to traditions and customs, from feuding to the role of the church. One of the more unusual subjects he commented on was the belief in vampires, which, like their Transylvanian cousins, sucked the blood from the living and eventually caused their death. Carnarvon was shown a house where the owner, a shoemaker, had returned from the grave every night except Saturday night and, as well as making a few shoes had made his wife pregnant. When accused of infidelity to her husband's memory, she told them the cause. "At this horrifying disclosure," wrote the Earl, "the villagers sallied forth to attack the vampire in his tomb, undertaking the enterprise on a Saturday morning, on which day alone the vampire's devil-imparted strength forsakes him, and the grave has power to hold his body. They found him working in his grave, making shoes. "How did you know I was a vampire?" exclaimed the still living tenant of the tomb. A villager, in answer, pointed to a youth whose cheek a month before had been bright with health, but on which the ghastly paleness of disease and coming death had fixed its mark. The vampire immediately spat at him. The moisture from those accursed lips burnt the man's capote (jacket) as though it had been fire, but it could not hurt the man himself, because it was blessed Saturday." The Earl continues the story with the Vampire threatening the entire village with vengeance so the villagers tore him to pieces, cut out his heart and divided it into portions which were distributed and eaten by the villagers – this being the sure and proven method of disposing of his kind.

The twentieth century continued to have visitors. Certainly in the first half, the area seems to have retained its customs and traditions that make it such a unique place. **Kevin Andrews**, an American archaeologist, spent four years in Greece right in the middle of the vicious civil war that bedevilled the country in the aftermath of World War Two and wrote up his experiences in "the Flight of Ikaros". He came to Mani from his studies in Athens by ship, docking at Gerolimenas in the south. and was clearly affected by his initial impressions – see the quote on page 114.

This description of how the Maniat males were armed is echoed by another twentieth century visitor, who unlike JBS Morritt a hundred and fifty years earlier, did stay in the area. In **Sir Patrick Leigh Fermor**'s travelogue, "the Mani", he gives a lengthy description of their dress, though the picture he paints is not contemporary but rather a summary of prints he had seen from earlier times.

"*Baggy trousers with many pleats just below the knees with legs either bare or greaved in embroidered gaiters, their oriental slippers some-times turned up at the tip. Over their shirts they wore a short bolero as stiffly galooned with bullion as a bullfighter's jacket. (Petrobey Mavromichalis, when Leake visited the Mani, wore a coat of green velvet charged with gold lace). Their great moustaches would sometimes meas-ure eight inches across and their hair fell in thick black waves over their shoulders. At a raffish angle on the side of their heads was perched the soft, 'broken fez' with its long black tassel of heavy silk. Over the sash their middles were caught in with belts equipped in front with a slotted marsupial flap of leather to hold their arsenal of weapons: the almost straight pistols whose butts tapered and then swelled into knobs at the end like wrought silver crab-apples;*

khangars, those long knives with branching hafts of bone or ivory that spread like two out-curving horns; and, their chief weapon for close-quarter fighting, the yataghan, its ivory hilt dividing like the khangar, the long subtle blade curving and straightening again as fluidly as a flame. Often, too, they would carry cross-hilted scimitars whose blades described a semicircle......Their long-barrelled guns, which resem-bled Afghan jezails, were so heavy that they could only be aimed when resting on a rock or a branch."

One of Leigh Fermor's encounters in the late 1950's clearly illustrates the level of poverty. On the Tigani peninsula he met a mother and daughter, collecting rock salt.

"*They worked here all summer, they said, and sometimes in the winter too, sleeping over in the huge cave by the chapel of the Hodygytria.....It wasn't much of a life, the mother said. How much could they sell the salt for? It was the equivalent, in drachmae, of sixpence an oka. And how much could they gather in a day? On good days, she said, a bit more than an oka; on bad days rather less. It all depended. Then she threw back her head and let out a laugh of genuine amusement in which there was not a trace of bit-terness.*"

Finally, the historian and classicist **Peter Greenhalgh** and co author **Edward Eliopoulos** (who first came to the Mani during the war as a mem-ber of the Greek resistance) travelled extensively in the area in 1980 to produce a less literary but equally scholarly guide book to rival Leigh Fermor's book from 20 odd years earlier. In particular, Greenhalgh goes into great detail of the internal paintings of the Mani's numerous churches.

Towers and Tradition

Background

In classical times, the Mani was not very different from the rest of Greece. The real contrast with the rest of the country developed after the fall of the Roman Empire and the subsequent invasions that hastened the collapse of the Byzantine Empire and, ultimately, domination of the rest of Greece by the Ottoman Empire. Most significant was the fall of Mystras in 1460 causing many refugees to flee to the Mani. Survival in the now crowded peninsula depended on power and that in turn depended on ownership of land and water. Out of this constant struggle evolved a unique culture with its own traditions. It was undeniably violent but so was life elsewhere on the Peloponnese, especially for those who resisted Turkish domination, as Kolokotronis illustrates in his autobiography when he gives examples of the consequences of being captured alive by the Turks during his time as a *klepht*.

"Old Gianni Kolokotrones was killed at Androusa (Messinia) – his hands and feet were cut off, and he was then hung." The same fate awaited *"the old father of Panagioras"* who was eighty years old. He was captured alive after a stalwart defence of his tower at Kastanitsa – *"The hands and feet, however, of the aged warrior were amputated, and he himself was afterwards hung."*

Little wonder then that a klepht drinking toast was to "the good bullet" – the one that killed you outright.

A drastic preventative measure was also used among friends, – *"When any of us was seriously wounded in a battle and could not be carried away, we all kissed him and then cut off his*

head. It was thought a great dishonour to have the Turks bear away one's head." It is against this backdrop that the Mani acquired a reputation for fiercely defending their land against the Turks, succeeding in maintaining a degree of autonomy not experienced elsewhere in Greece.

Towers

The struggle for power in the Mani was therefore rooted in the need to obtain and control areas of valuable land and then to defend them against others with equal ambitions and the method of defence that evolved was the tower. This was explained by Colonel Leake when he wrote,

"Each person of power and every head of a family of any influence has a pyrgo (tower), which is used almost solely as a tower of defence: the ordinary habitation stands at the foot of it. ...in general these buildings are uninhabited except in times of alarm. To overturn the pyrgo of the enemy and to slaughter as many of his relations as possible, are the objects of every war. The tower has loopholes in the different stories and battlements on top, and he that can get a rusty swivel (small cannon) to plant upon them is not easily subdued. Most of the ordinary dwellings are built with loopholes in the walls; nor are the villages in which there is no inhabitant of sufficient opulence to build a pyrgo, the more peaceable on that account, but quarrel either among themselves or with their neighbours, and endeavour to overturn one another's houses just like their betters."

As well as serving an obvious military purpose, the towers were an outward sign of clan strength and unity. The height, strength and armament of a tower was an open display of power and the effort and resources required to build the tower showed the common purpose of the clan. Over the years, three kinds of tower developed; the war tower, the tower house and the tower dwelling. The war tower stood independent within a village or complex and was designed specifically for warfare. In peacetime they were manned by sentries but not usually inhabited by the clan. Their design of being tall and narrow was geared towards defence not habitation. The tower house however had a dual pur-pose, as a lower house, usually connect-ed to the tower itself, was where the local *kapetanios* lived. The logical devel-opment of this came largely post-1830 where the towers were much larger and wider, enabling the clan members to actually live in the tower. By this time the tower dwellings were only required to protect a clan involved in a local feud, as the Turks had finally been defeated. This local rivalry also shaped the design and function of the towers. There are some examples of isolated strongholds in both Inner and Outer Mani, for example the Mourtzinos fortification in Kardamyli or in the village of Agios Giorgios, on the road to Mezapos. The latter serves as a very good model of a small, isolated clan stronghold. Here well-built, fortified houses surround a tall, thin war tower like the circled wagons of American pio-neers in a defensive stance in the middle of a prairie. The view from the top of the tower would allow a sentry to give ample warning of hostile approach from any direction but there are very few firing loops or defensive features on the tower itself which suggests that, in this partic-ular example, the main fighting defences were the houses themselves while the tower served as lookout and 'command and control' centre from which to con-duct the defence. The flat, exposed site of this village made such a circular defence necessary whereas other villages used natural features such as hills, mountain slopes, ravines and escarp-ments in their defensive plans and these

tower house

war tower

tower dwelling

tower complex

features dictated the strategic siting of towers and houses. Where different clans lived in close proximity, strength and unity was often demonstrated by the building of more than one tower and by the size and strength of the surrounding houses. This is well illustrated in villages like Vathia, Kita and Lagia where interfamily feuding was commonplace.

Morritt, ever the romantic, when describing clan areas draws a parallel with Lycurgus – the Spartan 'law giver' (Lycurgus is the traditional founder of Sparta's "*enomia*" – 'good order' – and according to Herodotus he brought all of Sparta's laws and the military and political institutions to Sparta from Crete). "*Their order of government is this, the land is still parcelled out in districts on Lycurgus's own plan; on every one of these lives a family, supported by the villagers and people of that district, who are as free as their masters, with their guns on their shoulders; and thus the head family commands about four miles round about, and is indulgent to the others, who would otherwise destroy or desert it.*"

He then goes on to say,

"*These rulers often make war on one another, and the plunders then committed bring them into the bad repute their neighbours give them. They acknowledge one man as Bey, who is united by family to many of them, and if attacked by the Turks take their guns, retire to the mountains, and, with a force of six thousand or seven thousand men, carry on a war that is the terror of the Ottoman Empire.*"

Defensive Features of the Towers

1. Turrets which, because they protrude from the walls, allow defenders a view of or shot at any attacker who has positioned himself against the wall of the building.

2. Firing loops.

3. A window quickly protected from incoming fire by erecting a stone 'turret' on the two (sometimes three) stones protruding from beneath the window.

4. Similar to the above but permanent.

5. Same as point 3 but without being blocked up for war. The stones needed to build the turret would be kept inside the tower.

6. Usually built over a doorway of vulnerable part of the building, this feature allowed defenders to pour boiling water or similar on attackers or to simply fire down on them.

7. Small doorways made it more difficult for potential intruders to enter.

Stone Carving

An abundance of stone gave the Mani a ready source of building material. Limestone was used throughout the area to build houses, towers and churches – a tradition still carried on today. Stonemasons often showed off their skills by carving intricate patterns and images on individual blocks as well as carving semi-relief sculptures. This folkloric tradition goes as far back as the ancient Greeks, who looked to their gods for protection and help when needed – for example, every Athenian house had a statue of Hermes by the front door to ask for a safe journey and a shrine to Zeus in the courtyard to ask for protection of the house. In the same way a carving of a snake on a stone block set in the walls of a house was thought to bring good health and fertility to the household, a ship a safe journey or a fierce looking face relief from unwelcome visitors (of which the Mani had many throughout history). Sometimes these heads were representations of the head of the household, as if to say "I am always watching you – beware!" Carvings of this kind can be seen throughout the Mani on both houses and churches.

Defensive Features   *1.*

2.

5.

6.

Castles

Although the Mani is more renowned for its tower houses, the area also has numerous castles. During the 13th century, the Franks built a series of castles on the peninsula, largely to defend themselves against fierce Slavic tribes who occupied the mountains. However, neither has sufficient primary documentation survived, nor has enough archaeological work been carried out to provide definitive evidence to accurately date each castle. Certainly the Franks were not the only builders as the Turks, Venetians and the Byzantines themselves sought to secure crucial strategic points in the Mani over the years. This has left a lot of room for debate and conjecture. Perhaps the greatest uncertainty is over the location of the Frankish *Grande Maini* castle. Several candidates vie for this title – Tigani, Cavo Grosso, Kelefa and Porto Kaiyo – but none can claim it without dispute. For a fuller discussion on this issue and a general overview of the Mani's castles, the 2006 issue of **Inside the Mani** magazine has an in depth article written by John Chapman, who also discusses castles (as well as churches) in his website http://www.maniguide.info.

Families, Clans and Feuds

Numerous books have been written in Greek and English on this subject so to summarise the information into a few paragraphs is, to say the least, very difficult.

The nucleus of Maniat society was 'the family' which usually traced its descent from a prominent patriarch but the family rapidly evolved into a clan by marriage and by alliance.

The evolution of elite families in tightly confined boundaries with local autonomy required its own system of justice. The lack of any organised district government meant that a system of personal rendering of justice prevailed and this was known as "*aftothikia*" whereby matters were resolved by the family. *Aftothiko* literally means – "to take the law into one's own hands" and from early beginnings in the 15th century, it evolved into a highly structured process. Before enactment of any revenge activity, a family or clan would first consult its 'Council of Elders' (*Gerondiki*) and, if sanctioned, would then give warning of the decision to the offending family. The Gerondiki were not always the oldest members of the clan but constituted the most distinguished male members. From then on, all and any actions were considered just. This did not usually mean an all-out attack on the enemy but would more often take the form of ambush and murder and this was considered perfectly honourable. This method of warfare could result in a feud continuing for a great number of years with "tit-for-tat" ambush and murder until the virtual extinction of one family.

Vathia – notorious feuding village

This in turn led to the creation of "rules" to enable the normal cycle of life to continue, although that may sound like a contradiction in terms. The harvest was essential to survival so a "*treva*" or truce could be called to enable the crops to be gathered and sometimes "safe conduct" would be granted to a rival provided he was accompanied by a third party who was trusted by both sides to act as escort. The feud could end in a truce, sometimes by the intercession of a third party, or by the families themselves with a mutual pardon. This was done to prevent the virtual extinction of both families and the mutual pardon removed the obligation for vengeance.

In general, women and priests were not direct targets and could come and go unharmed. Thus the women's role also included the supplying of food, ammunition and powder to the family tower when under siege and running short of supplies. The Earl of Carnarvon recorded,

"*The Maniats never attacked a woman. In the fiercest wars, no shot from tower or ambuscade (ambush) seems to have been directed against her. Even when she served as a screen for her husband, the assailed party is said never to have returned fire upon her.*"

This was not entirely true for there were instances where the pregnant wife of a murdered man would be deliberately killed to prevent possible future vengeance from a son.

Aftothikia was given moral support by the church in the Mani – if only by keeping silent. It was the only form of justice available and the priests were usually natives of the Mani who had been raised within the tradition. Most had received only local training and had not attended any major religious centres, so their acceptance of Mani life was no different from other inhabitants. In reality, what could the church have done to prevent the

Towers at...   *Pyrrichos*

Briki

Pepo

Lagia

feuds? The Earl of Carnarvon asked the same question and wrote

"My Maniat friend observed that they (priests) would have been in danger had they interfered, but that they pursued a prudent course in saying that they had nothing to do with points of honour."

Besides, the Maniats themselves were usually very devout and adhered strictly to their Christian beliefs as Col. Leake observed when he wrote,

"No people are more rigorous in the observances of the Greek Church than the Maniats. A Kakavouliote (Maniat from Mesa Mani), who would make a merit of hiding himself behind the wall of a ruined chapel, for the purpose of avenging the loss of a relative upon some member of the offending family, would think it a crime to pass the same ruin, be it ever so small a relict of the original building, without crossing himself seven, or at least three, times."

The Earl of Carnarvon also remarked on this contrast between strict religious observance and casual disregard for killing.

"I was eating some fowl in one of their rude dwellings on a Friday. 'I would not do that for all that the world could give me,' said a young Mainote chief, who had been much with me, and whose hands were red with a hundred murders.

'But, observed my muleteer, with the freedom so common in these countries, 'you would think nothing of killing a man.'

'Oh no,' replied my Mainote friend, 'but eating meat on a Friday is a crime.'"

Not only did the church condone Aftothikia, but by acknowledging it as the only available system, on occasion resorted to the use of it themselves. Col. Leake recorded an incident that occurred two months before he went to the Mani, when the son of a priest had accidentally killed a boy who was related to another priest.

"The latter papas declared war against the former, which is done in Mani in a formal manner, by crying out in the streets. The first papas went to his church to say mass with pistols in his girdle; such being a common custom in Mani; but as usual in such cases, he laid them behind the altar, on assuming the robe in which the priest performs divine service. The other papas entered the church with some of his party, and the instant the office was concluded, walked up to his enemy, who was still in his robes, and fired a pistol at him, which flashed in the pan (failed to fire properly): the latter, then running behind the altar, seized his arms, shot his enemy and one of his adherents, and drove all the rest from the church. The affair was then settled by the interposition of the Bey himself, in whose village it had happened."

Another example of the church tolerating and even condoning activities which would seem to contradict religious training, was concerning piracy. The Maniats were famed and feared as pirates and the coastline of the peninsula was a place for shipping to avoid whenever possible. The peninsula had been subjected to raids throughout history and piracy was considered a legitimate response to this it also provided goods which would not otherwise be available and for which there was never the money to trade. Not only were the pirate boats blessed by the priests to encourage success but priests fre–

quently accompanied the boats on their forays and raids.

John Morritt also mentions piracy.

"They are all robbers, or rather pirates, and infest these seas with small armed boats which pillage all the small craft from port to port."

Such a violent existence, which also included fighting off invaders and raiders, took a heavy toll of manpower and the greatest asset to any family or clan was the amount of men who could fight on its behalf. The birth of a son, often called a 'gun', was a major event and the birth of a daughter was by contrast, a virtual disaster. This paramount need for men resulted in large families as Leake said when he stayed at the tower of Katzanos in Skoutari,

"Katzano has twenty five persons in his family, of whom nine are his children; he married at the age of nineteen, his wife was fourteen; they have had fifteen children."

If a wife failed to provide sons, the husband could marry again, without a divorce from the first wife, and if the second wife bore sons, they were considered legitimate.

The Earl of Carnarvon attended a wedding in Kita where he was told that the first wife had not had any children, so the groom was taking a second wife.

"On my asking some further questions, it appeared that his first marriage had indeed given him three daughters; but my informant repeated his statement that there were no children – so completely are girls counted as nothing in this country. One of my muleteers clinched the argument by the additional question of – how could a man wish to have anything to do with a woman who brought him no sons?"

This attitude conveniently overlooked the

Out of Season–   twister over Stoupa

snow near Milea

waves crashing over Stoupa's harbour wall

Stoupa beach in winter

role that some women had played in warfare – not least of all at Pyrgos Dirou in 1826 when women saved the day against a Turkish invading force of 1,500 men – only 13 years prior to Carnarvon's visit and only a few kilometres away!

Leake also reported that many women were good shots and one offered to put a musket ball through his hat at 150 yards range but he declined,

"*I had too much regard for my only hat to trust her, for she has had two wounds in battle, and affects to consider her husband as no braver than he should be.*"

He also told the story of a woman defending her tower against a Turkish force while covering the escape of a servant and her two children through a back door. In fact, the courage and fighting ability of women in the Mani was indisputable and the Earl of Carnarvon acknowledged this when he wrote about

meeting Petrobey Mavromichalis' mother,

"*a most interesting person, who had with her own hand fought against the Turks, and on more than one occasion had defeated them.*"

J.B.S. Morritt wrote a letter to his sister Anne while he was at Mystras in which he describes the role of women in wartime –

"*In case of an attack upon their country they arm both men and women, and their whole force amounts to about fifteen thousand. It would be a disgrace for them to stay behind when their husbands and sons are in danger. Fighting side by side, and with their wives and children around them, can you conceive a more formidable corps than the smallest clan so animated?*" In the same letter, he goes on to say, "*I must allow that the ladies, beautiful as they are, are rather farouche in their ideas of honour, as at one captain's where we had a ball they apologised for not having*

Maniat women commemorated at Pyrgos Dirou

better music, as a favourite fiddler having
made too free either with the person or
reputation of a fair lady here aroused the
vengeance of the softer sex, and shot him
through the head upon the spot."

Morritt was evidently quite smitten with
the Maniat women. While he was at Kardamyli, he saw some women practising at
throwing stones, which they used as
weapons. He went on to say,

"With all this they are beautiful, and, as
far as I hear, very virtuous, so their edu-
cation spoils neither their persons nor
their minds. Such is the state of the
ladies."

*Past Times : threshing circles ('alonia') can
be seen throughout the area*

When he stayed at Kitries he described his
hostess and her family to his sister.

"The lady is about twenty eight; her husband, who governed here, is dead and
she is mistress of the territory. While the
sex is degraded at three hours distance,
they are here free, simple and happy. By
what I am told, they are very virtuous and
it is the only instance in the Levant. For all
this, they are as beautiful as angels; it was
a new thing to us to have audience of a
fine woman, attended by a train of
damsels, most of them pretty, and her
sister, who was about eighteen, and as
beautiful as you can conceive."

This report of a woman as "mistress of
the territory" is in marked contrast to the
reports of Carnarvon and, to a lesser
extent, of Leake. Morritt did not travel
into Mesa Mani so that may explain the
contradiction.

There was another side of Maniat life that
appears to be almost a contradiction of
the fierce reputation acquired by the
Maniats as pirates, mercenaries and brig-
ands – the tradition of hospitality.

*terracing – every inch of land was used to feed a
large population
water cistern – water was always a valuable
commodity*

"Nor less sacred was the virtue of hospitality." wrote the Earl of Carnarvon, "Poor
themselves, and barely deriving a subsis-
tence from their rugged soil, they would

accept any privation or make any sacrifice for the humblest stranger who might claim their assistance."

Leake also encountered unreserved hospitality wherever he went and none more so than when he met an old priest at Kiparissos,

"whose only costume is a jacket with a pair of wide trousers of coarse blanketing of Maniat manufacture, receives me with an air of cheerfulness and hospitality;" After describing his obvious poverty, Leake goes on to say, *"He points, however, without hesitation, to the only fowl he possesses, as he desired us to "take off its head", imitating the action of a Pasha ordering an execution."*

Morritt is his usual effusive self on this subject. *"At the same time they have such an idea of hospitality that the houses of the rich and poor are open to strangers in the worst places, and the very men who would strip you to the skin as an enemy, if unknown, will if you claim the rights of hospitality give you every assistance, and stake their lives and families to defend and protect you as a friend."*

So the Mani was a barren, violent place where the struggle to survive forged a culture that held life cheap but at the same time was deeply religious; where hospitality was inviolate but piracy honourable; where women counted for little but, illiterate as they were, could spontaneously create an 'epic poem' at funerals *(miralogia)*. It is an awareness of these contrasts or paradoxes that makes this region so fascinating and helps explain some of what you might see on your travels – not least of all why a landscape studded with war towers also contains so many beautiful Byzantine and post-Byzantine churches with carved marble and frescoes that show great artistry and devotion.

Kiparissos – showed Leake unreserved hospitality

Churches and Frescoes

"*Very often, wandering the wilder parts of Greece, the traveller is astonished in semi-abandoned chapels where the liturgy is perhaps only sung on the yearly feast of the eponymous saint, by the beauty of the colouring of the wall-paintings and the subtlety with which the painter has availed himself of the sparse elbow-room for private inspiration that the formulae of Byzantine iconography allow him: a convention so strict that it was codified by a sixteenth-century painter monk called Dionysios of Phourna. He formalised the tradition of centuries into an iconographic dogma and deviation became, as it were, tantamount to schism. He it was who made the army of saints and martyrs and prophets identifiable at once by certain unvarying indices.*"

Patrick Leigh Fermor, The Mani, 1958.

Although Christianity came relatively late to the Mani, the Maniats certainly made up for lost time and the legacy of centuries of fairly prolific church building has resulted in the area being scattered with numerous "semi-abandoned chapels". Wherever you are in the Mani, a closer look around you will inevitably reveal a tiled church roof poking out above the olive groves or a chapel silhouetted on top of a hillside. The dates of these churches vary enormously and accordingly, so do the frescoes inside. Religious painting in both western and eastern Europe may not be the most expressive art form ever conceived and the restrictive nature of the movement mentioned by Leigh Fermor may explain its rather limited appeal – however the church and therefore church art was, and still is, integral to Greek society and the Mani is no different. Therefore it could be said that a visit inside an Orthodox church to appreciate its design and the paintings inside is as important an experience to the foreign visitor here as exploring the tower house villages in the Deep Mani, going into the

wandering past a semi-abandoned chapel...

Pantocrator

single-vaulted church

'cross-in-square' church

caves at Pyrgos Dirou or visiting the major sites of the southern Peloponnese.

Church Design

The most commonly used design was, and still is, the single-cell, vaulted church – the most economic to build. A single apse (1) is often flanked by a conch on either side where the *prothesis* and *diaconicon* should be in a three-apsed *bema* (see later). The *bema* (the sanctuary) is segregated from the main vault of the church by a *templon* (if stone or marble) or *iconostasis* (if wooden) (2). Single-vaulted churches vary in size from tiny chapels to quite large

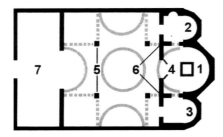

churches and are often privately owned by families.

The 'cross-in-square' plan was adopted in Constantinople in the late 9th century and spread across the whole Byzantine Empire. It is the most common form of church that has a dome. The lower half of the church is a cube on which a plan of a

cross is placed. In the centre of the cross, a dome (*cupola*) is supported on a cylindrical drum. The internal plan of the ceiling shows how each arm of the cross has vaulted ceilings while in the centre is the dome. This basic design is often added to – the diagram shows the most commonly added features. Three apses (1,2 & 3) are usually added on the east end and a narthex (7) on the west. The central apse (1) is larger than the other two, housing the altar. All three have a conch (a curved, semi-domed recess in the rear wall). Apse 2 is called the *prothesis* and is where the priest prepares the Eucharist and there is usually a second small conch in the north wall that provides a work surface for this purpose. Apse 3 is known as the *diaconicon* and is used for storing vestments, books etc. These three areas form the bema and is a part of the church forbidden to women and indeed non-clerical men. The dividing *templon* or *iconostasis* has three doorways into each of the three apses and whether wooden or stone has frescoes painted on. The wooden iconostasis (literally 'icon station') is more typical in post-Byzantine churches. Sometimes the cupola is supported by four columns but more commonly on just the two western columns (5) leaving the eastern end of the dome to be supported by the walls that divide the apses (6).

Church Paintings

It would require the work of a PHD thesis to go into the depth required to understand all there is to know about Byzantine and post Byzantine art. In the context of this book it is hopefully enough simply to give a brief guide to frescoes worth visiting in the area (taking into account the infuriating problem of churches being locked with no key-holder to be found) as well as first giving a taste of the "unvarying indices" that so restrict their content.

Faced with bare plaster in a newly built church, the painter had two conventions to follow– the location of specific images in specific places within the building and then once work commenced, how these images were portrayed. There is uncertainty over the degree of impact the code laid down by the monk Dionysios of Phourna actually had on contemporary and succeeding painters – some argue that the nature of the work intrinsically required conformity and tradition – but the fact that this eighteenth century (not sixteenth as stated by Leigh Fermor) document was only re-discovered in the early nineteenth century at an Orthodox church in Munich where the artists were referring to the "painters manual" as it is now known, suggests that it did have widespread recognition. In any case, simply browsing through the document gives a clear indication of the attitude towards the serious business of religious painting. Not only does it give technical details ranging from making paints and varnishes to more purely artistic concerns – the proportions of the human figure, how to put highlights on garments, how to paint flesh etc – but it also states how the artist should portray certain biblical scenes and figures. Here, the role of the beard takes on great importance (to help the congregation identify who is who?). To quote an example from the Old Testament, the Creation of Adam:

"*Adam, a beardless young man, stands naked; the Eternal Father is in front of him, surrounded by a bright light, and holds him by the hand with his left hand and blesses him with his right. Around them are little hills with trees and various animals, while above is the sky with the sun and moon*".

Equally from the New Testament and Christ Judged by Herod:

a single apse

a templon

an iconostasis

John the Baptist

" *A palace, and Herod, an old man with a rounded beard, sitting on a throne in royal robes; behind him are soldiers and Christ is before him. Two soldiers are clothing him in a white garment and a crowd of Jews is behind him.*"

Every significant event from the Bible is mentioned in this way along with added tales of various martyrs and saints. As already mentioned the specific location of particular images and scenes was another tradition to follow and the Painters Manual also catalogues these rules;

"*When you wish to paint scenes in a church with a dome, up inside the cupola make a circle of various colours, similar to those in a rainbow that appears in the clouds in rainy weather; in the middle of it paint Christ blessing, holding the Gospels on his breast, and inscribe it with the title "Jesus Christ the Pantocrator".*" Or for a single barrel-vaulted church with no central dome "*paint the Pantocrator up in the middle of the vault inside a circle, and to the east over the iconostasis the Virgin, and to the*

west the Forerunner". Other than the *Pantocrator* ('All Ruling') image there are numerous other examples of these location-specific rules. For example, on the templon (the stone wall dividing the altar from the main body of the church, called an iconostasis if wooden) the image to the left of the central door is usually *Panagia Hodegetria* – the Virgin with the infant Christ on her knee indicating 'the way, the truth and the light'– and on the right is Christ Enthroned showing Christ wearing an archbishop's mitre and robes, sitting on a throne attended by angels and saints. He is giving a blessing and has an open bible, which often shows the text: "My kingdom is not of this world...." To the right of Christ Enthroned you will often find John the Forerunner (Baptist) who is always depicted as being somewhat scruffy with wild hair and coarse clothing as befits a man living in the desert. In the conch of the central apse behind the altar the most common painting is *Panagia Platytera* – 'The Wide Wings of Heaven'. The Virgin has her arms spread wide to both welcome and offer love and protection to the

Panagia Playtera – ' the Wide Wings of Heaven'

congregation and has a medallion of the young Christ on her chest.

Another common theme depicted in numerous churches in the Mani are the *Ainoi* (the 'Praises' from psalms 148–151). In the centre is Christ Enthroned encircled by the sun and moon and signs of the Zodiac, a reference to "*praise him all his angels....... ye sun and moon....praise him all ye stars of light.*" Radiating outwards you will be able to identify other references to these psalms – "*praise the Lord ye dragons and all deeps......beasts and all cattle; creeping things and flying foul*" explains the strange beasts and the numerous musicians refer to "*let them praise his name in the dance, let them sing praises to him with the timbrel and harp*". You will also see notables chained together and guarded by swordsmen; "*Let the high praises of God be in their mouth and a two-edged sword in their hand: to execute vengeance upon the heathen and punishments upon their hand; to bind their kings with chains and their nobles with fetters of iron.*" Close to these scenes in the northwest corner is a two-tiered, domed building. The top tier depicts two, crowned Byzantine nobles and the lower tier shows a Muslim caliph and a man in western clothing wearing a stylish hat and a ruff. These represent the 'Earth's Judges' from psalm 148; " *Kings of the earth, all nations, princes, earth's judges all; both young men, yea, and maidens too, old men and children small. Let them God's name praise.*"

There are literally hundreds of churches and chapels to visit in the Mani to get a taste of how these formulae were passed on from generation to generation of painters. However, some are fairly inaccessible, some are permanently locked, in some the paintings have been plastered over and in others the building is so derelict that the paintings are barely decipherable. But thankfully some gems still exist and throughout the book these are highlighted.

Note: When visiting a church, you should not be displaying bare legs and women should not display bare shoulders as this can cause offence. It is also usual to leave a small donation.

the Crucifixion

the Holy Trinity

the 'Ainoi'

detail of the above

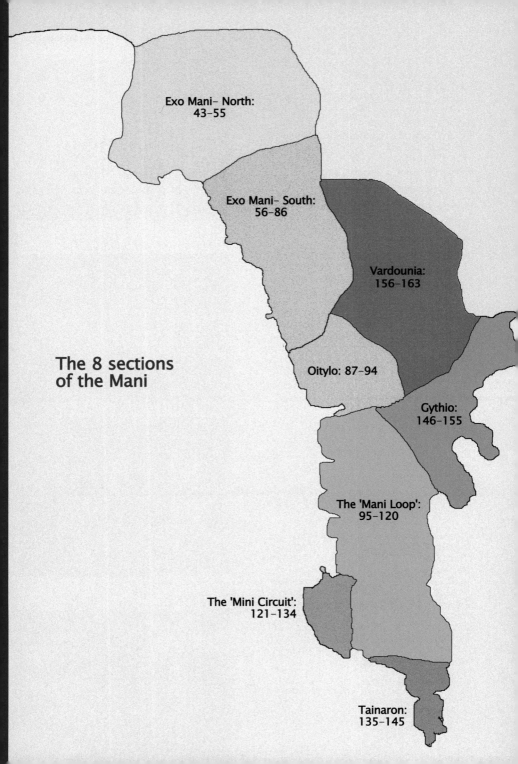

The 8 sections
of the Mani

Exo Mani- North:
43–55

Exo Mani- South:
56–86

Vardounia:
156–163

Oitylo: 87–94

Gythio:
146–155

The 'Mani Loop':
95–120

The 'Mini Circuit':
121–134

Tainaron:
135–145

Exo Mani-North

The northernmost part of the Mani, on the west coast, begins at Verga as, strictly speaking, Kalamata is not a part of the area. From here to Kardamyli, where the Viros Gorge defines the southern part of this section, there are a number of things to see and do. The choices are varied. The coastline from Avia to Kitries offers several opportunities for swimming and relaxing in a seaside taverna. Further inland, there are two spectacular drives up into the mountains to either Altomira and beyond or around Kendro, above Kambos. In terms of sightseeing, the main attractions are two castles, a couple of interesting churches and two dramatic gorges.

Kambos – the Koumondouros Tower with snow–covered Taygetos in the background

Exo Mani-North

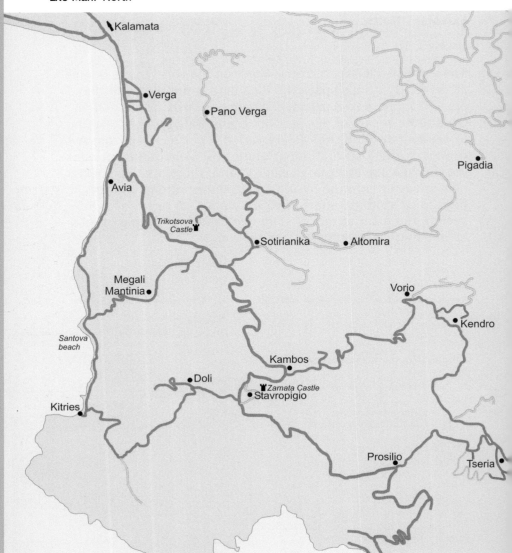

As you leave Kalamata, heading south to the Mani, you pass through **Verga** and, on your left by a bridge, you will see a large white marble statue of a Maniat Warrior. Running up towards the mountain slopes from here is an old stone wall with many *polemotrypes* (firing loops) built into it. Higher still you will see a derelict, round tower with more *polemotrypes* and larger openings for cannons. The wall used to run several hundred metres further, straight up the mountain and there was also a square tower on the other side of the road towards the sea but these have disappeared – probably due to 'quarrying'. The wall runs along the top of a dry riverbed and this combination presented a formidable obstacle to the Turkish attackers.

the Viros Gorge marks the southern border of this section
Santova Beach

This type of 'linear defence' is called a *verga* and hence the name of the area. It was built in a very short time under a system known as *maziki* (together) whereby everybody helped to raise the defence, in the same way that many towers were built at short notice with mutual collaboration within a family or clan.

In June 1826, the War of Independence was going badly for the Greeks and Ibrahim Pasha, the Egyptian general who was supporting the Turks with his army, was poised to attack the Mani. He had swept through the Peloponnese after the fall of Missolonghi (where Lord Byron had died of a fever) and seemed to be invincible. News of his approach caused the wall at Verga to be built hastily and then manned by the Maniats to thwart his intentions. He was defeated at Verga in a fierce battle that lasted for four days and then forced to withdraw to Kalamata when Kolokotronis approached over the Taygetos Mountains with a force of 2,000 men. The Pasha had simultaneously landed another force behind the Maniats at Pyrgos Dirou to attack them from the rear but this force was defeated by Maniat women who attacked it with stones, knives and sickles. (see 'Pyrgos Dirou').

a 'verga' at Verga

Kitries harbour

There is a strange footnote to this incident. En route to Verga, Ibrahim Pasha stopped at Messini where he had a disturbing dream. A local lady, *Kiria* Sykous, had a reputation as an interpreter of dreams and, when consulted, predicted impending disaster for Ibrahim. After his defeat he returned to Messini and ordered *Kiria* Sykous to be hanged in the square.

Soon after Verga the road divides just after the pastel-coloured Hotel Messinian Bay. The right fork runs along the coast as far as Kitries, the left fork is the quickest way to Kambos and on to Kardamyli and Stoupa. There are three roads that run down to the coast from this route at Mikri Mantinia, Kambos and Stavropigio – these will be mentioned later.

The left fork starts climbing up into the mountains in a series of long zig-zags and you have a dramatic view across the Bay of Messinia to the shore of the peninsula opposite and of Kalamata and Messini at the north end of the bay. After about 6 kilometres, you reach a small hamlet with a few houses and kafenion on the right. The turning here leads to both **Mikri** (small) and **Megalo** (big) **Mantinia** on the coast. Just past the bend at the end of the straight stretch of road is a turning to the left, sign-posted **Sotirianika** that leads to Trikotsova castle, the villages of Altomira and Pigadia and the church of Agios Nikolaos. Follow the road into the village, past the olive press

Agios Nikolaos, Sotirianika

on the right until you reach the *platia* (square). Cross the square and immediately you are faced with a T-junction. Right is signed to the church. To get to this wonderful spot, follow the road (and another sign), ignore a left turn, cross a small concrete bridge, ignore another left turn (where the walk on page 167 begins). The road now becomes a dirt track (but fine for a normal car). Ignore two further turnings on the right and turn left or park by a very derelict small building on the right. Sixty metres along this track on the left is the monastery.

The Church of Agios Nikolaos

The church is set in a beautiful spot with the derelict buildings nestling among trees and rocks below the wooded slopes of the mountains. Crude steps run between a spring and a derelict building that was also possibly once a church although it does have a *kamara* (vaulted room) below ground level. The steps lead up to a rather odd looking church with an arched doorway in the south wall and it is very apparent that this part of the building is a later addition, or 'exo-narthex', to the older 'cross in square' church. The original church has a very squat concrete dome and examination of the exterior and interior shows that this replaced an earlier dome, which had collapsed. The east end of the church has some cloisonne and dentil brick-work decoration that suggests a late Byzantine date. Inside the church, the exo-narthex is void of any decoration but there are the remains of frescoes in the arch of the west end of the original church and on the north wall. The iconostasis is made of concrete with plaster decorations and is obviously a much later addition. The frescoes on the south wall of the nave show four saints and above them, six

panels which tell the story of Adam and
Eve. The top three panels are damaged
but by looking at the feet, you can see
the creation of Adam who is joined by
another pair of naked feet when God,
wearing a grey tunic, presents Eve to
Adam. The centre of the bottom three
panels shows them with the apple tree
and then being banished but the first
panel has a third naked person who is
a mystery. On the opposite wall is a
very confusing scene. At the top is a
"Last Judgement" with Christ flanked by
saints etc. Below this it is possible to
make out the balance in which souls
are being weighed, a group waiting to
be judged and a 'river of fire' leading
down to the gaping jaws of hell with
various people en route. To the left of
the river are scenes of animals (foxes,
snakes and a griffin are identifiable)
carrying body parts towards the river
and below this fish are also carrying
body parts. The crucifixion on the
north wall shows a very flamboyant
horse with a long tail looped almost
into a knot and the two robbers crucified with their lower legs bent at the
knees and tied in an excruciatingly
painful position. The whole scene suggests a western influence although
Christ's feet have been individually
nailed to a cross bar rather than with
one nail through both feet crossed
over. This is a common feature in
Orthodox art with the result that
Christ's body on the cross is often less
contorted than in western art. The panels below the crucifixion are hard to
interpret and the left hand panel is
rather strange. A very ugly 'man' with
wings protruding from his shoulders is
shown atop a red building from which
several strange 'people' are floating out
of the windows. These are all white and
elongated without real shape and the
effect suggests they are phantoms.

The track that leads to the church continues around a bend and then opens
up into a fantastic *kalderimi* (stone

the templon, Agios Nikolaos, Sotirianika

the Last Judgement, Agios Nikolaos

the Crucifixion, Agios Nikolaos

bridge over the Koskarakos River

mule path) – worth a look and a photograph. The path leads all the way to the **Koskaraka Gorge** where a stone bridge spans it.

Back at the junction in the village the left and unsigned turning leads to the castle and up to Altomira. The castle lies at the end of a signed left-turn through the small hamlet of **Haravgi**. The road is concrete all the way.

Trikotsova Castle

The 'Kapetanakis Castle' can be dated to the early years of the 19th century. Documents in the museum in Kalamata name the castle's founder as Giorgios Kapetanakis, who was one of the leaders of the local Maniat clans, and they even mention the mason he hired to build the castle, a certain Niketas Mandrapelias. It was clearly built to watch over Kalamata and guard against a surprise Ottoman attack on the Mani before and during the Greek War of Independence. The main feature is a 3-storey tower surmounted by battlements and with four *klouvia* on the corners. Access to upper floors of this tower would have been a very difficult task for an attacker – as you will discover if you decide to enter it. Proceed with caution as the internal floors have long since collapsed though the vaulted ceiling of the ground floor is still standing. Forming part of the south wall is a small church, Profitis Illias. The views from here are spectacular and the strategic importance of the castle is obvious. The Kapetanakis family also had a tower at Avia and there was direct line of sight between both locations and one assumes, some sort of method of signalling. The same is true with the Castle of Zarnata to the south.

Retracing your steps, turning left

after Haravgi, the road starts to wind its way up and up to **Altomira**. The views get progressively more impressive and the landscape more agricultural. You will pass another left turn before the village, taking you up to **Ano Verga** and the beginning of the walk on page 165. Altomira itself seems largely deserted with a few houses in the process of renovation. After Altomira, the road rapidly deteriorates and is no longer suitable for a regular car – only a 4x4 can make the next village of **Pigadia**, through wonderful alpine forests. The village is very small but boasts a large square with a huge plane tree. The village only really comes to life in the summer months – either side of the peak period it is utterly peaceful and atmospheric.

Messinian Bay Hotel to Kitries

Though not as quick, the coastal route is a more picturesque way of getting from Kalamata into the Mani. There are a number of beaches along this stretch although Santova is the only one with sand. In the height of summer and especially at weekends, the road can get very congested and the sea fronting cafes very busy. It is more of a 'Greek' resort than Stoupa.

Avia is the first 'section' of this coast road and takes its name from ancient Avia that Pausanias says *"used to be called Ire and was one of the seven cities Homer makes Agamemnon promise to Achilles."* He explains that the name was changed to Avia in honour of Herakles' (Hercules') nurse who founded a sanctuary here to her former charge. He also says there was a sanctuary of Asklepios here but these have never been identified or excavated. There is a splendid tower house here and as you drive south you will see the battlements of the tower on the higher ground on your left. Just before you reach tavernas on both sides of the road, there is a turning to your left. There is no signpost but the concrete surface climbs to a T-junction where you turn right, drive a little further and take a turn to the left when you see that you are close to the tower. The tower and adjoining house were well fortified and the elevated position dominated the coastal route to the complex at Kitries further south. The '*klouvia*' on the tower are particularly well preserved and give it a most impressive appearance. It was owned by the Kapetanakis family who also owned Trikotsova Castle so this family was responsible for protecting the road into the Mani through the mountains and also via the coast. If you visit both sites you will see the strong similarity between the towers that suggests that the same builder was responsible for the construction of both. Just after Avia is the first road heading up to the main Kambos road, signed **Megali Mantinia.** The second turning left up to the main road lies immediately after you pass a wide riverbed that is the end of the Rindomo Gorge. This will bring you out just north of Kambos.

Kitries lies further down the coastal road, beyond sandy Santova Beach. This used to be a very important anchorage and walled complex and was the base for five of the Beys of the Mani. It was completely destroyed in an earthquake and almost no trace remains of this once extensive fortification except a large, arched gateway. Leake visited Kitries before the War of Independence and wrote,

"*The pyrgo of the Bey and adjoining buildings are large and agreeably situated on a height above the sea. Besides the Bey's pyrgo and its dependencies, the only buildings at Kitries are five or six magazines (shops) near the sea. In one of these I found a singular personage, a Turk keeping a shop in a country of Greeks.*" Lord Carnarvon visited Kitries in 1839 and recorded, "*We passed the ruined aque-*

Trikotsova Castle, Haravgi

view from the castle

Pigadia

The Kapetanakis Tower, Avia

ducts and fountains which marked the scene of much former splendour." His host, Petrobey Mavromichalis' brother, remarked that the government *"disputed him even the possession of his own house, battered as it was by Ibrahim Pasha's guns; and his means were too low to allow him to restore the ruins."*

Nowadays Kitries is a very peaceful and attractive fishing village with a small harbour and a couple of tavernas and, although nothing remains of the fortifications, it is well worth visiting for a long leisurely lunch by the sea. The coastal road ends here. Retrace your steps from the harbour and turn right up a steep road to reach **Stavropigio** via **Doli**. Before Doli you will pass through the hamlet of Kalianeika– a dirt track by the blue church leads to the fortified monastery of Rousaki. Unfortunately the church is kept locked. A tiny Byzantine chapel of Agios Nikolaos lies further along the road and is open though there is not much left of the paintings inside. As you approach Doli you will see a small blue sign – Agia Paraskevi – on your left pointing down a dirt road. This dirt road is badly eroded in places and unsuitable for an ordinary car so you should walk if you are not in a 4x4. The track finishes just above the church and you can see the cupola between the trees and shrubs. The drum is octagonal with arches and a slit window on each facet and just below the tiles of the dome is a second "fringe" of tiles. As you approach from the east, you can see it has a single apse with five narrow arches as external decoration in plaster or concrete – or both. The apse has a tikles roof and it too has a thin layer of concrete covering it. The church is kept locked.

There are the walls and foundations of ruined buildings around the church so it was probably a monastery once upon a time. One of the ruins has two large stone mill wheels so it must have been an olive press. Another ruin looks as though it might have been the base of a tower. The setting is beautiful with Kitries just visible far down below and the Bay of Messinia stretched out beyond. Return the way you came and continue into Doli. Doli is really two villages – Ano and Kato Doli. To enter Kato Doli, you turn left at the T-junction. The church here is dated 1800 and has some fine decorations externally but a new concrete bell-tower. There is a taverna in the village centre. The road goes through the village and down towards the shore but turns into a track after about one kilometre. It is signposted Kitries and Kalamata. If you turn right at the junction, after a short distance there is a road to your left signposted to Ano Doli. A copy of a print dated 1830 shows Doli (both parts) as having two churches with massive pointed spires. These have disappeared (if they ever existed – which is doubtful) and the church at Ano Doli has been 'restored'. It is dated 1805 on the smaller bell tower and there are frescoes above the doors. The rest have been plastered over.

Kambos

The village of Kambos ('plain' or 'plateau') is dominated by two features that are both visible from a long way off – the large modern church and the castle of Zarnata on the hill above the village. The village itself sits on either side of the main road with kafenia and a couple of small shops lining the road. There is a sharp right hand bend at the far end and just past this, on your right, there is a small Byzantine Church with a playground behind. The church is always open and is dedicated to the **Saints Theodoros** and they are depicted on a faded fresco in the tympanum above the south door. Outside, the church is fairly unimpressive but inside most of the wall space is covered with frescoes and although some are damaged and faded, there is easily enough to get an impression of how glorious the church must have been in its heyday. The dome is supported on two large columns and the Pantocrator is badly faded but between the four slit windows, the frescoes are in better condition. Only part of the decorated marble ring at the base of the drum is still intact. There is an old, carved wooden iconostasis, dating from the 18th century with three doors leading through to the sanctuary that is divided into three sections with arches between them. The 'Panagia Platytera' decorates the conch of the apse and the rest of the sanctuary is covered with frescoes of saints and martyrs. The most interesting features of the wall paintings are to be found on the ceiling of the main vault where there are a number of paintings collectively known as *the Ainoi* ('Praises' – see page 41). Close to these scenes in the north-west corner is a two-tiered, domed building. The top tier depicts two crowned Byzantine nobles and beneath them sits a Muslim caliph and a man in western clothing wearing a stylish hat and ruff. These represent the 'Earth's Judges' from psalm 148; "*Kings of the earth, all nations, princes, earth's judges all; both young men, yea, and maidens too, old men and children small. Let them God's name praise.*"

From the church it is possible to walk the short distance to the Koumoundouros Tower and the Mycenaean tombs (these are signed further along the main road but there is nowhere to park). Walk past the playground behind the church and turn left down a narrow path just after the village school. Follow this path, ignoring the right turn and veering left at a house where the path becomes walled in. Cross

Agios Nikolaos, between Kitries and Doli

Agia Paraskevi, outside Doli

Kambos – Mycenaean Tomb, Koumoundouros Tower and Zarnata Castle

Agioi Theodoros, Kambos

over a tiny bridge and after 150m, just before reaching the main road, head right to the ruined tower with a statue of Koumoundouros. The tower was originally a windmill (the round end) but was turned into a fortified building, constructed so that the entrance was flanked by part of the tower and defensive fire from upper windows could protect it. The Koumoundouros family were one of the leading *kapetani* in this part of the Mani and Alexandros Koumoundouros (1817–1883) was Prime Minister of Greece on no less than ten occasions, during the turbulent period that followed Independence. It was he who during one of his periods in office, used government troops to end the last great Maniat feud at Kita. There is a local tale that believes the tower to be connected to Zarnata Castle by a tunnel. In the early 1800s, Theodoros Kolokotronis was wounded while fighting here for the Fourth Bey, 'Koumoundouraki'. The Turks had deposed him as Bey in favour of Antonbey Grigorakis and had sent an army to subdue him. Kolokotronis recorded in his biography, "*The chieftains and other Maniats fought with us and I was wounded but we took possession of a tower and during the night we reached the fort.*" (Zarnata). Koumoundouros was forced to submit and taken as a prisoner to Constantinople where he died but Kolokotronis escaped capture. The *tholos* or 'beehive' tomb is below and to the right of the tower. The conical roof has collapsed but the entrance, surmounted by a massive stone lintel, is still intact and the interior walls show how the tomb was constructed with the courses of stones diminishing towards the centre to form the beehive. It was excavated in the late nineteenth century and its finds are now in the National Museum in Athens.

Continuing on from Kambos, past the signs to the tower (if you did not want to walk from the church then there is a lay-by further along the road on the right) the road snakes up to **Stavropigio**, a village that has narrow winding alleyways and many old houses that can only be explored on foot. The village also provides the best access to Zarnata Castle. On a right hand bend in the main road, you will see a small cafe on your left with a side road running straight up into the village. There is a T-junction a little further along this side street and here you turn left up a narrow street with old houses on both sides until you reach a small square with a church immediately in front of you. Pass this on the right side and continue a little further. Where the road starts to bend to the right, park the car and take the track running up the hill past some new houses. It is only a ten-minute walk from here to the summit.

Zarnata Castle

Like so many of the castles in the Mani, Zarnata has a complicated and

view from Zarnata Castle

uncertain history. Kevin Andrews noted that the lower levels of Zarnata's walls were ancient and were simply added to by successive occupiers. Therefore it is thought that Zarnata was the acropolis of ancient Gerenia. Certainly its medieval history is one of constant change in terms of its occupiers. The earliest record of Zarnata is that in 1427 the Byzantine ruler of Morea, Theodore, ceded it to his brother Constantine Palaeologos. The Turkish dominance of the castle following 1453 seems to have been anything but constant and during the next two centuries control was taken away from Maniats when a foreign power was enjoying a successful campaign – the Turks in 1670 and 1715 and the Venetians in 1685. The castle is fairly ruined nowadays but the short walk up to it gives a great 360-degree panorama. It is hard to imagine that in its heyday there were 500 houses making up the village of Zarnata. The only remaining evidence of Byzantine occupation are some sections of medieval wall and the Church of Agios Nikolaos in which some excellent 15th century frescoes can still be seen – the church is kept locked.

To get back to the main road you can continue in the direction you arrived through the village of **Malta**. The road takes you past the village church and then past the lone Mavrikos tower on a hill on your right. It is possible to climb up to it by a path which runs down the side of a chain–link fence at the side of the road and then weaves up the hill but it is very overgrown and thorny so wear long trousers. It was built in 1814 according to the date on the *zematistra* over the main door where there is also a carved head and the mouth of a cannon. There are additional stone cannons protruding below the battlements. Mavrikos is described as 'a notable of Malta'. It was obviously built for defensive purposes which is why the main door is on the first floor and could only be reached by removable wooden stairs. The ground floor is a storeroom or *gouva* with a vaulted ceiling. From here it is a few hundred metres to the main road where you turn left to continue

Koumondouros Tower, Kambos

Zaranata Castle perched above Stavropigio

Zarnata Castle

Mavrikos Tower, Malta

your journey south. After a series of bends you will soon reach the highest point of the road to Kardamyli – from here it is downhill all the way. The view down the the Mani suddenly opens up and a lay-by on the right is a good place to stop and enjoy it. The next village you come to is **Prosilio**, nestling in the hillside and dominated by its large and handsome church. The turning into the village also leads to **Tseria**, 5km higher up the mountain. Tseria is perched on the northern side of the impressive Viros Gorge and the views down into it are worth the drive. The satellite villages of Katafigio and Pedino lie just beneath Tseria itself. The road through Tseria is fairly narrow and so it is easiest to park as you enter the village and walk. Once you have passed the kafenion on your left you will come to a tiny square with a church. The church is dated 1836 while the cupola on top is dated 1844. There are some wonderful carved, stone decorations on the side of the church next to the tiny square. These include some dancers and musicians, a child-like drawing of a donkey being induced to move by a 'bait' (carrot?) being dangled in front of it on a stick and, just left of and slightly above the door, the Archangel Michael who is often depicted with a sword in hand and a fierce, grotesque face on the breastplate of his armour. Keep straight and take the left fork that bends round to the gorge. A *kalderimi* leads down to the riverbed. There are a number of possible combinations of walks that link surrounding villages via the gorge– for more details refer to 'Inside the Mani, a Walking Guide' or to the relevant Avavasi walking map. The gorge should not be walked after a few days of persistent rain. One area of Tseria is called Zaharias after the *klepht* leader who was murdered in a tower (see page 161).

The Gaitses villages

Driving from Kambos to Prosilio gives no indication of a cluster of villages secretly hidden high in the mountains around another gorge. They can be visited in a circular route, starting at either Kambos (coming from Kalamata take the last left before the sharp bend) or Tseria (take the right turn clearly visible on leaving the village). Either way, it is a beautiful drive on concrete all the way and takes around 30 minutes to drive non-stop. Going from Tseria, the narrow road winds its way across low hills, passing a honey warehouse on the left. Across the road from here is a ruined church. If you walk up the wooded hill above this church, you will find the Monastery of Panagia Chelmou, which is virtually invisible from the road. The church interior is wall to wall with frescoes that are probably 18th century and many of them are in a reasonable condition. Just below the monastery buildings is a clear, fresh spring that on a hot day provides welcome refreshment. Back on the road, Gaitses soon comes into view. This collection of villages seem to constantly change their name – they are also known collectively as Kendro although the first village you come to is individually known as Kendro too. The modern names are simplicity itself – **Kendro** (Centre), **Vorio** (North) and **Anatoliko** (East). As you enter Kendro, the right fork takes you into the village square where there is a kafenion. The right turn from opposite the parking area takes you round to Anatoliko. The left fork takes you past the rest of the village and on to Vorio. The next right turn on this road is the other end of the loop to Anatoliko and the modern taverna there is open all year round. To get a peek at the Rindomo Gorge take this right turn and then turn left down the dirt track (which is fine for a regular car) opposite a greenish chapel on your right. Wiggle along the track and turn left at a small white chapel. Crowning the hill opposite is the monastery of Profitas Ilias. The road now creeps close to the edge of the gorge and a track for walkers is signed on the right – if you walk a little way down and have binoculars you may be able to spot a series of stone-built water mills clinging to the side of the gorge looking straight ahead. (There are close-up photos of these mills in the museum in Kardamyli). The road now passes under the monastery and a little further on a track zig-zags up to it. The view down to the gorge is even more vertiginous from here. The 18th century paintings inside are unfortunately kept under lock and key and indeed sometimes the gate to get in is also locked. Vorio is a pleasant village so stop for refreshments in the kafenion by the large church. The road goes straight through the village and rejoins the road from Kendro (which you will be on if you did not take the gorge detour). The road now begins its descent to Kambos, passing the turn-ing to Orovas, a village of no particular note, en route. You arrive in Kambos by the main church and left at the high street brings you handily straight to two kafenia.

Back on the main road there is one more village after Prosilio before Kar-damyli – **Kalyves**. There is not a lot happening here but it does offer another perspective on the Viros Gorge. There is a large 'car park' when you reach the hamlet and just below it is a small church among some ruined houses. The frescoes here are quite badly damaged but on the wall by the door they seem to have a theme of martyrs and include an inverted cruci-fixion, a decapitation (John the Bap-tist?) and someone tied to a wheel that appears to rotate over a fire. From outside the church there is a stunning view of the gorge.

carving in Tseria

Vorio

Rindomo Gorge – on the right bank are remains of a series of water mills

bee-hives, Kalyves

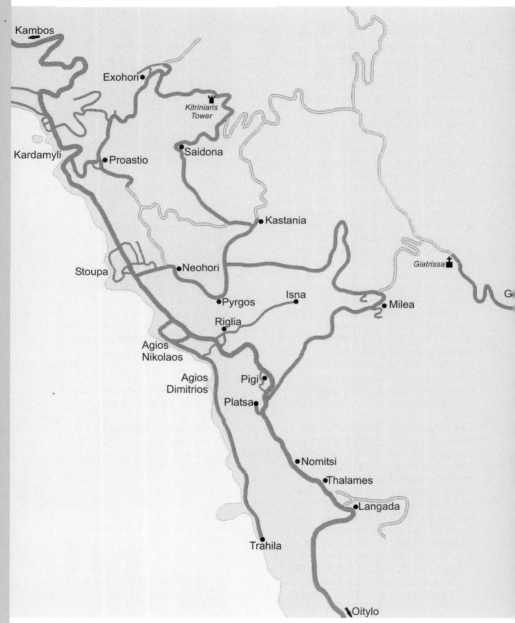

This section of the Mani is now the area's main foreign tourist destination. The combined coastal villages of Kardamyli, Stoupa and Agios Nikolaos offer contrasting styles of holiday. The relatively modern village of Stoupa and its two, great sandy beaches has led this development while Kardamyli and the fishing port of Agios Nikolaos have grown, in terms of tourism, at a slower rate. The hills inland are easily accessible and have plenty to offer. Exploration from the coast can be done by car or moped – from Kardamyli up to Proastio and Exohori, from Stoupa up to Neohori, Pyrgos, Kastania, Saidona and Milea and from Agios Nikolaos to Riglia, Pigi and Platsa. There is now a tarmac road linking Exohori to Saidona and Milea to Platsa.

Kardamyli

Kardamyli has a long history. According to Pausanias, it was originally named after Kardamos, the son of Lakon who was the first king of Lakonia and it always had ties with Sparta. In Homer's Iliad, he records that this was one of the towns offered by Agamemnon to Achilles to heal the rift that he had caused by taking the captive girl Briseis from him, so it would seem to have been a recognised town in Mycenaean times. Pausanias recorded that there was a sacred precinct in Kardamyli that was dedicated to the Nereids, the sea nymphs. And yet another link between Kardamyli and the gods is the so-called tomb of the Dioscouri, the heavenly twins, Castor and Pollux (mythology would have us believe that they were the product of a famous seduction, when Zeus, in the guise of a swan, overpowered Leda who eventually produced two eggs. Castor and Pollux were hatched from one egg, while the other produced equally distinguished offspring – Helen and Clytemnestra).

This double tomb is carved in the rock alongside the path that leads towards the acropolis from Pano Kardamyli. It is not known whose tombs these really are and Pausanias does not report on them (although he usually recorded the location of important tombs and any history they may have). He does report that in the town there was "*a sanctuary of Athene and a Karneian Apollo in the local Dorian style.*" On the acropolis above Pano Kardamyli there is evidence that it was used from Neolithic times until medieval times but it has never been properly excavated. Strabo mentions, "*Kardamyli, which is situated on a rock fortified by nature.*" Herodotus referred to Kardamyli only briefly, to identify the location of Asine (Koroni), but this signifies that Kardamyli was well enough known to be used as a point of reference.

From the 1st Century BC until the 2nd Century AD, Kardamyli was the main port of Sparta. Gythio had been the main port but had joined the anti-Spartan League of Free Lakonian Cities. Sparta was linked to Kardamyli by a path over the Taygetos Mountains. The island just off the harbour is called Meropi and has a small Venetian castle and a church dedicat-

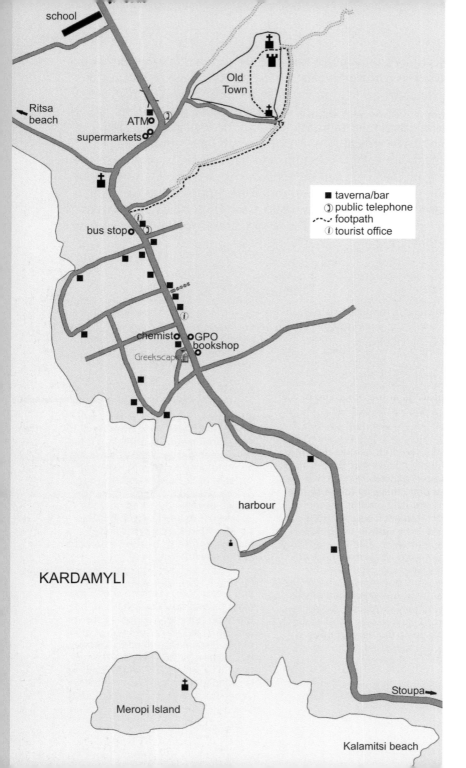

school

Ritsa
beach

ATM

supermarkets

Old
Town

bus stop

■ taverna/bar
☾ public telephone
- - - footpath
ⓘ tourist office

chemist ●GPO
bookshop

Greekscape

harbour

KARDAMYLI

Meropi Island

Stoupa→

Kalamitsi beach

ed to the Virgin Mary. Leake says there was a monastery there in his time.

The village itself is charming. Handsome houses with several tavernas, shops and kafenia flank the high street and there are other places to eat and drink off the main street towards the sea. At the southern end of the town is a rough road that takes you down into the harbour. It is extremely picturesque and the harbour jetty has what used to be a fortified customs house and a small church built on it. The chimney that dominates the skyline was once a factory producing olive soap. The main beach, Ritsa, lies down the concrete road that runs down the side of the main church. The long pebbly beach has some shade and there is a taverna at the far end (which also rents sun beds and umbrellas); beyond that, the campsite has a cafe too. Even in the height of summer it does not feel too crowded. Kardamyli's other beach is at the other end of the village. Once you have passed the last two tavernas on the right beyond the high street the road bends to the left. Where the wall that defines the lay-by ends, a path begins that takes you all the way down to Kalamitsi Beach. You can also drive there by following the road further past the entrance to the Kalamitsi Hotel and turning right where the road sweeps right. Again the beach is pebbly with lots of rocks for good snorkelling. There is no cafe or taverna on this beach.

There are numerous possible walks starting or finishing in Kardamyli – the council provides a map of way-marked paths or refer to **Inside the Mani, A Walking Guide.**

the tombs of the Dioscouri, Kardamyli

the Mycenaean acropolis behind Old Kardamyli

Ritsa Beach, Kardamyli

Kalamitsi Beach, Kardamyli

We chose the Mani

The Pioneers

It is not an easy decision to leave everything that is familiar and pack up your family and move to a foreign country with a completely different language and culture. Deborah and Erhard had already done it once, to do it a second time was like walking on steps that they had already trodden.

Deborah and Erhard and their family moved here last September from the south west coast of Ireland. Erhard came first and bought a large plot of land through Greekscape. The movement of the Gulf Stream and the steady worsening weather had finally played its toll on their well being. The journey took them 10 days travelling with two camper vans and a horse box. As well as the horses, of course there were 2 dogs, 3 cats and 3 children and all their personal belongings. Their approach into Kardamili was a sight to behold.

We had arranged a long term rental house for them with a large garden right in the centre of the village of Proastio and as they all de-camped on that summer evening the villagers were extremely curious to meet them, particularly the children and the teacher from the local school.

Proastio is the only village that still has its own village school but numbers were dropping and if they didn't have two more children by the beginning of September the school was threatened with closure. George (6) and Fionnuala (8) had saved the day. As for Emma (16) she just came along for the ride. She reckoned a "gap year" in Greece before going on to do 'A' levels could be an interesting experience.

With the olive picking season fast approaching Erhard had to move pretty quickly. He knew nothing about olive picking and he had 200 trees to pick. However, there were plenty of villagers to offer advice and he struck up a close friendship with one of them. When it comes to picking olives it's 'all for one and one for all.' Erhard first had to help Vassilis with his olives and he soon learnt the rudiments.

Spread large sheets on the ground. Beat the olives off the trees with a large beating fork. Collect olives from sheets and put into large sack. Tie up large sack. Hump all large sacks onto the back of trailer. It's not work for the fainted hearted but by the end of the season bodies are fit and tanned and well toned muscles have been developed.

As for Deborah she had her work cut out settling down the children into their new schools. Emma decided to bite the bullet and attend the Secondary School in Kardamili. She told me it was really tough at the time not knowing what anyone was talking about. However, a bright girl, she soon started to get a grasp of the language and make friends.

As for the two youngest ones their freedom is unparalleled. They start school at 8.30 a.m. and finish at 1.30 p.m. Then it's playing with their friends in the village, going for a ride on the horses or popping down to the beach for a swim.

Unsurprisingly, they love it here and Deborah likes the fact that they are in a small family grouped school. The children ages range from 5 – 11. However, there are only 20 of them, one full time highly dedicated teacher and several volunteers.

You could really feel the children's sense of belonging in this small village community school.

Recently Deborah and Erhard bought some more land adjacent to their own plot with 200 more olive trees. Deborah has worked all her life with horses in England and in Ireland, where she ran her own riding school. They now plan to extend the farm and start up a riding school and trekking centre. They are also busily learning the language which is a high priority. Deborah, Erhard and their family are now a familiar sight in the village and they are all extremely happy they have made their escape to the Mani.

Written by Lydia Ellis
Managing Director
Greekscape Real Estate

"Travel must be adventurous to feel the needs and hitches of life more nearly: to come down off this feather bed of civilization and find the globe granite underfoot and strewn with cutting flints" The bumps are vital. They keep the adrenalin pumping around"

From the book "Winding Paths"

The Troupakis Fortified Complex and Museum– Pano Kardamyli

The "family complex" in Pano Kardamyli is a good example of a typical Outer Mani walled and fortified, defensive family grouping which served as a "clan" stronghold and power base. It lies to the east of the main road through the village, behind the newer houses and is well worth investigating. To reach it, walk along the narrow road that leads from the War Memorial in the small square at the north end of the main street or drive, following the signs opposite the supermarkets.

The Troupakis family grew to prominence and power in Androuvitsa (Exochori) and then created the complex in Kardamyli because the harbour gave them access to the sea. The family are thought to have been refugees from Mystras when the city fell to the Turks in 1461. As fugitives, they moved to caves in the Taygetos Mountains at Androuvitsa along with many others from Mystras. The Maniats had long been accustomed to taking refuge in caves in times of trouble and there are many examples of fortified caves throughout the peninsula. The local dialect word "Troupa" means a "hole" and this troglodyte existence gave the Troupakis family their name. The complex was started in the 17th century and in the early 18th century was established by 'Kapitanios' Panayotis Troupakis who had four sons; Michalis, Petros, Theodoros and Ioannis. As the oldest son, Michalis inherited the main section of the complex by the Church of Agios Spiridon, with his brothers living in adjacent, mutually defensive properties. Michalis became the second Bey of the Mani in 1779 and as well as Kardamyli, he acquired Zarnata Castle at Kambos and the defensive complex at Kitries. Kardamyli remained, however, Michael's administrative centre, residence and main garrison. His 'reign' as Bey ended in 1782 when he was beheaded by the Sultan. Michael's son, Kapitanios Mourtzinos Troupakis, became head of the clan and gave his name to the "Mourtzinos War Tower" which still stands in the complex. Above the door of the War Tower is the date 1808 which is when it was rebuilt following its destruction during a three-month siege by a rival family. This occurred in 1805 and resulted in Mourtzinos being exiled to Zakynthos for three years until given amnesty by the Turks and allowed to return to Kardamyli. Here he restored the complex and reclaimed leadership as *kapitanios*. In 1813, a visiting Englishman, J.R. Cockerell gave this description of Mourtzinos and the complex.

"His castle consists of a courtyard and a church surrounded by various towers. There is a stone bench at his door where he sits surrounded by his vassals and his relations who all stand unless invited to sit. The village people bring him presents, tributes as it were, of fruit, flowers etc. On a lofty rock close by is a watch-tower where watch is kept night and day. The whole gave us the picture of feudal life new and hardly credible to a nineteenth century Englishman."

The watch tower referred to is "Petreas'" Tower which stands on a rocky hilltop south of the complex and gives an all round view of the approaches to Kardamyli, including the sea. The seaward aspect is further improved by a small watchtower above the harbour. Another reference also gives an insight into the position and power of the kapitanios:

"He rang a large bell every midday before the meal and every evening

before supper, thus publicly inviting those who were in need or those willing, to dine; and not a day passed that at least fifty to one hundred people, strangers to the family, were fed by him."

In 1821, on the eve of the Greek War of Independence, Theodoros Kolokotronis established his headquarters at Kardamyli and here was joined by Petrobey Mavromichalis, bringing with him his Maniat army north from Areopolis. According to local legend, they played chess in the courtyard next to the church of Agios Spiridon, using soldiers as the chess pieces on a board marked out in chalk. Kolokotronis doesn't mention this in his memoirs (maybe he lost) and his relationship with Mavromichalis seems to have been very guarded as we can see from his own words,

"He (Mavromichalis) behaved himself tolerably well towards me and it is not true that he betrayed me to the Turks, for he had not the power to do so even if he had the will, for besides my friendship with Mourtzinos, it is a custom in Mani to help everyone who goes there for a place of refuge."

From Kardamyli they marched on Kalamata and there defeated the Turkish garrison in the first victory of the war that finally liberated Greece. To quote Kolokotronis again, *"On the 23rd March we fell upon the Turks at Kalamata. They were led by Arnoutogles, a man of some importance in Tripolitsa (Tripoli). We had two thousand Maniats, with Mourtzinos and Petrobey."*

Mourtzinos's only son, Dionysos, also distinguished himself as a great fighter in this war and in 1830 became War Minister in the newly formed Greek Government.

The renovation work to turn the complex into a museum was finally finished in 2005. In 1967 the last surviving family members, Maria and Evangelia Boukou-

the Troupakis Complex: scale model in the museum

exhibits in the museum

the museum, once the living quarters for clan members

Agios Spiridon

valea, donated the buildings to the Greek government specifically for this purpose and with a hefty EU grant, this aim was achieved. The main exhibits in the museum must be the complex itself and an explanation outlining the work involved in the renovation is in the vaulted ground floor of the living quarters, where a scale model describes the function of each building. The two floors above house a limited number of exhibits and commentary on traditional Mani life – all very tastefully presented. The view to the ancient acropolis inland and down to the coast from the steps leading to the main tower, are exceptional. At the time of going to print there was no entrance fee.

The church, Agios Spyridon, is from the same period and was used by the family. It is kept locked and in any case is more attractive from the outside with intricate carvings on the bell tower.

The two most immediate villages above are **Agia Sofia** and **Petrovouni**. Both are reached from the main street in Kardamyli by turning left just after the bookshop. En route to Petrovouni you will pass a green walker's sign on your left. This leads to a wonderful kalderimi that winds its way up to Petrovouni (in just 10–15 minutes). The hamlet is perched on the edge of the escarpment overlooking Kardamyli and is centred around a small square, off to the left of the road, with a small, restored tower house and some old houses.

Agia Sophia

On the corner of the road, opposite the entrance to the square, is an old house with an arched door at ground level and two arched windows higher up. It is worth noting the carvings on the wall between the windows – a very good Byzantine double-headed eagle at the top, a cross and hieroglyphs below this and a crude lion or dog, a half sun and a rosette. By wandering through the hamlet from the square, following the red way marks along cobbled alleys, you will soon get stunning views down to the coast. Keep following the path to get to the kalderimi coming up from below. From this point the track leading down the side of a ruined house (with what must be one of the best views in the area) leads to a junction in walking paths and what used to be the local launderette. From this shady junction you can loop back to the car by following the sign to Exohori but then bearing right past a colourful house until you meet the main road. Turn right to get back to the car.

Heading inland from the square you pass the post-Byzantine church of Panagia Zoodigos Pigi – the Virgin Mary as "the life-giving fountain" – on the right. From here the road runs alongside a small gorge, on the opposite side of which you can see the post-Byzantine church of the monastery of Koimesis Theotokou (Dormition of the Virgin) but known locally as Karaveli. To reach it, take the first dirt road leading off to the left as you come round the apex of the gorge and this leads past a stone threshing-circle to the monastery. As you approach the church from the east you can see it has a single, semi-hexagonal apse and is surmounted by an ornate cupola with relief decorations all the way round the drum. This has fourteen arched facets, each with a small tympanum and a stylised angel inside. Above each arch the design alternates between a circle and a small tympanum and above these is a highly decorated band which runs round the dome.

Return to the road, turn left and continue towards **Agia Sofia**. The road follows the contours inland to negotiate another gorge and then heads back towards the coast until you reach the village of Agia Sofia which sits on a spur overlooking Kardamyli. On the end of the spur stands the post-Byzantine church of Agia Sofia that gave its name to the village that is also known as Gournitsa. Most of the houses in the village are old. Some have been restored while others are derelict. As you drive in, there is an open area with a ruined building with only two walls remaining and you should park here because driving in the village is virtually impossible. As you make your way towards the church, you come to a wide-open area of rock and scrub and some of the rock faces clearly show evidence of earlier quarrying. The church is kept locked but inside is covered in frescoes, the most striking being a wonderful painting of an elephant. The local keyholder can no longer be contacted and so to get in, the priest in Kardamyli needs to be found.

The church is taller than most, which might explain why there are so many tie beams between the various internal walls. All of these beams have been plastered and painted with various decorations. There are two very large marble columns supporting the dome. The church sits right next to a cavernous water cistern whose lid is visible amongst the rocks. To get a closer look, go through the gate towards the old priest's house and scramble right. The opening, set in the cliff face, is obvious.

water troughs, Petrovouni

tower house, Petrovouni

kalderimi from Petrovouni back down to Kardamyli
the church of Agia Sophia

Proastio

Proastio ('suburb') can be reached either by continuing up the concrete road from Petrovouni and turning right at the junction, or the quicker route is to head south from Kardamyli, past Kalamitsi beach and then immediately left. It was one of the oldest and most important settlements in N.W. Mani according to a survey conducted in 1479. In 1618 there were 100 families living there and throughout the 17th century it suffered from periodic attacks by the Turks. After the Turkish-Venetian War in Crete (1645 - 1665), when the Maniats had openly supported the Venetians, the Turks increased their attacks on the Mani and in 1670 they burnt Proastio as it had become an important Maniat military base. A record dated 1743 shows that Proastio was the seat of a Bishopric and there are more than 40 religious buildings – monasteries, parish and family churches – in and around the village. The village is interesting to explore on foot (and to play "How many churches can we find?") and three kafenia offer a chance to relax after such activity. These shops have renowned wooden wine barrels full of cheap but very good rose wine, which not only can be tasted on the spot, but if you take some plastic water bottles with you, can be taken away too.

Recommended churches to visit in Proastio:

Church of Agios Nikolaos

From the Kalamitsi entrance, the main road enters the village with the largest kafenion on your right and a mini market on the left. Just around the next bend, the road widens into a small square in the centre of which is the church of Agios Nikolaos. One of the lucky few, this church has enjoyed a recent restoration, revealing its mid-Byzantine cloisonne brickwork on the eastern end of the church (it was once completely covered with external plaster). The addition of an extensive narthex was probably carried out in the 16th century and the Venetian-inspired bell tower is probably early 18th century. An inscription states it was repaired in 1789. As is typical of the Mani, there are numerous folkloric carvings on it. One consequence of the restoration is that it is now kept locked. The keys can be found at the kafenion at the end of the alley opposite, which may involve finding the local priest.

Church of Agioi Vasileios and Spyridon

Continuing along the main road towards Exohori, a short distance after Agios Nikolaos, there is a small road off to your right that is sign-posted to Neohori and Kastania. Follow this road past the cemetery and the sandstone quarry and you come to a church on your left on the side of the road above a low bank. This is a twin church dedicated to Saint Vasileios on the north side (left hand door) and Saint Spyridon on the south side (right hand door). A small low door connects the two churches inside which were originally two barrel-vaults but at some time the southern vault collapsed and was replaced by the wooden roof which is there now. The northern external wall has been strengthened by buttresses to prevent the same thing happening to that vault. Unlike many other twin churches where one church was 'added' to another, these two were built at the same time in 1754 by the Pourgalis family and the frescoes were painted by Anagnostis Dimangelakis of *Koutifari* (now Thalames).

Monastery of Agioi Theodoroi

Further on along the same road you pass a tower off to your right and then reach a small concrete road which runs up a slight slope to your left, signed to the monastery. It was dedicated to the Sts. Theodoros and was established in the 13th Century. Documents claim that at one time is was the home to over 100 monks. The main church is dedicated to the Koimesis Theotokou (Dormition of the Virgin) and is kept locked. The smaller, older church is in very bad condition and visibly worsens each year. A last-gasp attempt to save it from total collapse has required scaffolding and internal joists to support it. It is unclear whether the Ephorate of Byzantine Antiquities in Kalamata intends to rebuild it.

Agios Nikolaos, Proastio

Agioi Vasileios and Spyridon, Proastio

Church of Agia Triada (the Holy Trinity)

This church is some 250 metres to the east of the large central church of the Eisodia tis Theotokou (refer to the map). You'll come across a large walled open space with fruit trees. There is a large arched gateway with faded frescoes and a long path running to the church. It was built in 1740 by, amongst others the Troupakis' from Kardamyli and the local bishop, as an inscription inside informs. It is a whitewashed, vaulted building and from outside it has no particularly distinguished features. Inside it is decorated throughout with frescoes from 1745 by Anagnostes Selemperdakis and Nikolaos of Nomitsi. The former is believed to have painted the church of Ag. Nikolaos in the centre of Proastio. One unusual image to look out for is a scene depicting the Archangels Michael and Gabriel who have just rescued a boy from the lake who had been thrown in, with a millstone around his neck, by three monks in a boat.

Agioi Theodoroi, Proastio
Agia Triada, Proastio – the rescue of a boy by the archangels Michael and Gabriel

Agios Giorgios

As you leave Proastio on the Exohori road, there is a walled enclosure with a church on your left over a small gorge. To get to it on a reasonable dirt road, turn left after you have passed the school on your right and the olive press on your left. The walled enclosure and outbuildings surrounding the church indicate it was once a monastery. The church is always open and the image of its patron is on the left by the templon. Most of the frescoes are faded and/or damaged and the original roof has been replaced but you can still see the martyrdoms of various saints, scenes from the life and passion of Christ and other stories from the bible.

On the main road, opposite the turnoff to Agios Giorgios, you can see the cuts and "shelves" where the rock has been quarried for limestone blocks. About 50 metres from the road (follow the track and bear slightly right) is a small Mycenaean tomb. A short tunnel, the smooth sides of which taper towards the top, was cut into the rock. The entrance to the tomb is closed by a mesh screen but you can see into the tomb chamber which is circular inside with low walls that taper slightly towards a flat ceiling. It is not a terribly exciting site but it bears witness to an early occupation of the area.

The main road continues up to Exo-hori, passing the tiny hamlet of **Lakos** en route.

Exohori

Some maps refer to two villages – Exohori and Androuvitsa – while others refer to Nikovo, Kolibetseika, Pripitsa and Hora too. More recent maps refer to the first village as Exohori and the second as Hora. Historically, Androuvitsa and Exohori were part of one 'hora' as a Venetian doc–

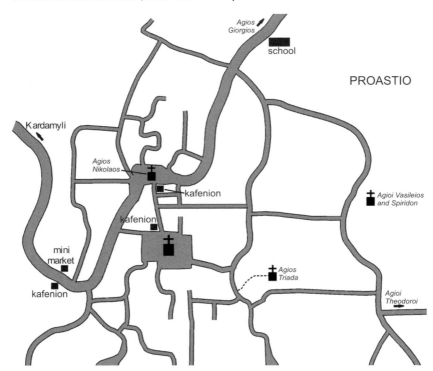

ument of 1618 records. This Hora was the seat of one of the local governors, the kapetanios, as early as the 13th century and in the 14th century a section of this region was given to a Frankish Nobleman, Nicolas Acciaiuoli. In the 15th century it was a fief of the Palaiologos family who were the ruling Byzantine family. During the 17th century, the area suffered from Turkish raids as did Proastio. Leake records that the Kapetanios of Androuvitsa in 1805 was Panayotis Troupakis who governed 700 houses in the district. This suggests that the Hora extended to Kardamyli where the Troupakis family had their stronghold. The first building you pass in Exohori is the olive press on the left and a little further along is a taverna with a large terrace (on the right). Most of the village lies to the right of the road. Like Proastio, there are numerous churches and chapels to discover throughout the village. After the taverna, and a couple more bends, you reach the old school building on the left. This is now a museum, officially open from June to September. It houses several interesting displays, ranging from artefacts from days gone by (including a range of old carpentry tools as the village was renowned for this skill, supplying the area with furniture, barrels, washboards, troughs – indeed just about everything) and weaving paraphernalia to a cabinet full of guns (including a German machine gun) and a display chronicling the history of the Greek drachma from 1900–2000. There is no admission fee so the museum sustains itself by selling gift packs of olive oil and olive soap, books, calendars and a DVD.

Note: If you are wondering why the school is no longer used it is due to a lack of clients. Severe depopulation has been the norm throughout the Mani as better lives were sought in Kalamata, Athens or overseas. Out of all the hill villages mentioned in this section from Exohori to Platsa, only Proastio still has an operating junior school. All of the other villages did have their own school at one stage but have

a garlanded St George, Agios Giorgios, Proastio view from the monastery to snow-covered Profitas Ilias

Mycenaean Tomb, Proastio

the museum, Exohori

been closed within the last few decades. Daily buses now ferry students down to the junior school in Stoupa or the high school in Kardamyli.

From the school you can clearly see Hora running along a ridge ahead of you. Just past the school a sign indicates a concrete road to 'Kato Hora' down to the left. This can be driven and on the other side of the small gulley there is a convenient area to park. Directly above you is the 18th century Sotiros (Saviour) or Metamorphosis church. Its bell tower, which seems to have lost its top layer, has numerous carved stones in it. Inside, the frescoes are faded but there is enough to give the date of 1736. The keyholder lives right by the church. Another church with a story to tell lies at the end of the ridge. Agios Nikolaos is where the English travel writer Bruce Chatwin requested his ashes to be scattered upon his death in 1989. Chatwin had spent some time in the Mani and this church was one of his favourite picnic spots. In taking the short walk there it is easy to see why. From the car-parking area walk up into the village and turn left down. After a few houses turn left along a narrow dirt path at a house with two large millstones outside. The slightly overgrown path soon brings you to the tranquil location of Agios Nikolaos. The church is locked but for once this is not frustrating as the setting – it is the setting which is

atmospheric. The exterior walls hold some ancient marble pieces.

Back on the main road, it now bends away from Hora. To get a good look at the Viros Gorge turn left at a blue sign that says gorge in Greek ('*farangi*'). The road leads to the top end of Hora where the Hotel Viros Gorge commands spectacular views and its restaurant is open to all. The village visible on the other side of the gorge is Tseria. If you want to walk there and back, follow the road leading downwards into the gorge and climb up a well-preserved *kalderimi* on the other side.

The main road is now tarmac all the way to Saidona which saves an enormous amount of time if you are spending the day exploring the villages away from the coast as well as giving an aerial perspective on the coastline.

Back on the coast there is nothing in the 7km that divides Kardamyli and Stoupa except Foneas Beach. It is possible to drive down to the pebbly beach but parking is limited so you will probably pass a few cars on the sharp bend above it. There is a cantina down on the beach, serving drinks and snacks. The water is fantastically blue and the steep cliffs provide plenty of natural shade.

Another beach lies just before Stoupa. Delfinia Beach is clearly signed as a campsite shares the same name. Once again, parking is difficult so if you are after a less crowded swim, the price to pay is a walk down the track from the main road, past the campsite. There is no cafe on the beach, which is a mixture of coarse sand and pebbles, and there is little shade.

Agios Nikolaos, Hora

Next to the kafenion is a private museum in a ground floor, vaulted room packed with a mish-mash of past paraphernalia. A sign in the olive tree outside proclaims that it is 500 years old (the tree, not the museum). Further along the main church has bits of marble (including a couple of capitals) in its grounds and in its walls. The second entrance into the village is further along, the main road, where again, the car should be left. Continuing on, you soon pass another olive oil factory on the right, where visitors are welcome to have a look around and buy direct.

the kafenion at Neohori

spring cleaning in Pyrgos

Beyond this is a right turn by a concrete bus shelter, signed to Milea. Keeping straight takes you to Kastania and Saidona.

Kastania

As you approach the village, the initial impression is "Where is it?" It is only when you have passed the final bend that it comes into view, tucked into a small valley. The defensive implications for this location are obvious. It is a beautiful village and worth taking the time to explore its narrow lanes and old churches (refer to the map). At approximately 500m altitude, it is noticeably cooler than on the coast, especially in the height of summer in the evening. The road leading to the top end of the village is fine though a bit steep in places, so the car could be left at the top or at the bottom. The taverna is at the top and has parking space by it.

Kastania

the Dourakis Tower, Kastania

Theodoros Kolokotronis took refuge here during the persecution of the Klephts in 1803, hoping for help from the local chieftan,

"*to my old friend Captain Konstantes Douraki, whom I trusted greatly because I had taken care of his family in former times, and because he was, as it were, my co-father-in-law, for I had betrothed my daughter to his son*". Nevertheless, his friend planned to betray him for '*grosia*' (money).

"Douraki, when he looked upon the grosia, determined to betray me for the Maniats will do anything for grosia".

Dourakis put opium in his wine but Kolokotronis was warned and knocked it over. He then announced his intention to leave.

"He tried to persuade me to go into his house and take wine with him before I left and went in to prepare it and at the same time he ordered some men to fall upon me and secure me whilst we were drinking together, but his brother prevented me from going in and he also kept the dogs from barking whilst we got away."

He then escaped, aided by Dourakis's brother, and fled to Kastanitsa on the other side of the mountains.

The five-story Dourakis tower house dominates the whole village and is

located on the square where there are two kafenia and the church of the "Koimesios tis Theotokou". Before reaching the square you will have passed the small, cruciform church of Agios Ioannis (St. John), on the left as you enter the village. It has some beautiful cloisonne decorations on the outside and is probably early Byzantine. At the top end of the village is the church of Agios Petros with more wonderful cloisonne brick-work decoration and old *tikles* roof-tiles. Unlike Agios Ioannis, it is possible to get into the church: if it is not open the key is left in a niche by the front door. Inside, the lack of natural light adds to the atmosphere. The original building probably dates from the 11th century, after which the narthex and bell tower were added. There is a lot of carved marble to admire on the templon, the support-ing columns and around the base of the cupola. The naos has a great mix of medieval frescoes and an 18th century iconostasis. Just a stone's throw below Agios Petros is Agios Nikolaos. This unusually long, vaulted church is made up of a large naos with a narthex tagged on to the west. It is not locked and inside there are extensive 18th century, rather naive frescoes. *The Ainoi* are depicted on the ceiling with the zodiac surround-ing Pantocrator, the beasts on the north wall and the judges on the south wall. Just below is the tiny Church of the Panagia, no bigger than 2 metres by 3 metres internally. It is not locked and the late Byzantine paintings have suffered from damp although St George and St Dimitrios are discernible enough on opposite walls. Another Agios Nikolaos exists just off the main square – a church not much bigger than the Panagia. Signs point the way but it is pot luck whether it is open or not. Inside are various depictions of the life of St Nicholas.

taverna

Agios Petros

Agios Nikolaos

Panagia

Dourakis Tower

kafenion

kafenion

KASTANIA

Agios Nikolaos

Agios Ioannis

Saidona is 8km further on. En route you will see the church of the Zoodigos Pigi nestling amongst the cypresses to the beneath you. Saidona is the village you can see perched high in the mountains north of Stoupa and at night the lights from here seem to be suspended in the sky. Before entering the village, there is a war memorial on the right opposite a parking area on the left. It is extremely poignant to compare the number of people from the village who died in the Second World War (a force of Italians set fire to the gorge below Saidona and destroyed much of the village) with the number who lost their lives in the succeeding political struggle of the Civil War. The memorial also lists those who died in other villages during this turbulent time. The road forks as you enter the village. The lower road takes you to a sensible place to park to explore– there is a taverna here too. The right fork leads to the Exohori road. If you park along here and walk down some fairly uneven stone steps, there is another taverna on your left with a small terrace under a vine where you can enjoy simple, tasty food in total tranquillity, even in August.

Heading to Exohori, if you are in total shock at being on what suddenly appears to be a motorway with crash barriers to boot (although it is unlikely you will see any other vehicles), there are two opportunities to stop and stretch your legs. Both are fortified monasteries and both are set in wonderful locations. The first, the totally hidden Agios Samouli, is reached by parking in a small lay–by on the first left bend after the turning up to the Vasiliki Forest. Head up a wide track leading up a gully and after 100m take a narrow dirt path heading steeply up the right bank. Samouli is a short walk away. The church was protected by a defensive wall and a tower and is open, though the paintings are badly faded. The second is a little further on where signs declare that you are leaving the Municipality of Saidona. Park on the left just before the

Koimisis tis Theotokou, Kastania

Agios Petros, Kastania

the 'Ainoi', Agios Nikolaos, Kastania

Samouli Monastery

Kitriniaris tower and walk back to the bend. Hop over the crash barrier and follow the path that leads up the left side of the valley– the Monastery of Vaidenitsa is visible ahead of you. A perfect spot, especially in spring when wild flowers and the gurgling stream put the icing on the cake. The church is kept closed by a removable rusty nail but is totally white washed inside,

Kolokotronis was involved in a feud at the Kitriniaris tower in support of the Dourakis family from Kastania.

"Kaptain Konstantine Douraki, who had been a friend of my father, had begun a feud about this time with Kitriniari, and we sent him reinforce-ments. The Maniates had caused him (Kitriniaris) to be in great straits, and he therefore desired to deliver the place up, and asked for me. His design, however, was not to surren-der, but to kill me if possible by an act of treachery. He came himself outside the gate of the tower in order to surrender it, but he had placed some men inside, and these men dis-charged six guns full at me. I was struck, but not hurt; I fell down under the roof of the tower gate, and my own men thinking that they had killed me, wanted to slay the relations of Kitriniares; others however called out, 'No, let us look after Theodoros.' The brother of Kitriniares came up, and I took him by the shoulder and protected him, and at night I threw fire into the tower, and it was then delivered up."

Kolokotronis was then asked if he intended to kill those who had betrayed him and he replied, *"God has preserved me, so I grant them their lives."* This incident makes the subsequent betrayal of Kolokotronis by Dourakis at Kastania even more incomprehensible.

The 'motorway' continues on to Exo-hori.

Milea

From the concrete bus stop junction to Milea (or Milia) the road continues for 11km along a road that skirts around a deep valley, passing through Kariovouni (once known as Arachova) en route. The village you can see beneath you, perched on an outcrop is Eliohora. Milea is an old village split into three sections – a lower section below the road, a mid-dle section slightly further on and an upper section on a hill above. This village *"and its dependencies con-taining 200 houses"* was listed by Col. Leake as being governed by Kapetanios Kyvelaki and he also quotes the poet, Nikitas Nifakos as describing Milea in this way –

"From hence (Arachova) *let us pro-ceed, by the wolf-path, to the rob-bers of kids and goats, the walkers at night, and record the name of the town of the kid-eating rogues, the mule-stealers, the goat-slayers, the thrice-apostate Milia, from which Garbelea is one quarter of an hour distant."* Clearly, the poet was not too enamoured.

The Koimisis tis Theotokou church in the small square in the lower section, Kato Hora, has a bell tower dated 1776 decorated with carvings and with a wonderful device of connecting metal rods for ringing the church bells. You will see a sign for Kato Hora on your right and this narrow road takes you down to the square and the church. Going east from this square is a narrow road and if you follow it on foot, you come to a small plain-looking church named after Agios Nikolaos. Local enquiries should produce a keyholder and it is worth the effort because the entire surface of the interior walls and arched ceiling are covered with frescoes. Some are slightly damaged or faded but the majority are glowing with vibrant colours and those on the templon seem to have escaped the usual damage from smoke from oil lamps. There are scenes from the life of Christ, the crucifixion and the res-urrection and the usual collection of saints and martyrs. Return to the 'main' road and continue south east to the next section of the village. In the square the Koimisis tis Theotokou church has a won-derful Pantocrator, and many other paint-ings, including a picture of Abraham about to sacrifice Isaac. The key can sometimes be found at the nearby kafe-nion. Looking from here due east into the mountains you can see a large building high on a ridge. This is the monastery of Panagia Giatrissa and you will have just passed where the walk up to it, on page 174, begins.

If you take the road to the east of the square you come to an old school on your right just below the road. Park here and follow the broken kalderimi which passes to the left of the old school and leads down to a small rather scruffy-looking church with a derelict building on the left. This is Agios Ioannis Prodromos or John the Baptist and appears to have been the katholikon of a small monastery. The church is flanked by stone walls with fir-ing loops forming a grassy courtyard with the monastery building forming the northern boundary. The church is small with a disproportionately tall, octagonal dome. The tiles of the roofs have been laid on top of the original *tikles* roof. The walls are covered in rough cement, which covers any clues there might have been as to the date of the church. The interior has been fully painted and the last line of an inscription over the door shows the artists to be Christodoulos Kalergis from the island of Mykonos. Most of the depictions in the paintings are standard themes but to the right of the door on the back wall is something a little unusual. It shows a

Vaidenitsa Monastery

Milea

Agios Ioannis Prodromos, Milea
The monk Zosimos, Agios Ioannis Prodromos, Milea

monk, Zosimos, giving the Eucharist to a wild and emaciated "Osia" (Holy) Mary. She was a prostitute who went on a pilgrimage to Jerusalem where she was prevented from entering the Church of the Holy Sepulchre by a supernatural force. She heard a voice tell her to go into the desert and repent and so she lived a hermitic life in the desert to atone for her sins. Zosimos gave her Holy Communion but when he returned a while later he found her dead. Two lions helped him to dig her grave and are sometimes shown in paintings of her although they are absent in this example. The church should not be locked. Just past the school, a narrow paved road takes you up to the upper or third section of the village and a small square with kafenia, shady trees and another large church. At first glance, this is modern but the on-going removal of exterior cement has revealed another Byzantine church with a later exo-narthex. The frescoes are later and many are damaged but include that enigmatic character, Simon the Stylite, who spent forty years perched on a classical pillar in Syria preaching to the masses who flocked there to see him (the church keyholder is in the small kafenion in the square).

Another 'motorway' now links Milea to Platsa.

Agios Nikolaos

South of Stoupa on the coast is the picturesque fishing village of Agios Nikolaos (still often called by its older Slavic name, Selinitsa). There are three exits off the main road to the coastal road that links Selenitsa to Agios Dimitrios and Trahila. Alternatively, there is a gentle coastal path from Stoupa which takes less than an hour on foot (see the maps of both villages for where the walk starts and finishes– you can not get lost in between). Life is centred around the harbour– a great place to sit, eat and drink while watching the boats coming and going. In the summer the road is closed to vehicles in the evening. The beach is over a kilometre further south. Pantazi Beach is a mix of coarse sand and pebbles with plenty of shade provided by tamarisk trees. There is one taverna and, these days, no camper vans actually park on the beach as the council placed a stone wall around the back of the beach to prevent illegal camping.

Agios Dimitrios

Agios Dimitrios is a small village with a little harbour, which once was the anchorage for Kapetanios Christeas of Stoupa and Platsa. The harbour was protected by the tower which formed part of a small complex on the headland above. In 1795, J.B.S. Morrit, a traveller, wrote;

"*The tower of Capitano Christea was a small distance from the port and adjoining it were outbuildings and a long hall of entertainment. We dined with the family at 12 o'clock and after dinner went to the great room of the castle. In it, and on the green before it, we found near a hundred people assembled and partaking of the chief's hospitality.*"

Morrit also identifies this as the site that Pausanias called Pephnos where

"*There is a little isle off shore no bigger than a big rock....The people of Thalamai say this is where the Dioscouri were born... On this little island there are bronze statues of the Dioscouri a foot high standing on the island in the open air. When the sea sweeps over the rock in winter it never moves them. This is a wonderful thing, and also the ants here have*

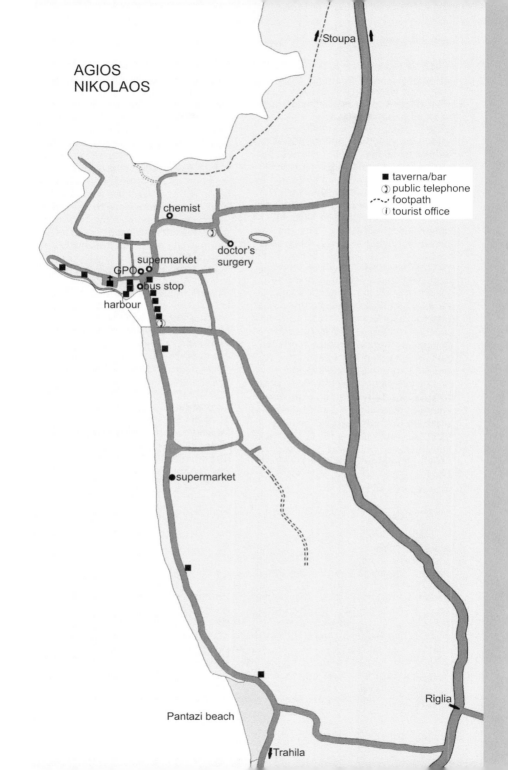

AGIOS
NIKOLAOS

Stoupa

chemist

taverna/bar
public telephone
footpath
tourist office

doctor's
surgery

supermarket
GPO
bus stop
harbour

supermarket

Riglia

Pantazi beach

Trahila

a whiter colour than is usual." (For Dioscouri – see Kardamyli).

The village has a taverna overlooking a small pebbly beach.

The road continues and deteriorates a little to **Trahila,** where it terminates. Trahila has an end of the road feel to it and has not really been affected by the growth in tourism just down the road. There are a couple of 'old-style' tavernas overlooking the harbour, and even in August you have the sense of having moved back in time.

To get back to the main road turn right at Pantazi Beach. Continuing south, a fairly immediate left takes you to **Ano Riglia** and **Isna** (the turning to Lower Riglia is a little further back). Both Riglias are picturesque villages to wander around and Isnia (or Eliohora to give its non Slavic name) is dramatically perched on a rocky outcrop. A green walkers sign points to a path down into the gorge below. This walk leads to Milea and then on to Yiatrissa– part of a pilgrimage route.

The main road now starts to wind its

way upwards. **Pigi** nestles in a valley just before you reach the plateau. The road in off the main road is unsigned but is by a public phone box and walkers' sign. To drive in involves a self-activated traffic light system as the lane is very narrow. Press the button on the pole to your left as the road narrows – this lets someone at the other end know you are coming. Alternatively, park further up the road where there is space after a tight bend and walk down the steps into the village. There is a taverna on the main square which seems to vary from year to year in terms of being operational or not.

Platsa

Platsa must have the grandest square in the area. A 20th century church dominates the space which is surrounded by large, 'neo-classical' town houses. On one side there are two kafenia and on the opposite side, the old school house is now an atmospheric bar. The village taverna is at the end of a left turn before you reach the square. It has great views down to the coast so get there before the sun sets. Platsa was a stronghold

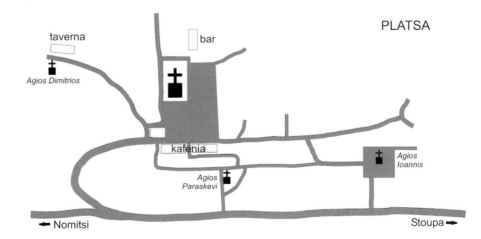

PLATSA

taverna

bar

Agios Dimitrios

kafenia

Agios Ioannis

Agios Paraskevi

← Nomitsi

Stoupa →

of Kapetanios Christeas. Agios Dimitrios on the coast below was its harbour – protected by the Tower built there by the Christeas family. There are no dominant towers in Platsa but it is easy to see that the old houses were built with defence in mind and indeed Platsa was attacked by the Turks several times during the 17th century. Leake reported in 1805 that a Christodhulos Christeas of Leftro governed Platsa, which contained over 1000 houses (making it one of the largest settlements in the Mani). The Christeas family name still exists in Platsa. Its narrow

the harbour at Agios Nikolaos

the Christeas Tower, Agios Domitrios

lanes are interesting to explore and once again there are a number of churches to have a look at – refer to the map. Agia Paraskevi ('Saint Friday') is a small barrel vaulted church with a transverse barrel vault half way across its length and no dome. The outside is decorated with cloisonne brickwork bands in an X or diamond shape pattern, though the stonework is generally rather rough and ready. Above the west door are three cloisonne decorated niches. It is probably 13th century and inside there is a mix of paintings in terms of date. It is not locked. Agios Ioannis is also accessible as the key is usually kept just above the door. There are two internal columns, one of which has been recycled from a much earlier, possibly classical building. Some of the frescoes have been whitewashed over but the zodiac (part of the Ainoi), and the crucifixion are just about detectable and the bema paintings have also escaped being whited-out. Agios Demetrios is a largish single-cell barrel-vaulted church which has no particularly interesting architectural features and no paintings but has a number of interestingly carved marbles inset into the floor and internal steps to the bema. The view from the door of the church northwards over towards Stoupa is worth the short walk. The church of Agios Nikolaos, Kabinari, is south of the village down a dirt rack off the main road, just past a taverna with equally great views. The local football team play nearby. The church is one of

Trahila

Agios Ioannis, Platsa

the oldest surviving churches in the Mani. Originally built in the 9th or 10th century with three adjacent barrel vaulted chambers – probably based on the plan of a three-naved basilica. The dome was added later. Interior doorways allow access between the three chambers but they also have separate exterior doors in the west wall. The two flanking chambers are slightly narrower than the central chamber. The left hand chamber is in the worst condition. There is no plaster on the ceiling but a few faded frescoes remain on the wall. The templon is carved marble. The right hand chamber has some very good frescoes depicting the life of St. Nicholas. There is one curious fresco of some sailors aboard a ship which is in danger of running onto rocks. They have reversed their oars to 'fend off' and their distress is clearly shown in their faces. St. Nicholas is depicted on board the ship in his role of Patron of Fishermen while a sailor dangles upside-down from the mast, with his leg caught in a rope with a black, winged 'devil' hovering close by. The frescoes in the main apse are of exceptional artistry although suffering from age and oil lamps and of a unique style in the Mani – possibly an artist from Mystras. The church is locked but the priest in Platsa has the keys (if you can find him).

There are a number of churches and old houses, many of which are derelict, in **Nomitsi.** However, the churches do not really compare to those in Proastio, Kastania or Platsa and to avoid church overkill, details will be omitted bar two. You can not miss the church of the Anargyoi as you almost crash into it as you leave the main street of the village. *The Anargyoi* translates as 'without silver' and refers to saints Cosmas & Damian who were twins who gave their

medical skills to the poor for free. The church is probably 13th century. There is a stone templon and a variety of frescoes, the oldest of which are of the medieval period although the state of repair is extremely poor. There are faded depictions of military saints in medieval Byzantine armour, a hardly discernible Crucifixion above the door and other fragmentary remains: Agios Giorgios is spearing a coiled and scaled serpent/dragon. If the church is locked, try asking at the taverna opposite, which itself is a great place to have a no-frills meal in the evening. The other church is further along the main road just out of the village is a little gem – the 11th century Church of the Metamorphosis. There are some faded frescoes (which desperately need preservation) but more impressive are the carvings on the templon and four supporting columns.

Thalames

Almost as soon as you leave Nomitsi, you are in Thalames. Pausanias records Thalames as being one of the Free Lakonian Cities where there was a sanctuary and an oracle of Ino. "*The oracles are given in sleep: whatever people ask to be told, the goddess reveals it to them in dreams. There are bronze statues in the sanctuary in the open air, one of Pasiphae, the other of the Sun. It is impossible to get a clear look at the statue in the temple itself because of the wreaths, but they say it is made of bronze like the others. Fresh drinking water runs from a sacred water-spring; Pasiphae is a title of the Moon, not a local divinity of Thalamai.*"

Plutarch says the oracle was Pasiphae's, not Inos and this makes more sense. Robert Graves in "The Greek Myths" says the Kings of Sparta frequently consulted this oracle. Ino

was a goddess of the sea who saved
Odysseus from drowning when his raft
was shattered by a storm sent by Poseidon. The site of the 'sacred water spring'
is thought to have been the 'Jew's Well' in
the square on the main road. You can see
a covered fountain just below the taverna
'O Platanos' (the Plane tree) and 50
metres north of the fountain, just below
the school, is the Jew's Well. Steps lead
down to two arches, through which you
can see the well. The large stone blocks at
the base of the outside wall and inside the
well itself are said to be of ancient origin.
One of the stones set in the outer wall
looks like a fragment from an old grave-
stone. The fountain below the taverna had
a series of inscribed and ornamented
classical, marble stones built into the
facade of the arch which covers it but in
1996 two of these marbles were stolen
and now the rest have been removed for
safe keeping. Next to the fountain is the
pedestal of a statue and the inscription is
a dedication to the Roman Emperor Marcus Aurelius. You can clearly see that the
pedestal supported two statues and close
inspection of the inscription shows that,
to the left the words have been deliberately obliterated. The owner of the museum opposite believes it to have been a
dedication to Caracalla, (see Kiparissos).

The ancient city of Thalames is thought to
have stood north east of the Jew's Well,
on the high ground behind the school. To
the left of the school, a narrow concrete
road leads up behind the village. Off to
the right of this road there is another old
well with crude steps leading below
ground level. It is not easy to see from the
road but there are some stone troughs
right by the well which can lead you to it.
50 metres to the northeast of this is the
possible site of the temple of the goddess, tentatively identified by some Hellenic masonry. A few hundred metres further up this concrete road there is a small
Byzantine Church on the hillside, which is
similar in size and construction to the
Metamorphosis church at Nomitsi, and

Agios Nikolaos, Kabinari

the church of the Anargyoi, Nomitsi

the 'Jew's Well', Thalames

Profitas Ilias, Thalames

some frescoes remain. It is dedicated to Profitas Ilias and is early 13th century. The frescoes inside are also said to be 13th century.

Back in the square, the 'Museum' opposite the school is a private collection of miscellaneous items including agricultural and domestic implements, early prints, a few weapons, church artefacts, Lord Byron first editions and autographs and more. Across the square, the Morea olive oil press is open to visitors and the taverna does surprisingly good pizzas.

Langada

Two kilometres beyond Thalames is Lagada. This is a fascinating village, which, unlike most of the Exo Mani villages, was divided into family or clan areas like the villages of Inner Mani further south. Lagada had three main divisions. The Bloutsos family were centred in 65 houses around the main square with the beautiful church of Agios Sotiras. The area around the Kapitsinos War Tower in the south of the village consisted of a further tower dwelling (only half of which remains), a round tower and 90 houses belonging to four allied families. Above this was the Tsicholianika area with twenty houses and a church. The old houses are obviously built with defence in mind and walking through the narrow lanes is fascinating. The main square of the village

Langada

is dominated by the church of Agios Sotiras, which is probably 11th century. It used to be encased in concrete and plaster but this was removed in the mid 1980's to reveal stonework decorated with the most wonderful cloisonne brickwork, especially on the belfry. The inside of the church has also been plastered over but tentative exploration has revealed some frescoes beneath this. There is still a great deal of work to be done to expose these frescoes once again and there is a written appeal and collection box for donations to carry on and complete this task. The local *papas* will open for you and can usually be found in the cafe nearby.

A narrow lane leads from the northwest corner of this square up to the church of Agia Sofia, which, although in a semi-ruined condition, is worth a visit because of its unusual architecture. The narrow lane turns into a very well made kalderimi and the church is a short walk further on your right hand side. The original outer covering of the roof is missing and close to the belfry you can see two curious humps which, when you enter the church, turn out to be two domes set in the ceiling of the outer narthex and the narthex. Some restoration work has begun. On leaving the village a taverna on the right claims that "all food is 3 euros". A cheap way to enjoy great views down to the coast.

From Langada the road follows the contours around a gorge and on the coast below you can see Trahila, protected by the small headland jutting out into the sea. Approximately 5 kilometres from Langada is the village of **Agios Nikon**. The village is named after Saint Nikon the Repenter – the soldier, monk and missionary who is credited with converting much of the Mani to Christianity.

Oitylo

This section is defined to the north by the county border between Messinia and Lakonia and to the south by the Areopolis/Gythio road. The dominant feature of this area is the glorious bay of Oitylo, once a harbour for shipping and piracy, now a growing resort aimed at attracting tourism. There is a pebbly beach at **Neo Oitylo** backed by a number of cafes and tavernas and further along the coast the smaller bay of **Limeni** has a couple of fish tavernas overlooking incredibly turquoise water, making a perfect place for lunch. The village of Oitylo and Kelefa Castle, opposite Oitylo across a gorge, crown the bay. Further inland there is another possible 'mini-mini' circuit to drive around to get off the beaten track and into the hills, starting at Kelefa and ending up at Oitylo (or the other way round).

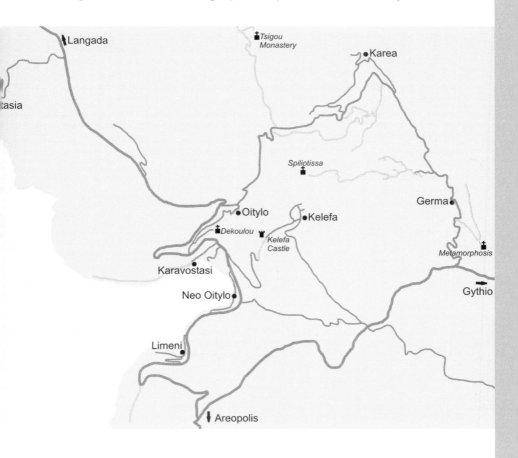

The first hamlet in this section offers the first swim stop south of Agios Nikolaos. **Hotasia** is reached by turning right at the welcome to Lakonia sign once you have passed through Agios Nikon. The road winds down to the sea. Before reaching sea level the only taverna here is on your left where there is ample car parking space. Continuing down the road to the sea, a weather-beaten sign indicates a left turn down a concrete road past a couple of new houses to the sea. There is no beach but rather a concrete shelf to get in and out of the water – the rest of the rocky coastline offers great snorkelling and the sheer cliffs behind give a dramatic backdrop to the setting.

Back on the main road Oitylo is another 5km. The road gently starts to drop as you near Oitylo. Just before a tight right-hand bend, up on the left is a small workshop that is keeping the stone-carving tradition going. A charming couple, Ioannis and Juliana, produce a variety of work, ranging from relief sculptures to small ashtrays and oil lamps. Visitors are more than welcome and Juliana speaks excellent English. She also weaves her own colourful rugs on an ingenious, home-made, space-saving loom.

Oitylo

To get into the heart of the village turn left onto the Gythio road, just past a large open area with cafes on

Oitylo, viewed from Kelefa Castle

your right, and take the right fork into the *kentro*. To explore the village it is easiest to park by the large square. The T-junction reached by walking between the square and the taverna further along offers two choices – right into the narrow lanes of the older part of the village where a fair amount of restoration work is going on or left towards the new church. Though it may not be the most interesting Mani village to wander around, Oitylo has an ancient past. Pausanias records Oitylo as one of the Free Lakonian Cities and Homer stated that Oitylo sent ships to support Agamemnon at Troy.

"*The sanctuary of Sarapis and the wooden idol of Karneian Apollo in the market place are worth seeing.*" was the only physical reference Pausanias made. It has been suggested that at this time, the majority of the city was below the ridge on the lower slopes above the sea with only an acropolis where the modern town lies. Marble spoilia are dotted around the village, for example lying on the small square in front of the old town hall (*koinotita*) or in derelict buildings near the new church.

Oitylo was always an important town, strategically because it linked North and South Mani and commercially through trade, piracy and a very profitable slave trade (Jules Verne called it the 'Great Algiers'). It was the 'capital' of the Mani before the rise to prominence of Tsimova (Areopolis) and Limeni, so it was a focus of attention for Turkish control of the area and Kelefa Castle, across the gorge, became a major garrison during the brief periods of occupation. The constant attacks of Turkish forces during the late 17th century and some desperate family feuds caused a mass migration from the Mani that included 1,700 people from

Oitylo and Kelefa village. Patrick Leigh
Fermor gives very detailed information on
these migrations and the settlements the
Iatrani and Stephanopoli clans established
in Tuscany and Corsica respectively. Most
of Oitylo's towers have been destroyed
but the strongly fortified houses illustrate
the constant defence put up by the local
inhabitants.

From the main square it is possible to
drive right through the village to rejoin
the main road – continue in the direction
you entered the village past the taverna
and later a plaque commemorating the
migrations to which Leigh Fermor refers
and out on a tarmac road. You will now
get your first views of the bay below. A
sharp left turn before you reach the main
road leads to the Monastery of Dekoulou.

Hotasia

stone carvings, Oitylo

Dekoulou Monastery

If you did not detour into Oitylo, the road
soon reveals the dramatic bay of Oitylo.
As you start descending with the sea to
your right you'll pass a tarmac road on
your left. This is a second way into Oitylo.
It is also the way, if you turn down a dirt
track on your right half way along this
road, to the Dekoulou Monastery. The
church here is spectacular inside as the
paintings have been very well preserved
by the Dekoulou family and of all the
churches in the Mani, perhaps this is the
one to visit to get an impression of how a
fully decorated post–Byzantine church
interior would once have looked. The
frescoes date from 1765 and cover every
inch of wall space with parades of saints,
martyrs and pictographs showing various
Old and New Testament stories. There is
an excellent version of the *Ainoi* – including a wonderful elephant. The artist is
working from hearsay and paints it with
not very large, almost human ears, a long
trumpet-shaped trunk, tusks growing
sideways out of its mouth and almost
cloven feet.

The west wall is covered with the crucifixion and below this, a large, dramatic ren-

Dekoulou Monastery

image of an elephant, Dekoulou Monastery

dition of the Last Judgement that serves as a warning to the congregation of their fate if they stray. Christ enthroned is flanked by the Virgin and John the Baptist and hosts of Saints. Below this, an empty throne with the symbols of the Passion (cross, spear and sponge), flanked by Adam and Eve depicts the 'Second Coming'. A river of fire flows down to the gaping jaws of hell – depicted as a fish-like beast. In the centre, the hand of God holds a balance on which the souls of the dead are weighed. Those that are 'saved' are to the left of the picture and include the 'good thief' crucified with Christ in fulfilment of the statement that he would go to Paradise. The Archangel Michael is prodding devils with his spear and they are in turn grabbing the condemned souls and hurling them down into the fiery pit. Adjacent to this, partially obscured and faded, is Satan himself, the Great Beast with twisted horns. Over to the right is a human depiction of the sea, a woman 'riding side-saddle' on one of many fish all carrying human body-parts in their mouths and holding a ship in her hand – depicting the passage 'and the sea shall give up her dead'. The whole picture is extremely 'busy' and well worth taking the trouble to see. The ornate wooden iconostasis has recently returned from restoration in Crete. The key holders live in the house next door – be prepared to brave their noisy dogs and, to be sure someone is in, it is best to go in the afternoon after school. The other ruined buildings by the church were once monks' cells.

The monastery hosted an ultimately unsuccessful diplomatic meeting in 1770 when the Russian envoys Alexis and Theodore Orlov came to the Mani with a force of 1000 men to help in the struggle against the Turks.

Putting aside their disappointment with such a paltry army, the Maniats planned a campaign, only for the whole thing to go wrong. It ended in the Mavromichalis's and Orlovs falling out and Turks sending in a vicious Turko-Albanian army to restore supremacy in the whole of the Peloponnese.

Back on the bay of Oitylo, there are three possibilities for a drink or lunch by the sea. The first is an immediate right turn when down on sea-level, signed **Karavostasi**. There are a couple of tavernas here along with some new hotels. It is also possible to take a boat trip from here that explores Palaeolithic caves and gives a commentary on local history. Call Dimitris on 6932 233310/1. The second potential cafe stop is on the main beach of **Neo Oitylo** where several tavernas stretch along the water's edge. A short cut to up to Kelefa Castle or on to Gythio (bypassing Areopolis) lies half way round the bend once you have passed the beach of Neo Oitylo – at a kind of crossroads with a stone bus shelter on your right, take the left concrete road heading up and turn left for Kelefa at the top of this road or right then left onto the main road for Gythio.

The final opportunity for lunch is further along at the bay of **Limeni** – a right turn takes you along a road running parallel to the main road and then rejoins it as it starts to climb up to Areopolis. There are two fish tavernas here and diners often view turtles swimming in the bay. Limeni was the harbour for Areopolis and strategically important for that reason. The Mavromichalis family grew to prominence in this area and, under their control, Areopolis and Limeni became the main town and main harbour of the Inner Mani – often in dispute with

Oitylo and its harbour, Karavostasi. The
harbour was protected by a round tower
(disappeared), several fortified caves and
defensively built houses. The tower house
of the Mavromichalis family, resembling a
Norman church, was intended to be a
museum but a theft of exhibits brought a
prompt closure. There was also a small
convent here, now derelict, but some of
the frescoes are still visible in the chapel
that has no roof. The Russian attempt to
help the Greeks overcome the Turks in
1770, The Orlov Event, started with a
landing here. When Leake visited as a
guest of the Mavromichalis family, the
convent was still in use and he commented that it had "a little garden about it".
Petrobey Mavromichalis is buried in the
small church on the north shore of the
harbour where there is a monument and
bust over his tomb. Leake stayed as a
guest of Petros Mavromichalis before he
became the Bey and wrote that he was "a
smart looking man of between thirty and
forty, dressed in green velvet and the
genteelest Maniat I have yet seen." He told
Leake the story of how, in 1792, his
father rescued a British ship in distress
near Pyrgos Dirou and piloted them back
to Limeni with a small vessel. He then
mounted a guard over the ship to prevent
any attack or looting and protected the
ship until it sailed again nineteen days
later.

There are numerous tales of piracy from
Oitylo and Limeni. One such example
involved two renowned pirates and close
friends, Theodoros and Anapliotis. After
disagreeing on how to divide their loot,
each one separately planned the kidnap of
the other's wife. Theodoros took Anapliotis' wife to a pirate from Malta whose ship
had docked at Oitylo. They were having
difficulties agreeing upon the price. The
pirate closely observed the woman and
finally said that two hours earlier he had
been brought a more beautiful woman for
half the price and ordered his servant to
bring that woman on the deck. When
Theodoros saw her, he stayed quiet as he

the Last Judgement, Dekoulou Monastery

boat trip from Karavostasi

the Bay of Oitylo

Limeni

recognized his wife, whom his opponent had already succeeded in kidnapping and selling. Instead of trying to rescue his wife, he asked the pirate to buy her too at any price, so that they were both imprisoned – by doing this he avoided Anapliotis' sarcasm. As soon as Anapliotis had learnt about the incident, he equipped a ship with a cannon and Theodoros joined him to go and threaten the Maltese pirate, who was forced to set the women free!

Kelefa

By car there are two ways up to the Turkish castle that overlooks the bay of Oitylo. The short cut has just been mentioned (at the time of print, the promising concrete road that snakes up from the centre of Neo Oitylo runs out significantly short and so would not be advisable in a regular car). The other way is to continue on to Areopolis, turning left at the junction just before the town and then left again down a road signed Kelefa after a couple of km. As you approach the village of Kelefa turn left down a new tarmac road that passes the village cemetery.

The castle was probably built by the Turks in 1670 after they had defeated the Venetians in Crete and turned their attention on the Mani and Oitylo. It is a large rectangular enclosure with high walls and bastions on the corners and could hold a garrison of 500 men. It gave the Turks a commanding view of Oitylo while dominating the harbour on the coast below and formed

part of the chain of castles from Zarnata to Porto Kayio. The castle was captured by a Maniat and Venetian force in 1685 and repulsed an attempt by the Turks to regain it during the following year. They (the Turks) finally re-captured it in 1715 and rebuilt it. Much of the thick, curtain wall survives with three round towers on the western side facing towards the sea. The southern wall still has the parapet and battlements from which the Turks kept an eye on Oitylo and from which they could bombard the town with cannon across the gorge once known as *milolangado* after numerous water mills it had. The interior of the castle is very overgrown in places and the undergrowth conceals the walls of various buildings within.

The mini-mini circuit can be started from Kelefa and only takes half an hour of driving. Head back to the main road, turn left and just after the beehives and honey vendor, take the left turn signed Germa and Karea. Before you come to the first village, a blue sign indicates a right turn on a sharp right-hand bend for a brief detour to an interesting church. Head up past a derelict house on your right and park on the right where a dirt track begins, just before a sharp left hairpin. Walk down the track to the church of the Metamorphosis of the Saviour (Transfiguration of Christ). Not only is this church in a lovely spot but if you didn't visit Dekoulou, this church also gives a good idea of how a fully decorated church originally looked in terms of frescoes (it is

Kelefa Castle

always open). They were painted in 1725 by the Klirodeti family who were also responsible for the work in Agios Nikolaos at nearby Germa. Their condition is so good that numerous scenes from the life of Christ and martyrdoms, including four martyrs boiled to death in a bronze cow, are easily discernible.

Germa is a little further on and is a very small hamlet. To get inside Agios Nikoloas, an excellent example of an 11th century church, knock on the door of the white bungalow next door to raise the key hold-er. The frescoes inside were only recently revealed, as, as is so often the case, they had been plastered over. The frescoes are not Byzantine but date from the mid 18th century and the Klirodeti signature is at the end of a frieze above the templon. There is a colourful, if rather naive looking version of the Ainoi with the zodiac in the narthex.

Another detour to an equally extraordinary church lies down a left turn soon after Germa. The sign to the Panagia Spliliotissa (the church of the Virgin of the Caves) does not indicate at all how far away it is. It is in the middle of nowhere down a dirt track that should not really be taken in a normal hired car. If you do though, it takes around 15 minutes to get there driving at a sensibly slow speed. Ignore all turnings off it (including a sign to 'Kelefa') as well as some large potholes. Its location is stunning as the tiny church is cut into cliffs that drop down into the Oitylo gorge. To get to the church walk across the recently paved square (used for the annual *panagiri* or festival), through an archway, down some steps through another gate and then draw breath as the steps down to the church are extremely vertiginous, though a handrail and wall help to provide security. The short walk down passes a shrine full of bones of monks who once inhabited the monastery. Leake visited in 1805 and mentions cultivated terraces and gardens once tilled by the monks. The cave part of the church is extremely low. It is possible to walk here up the 'water–mill gorge'

Kelefa Castle

Agios Nikolaos, Germa

walking the Milolangado gorge

'Panagia Spiliotissa'

from the coast, though it is a fairly tough hike. If the gorge still has some water, allow 2.5 hours to get there, 2 to return. If the gorge is dry, then 2 hours to get there and 1.5 to return. These timings allow for a leisurely pace with plenty of photo/flower stops. The walk starts at the small beach at Karavostasi in the north corner of Oitylo Bay. Follow the vague dirt road southwards along the edge of the beach. After 180m ignore the asphalt road on your left and continue along the pebbly beach. After 140m you will reach the riverbed of *Milolangado* – follow it left into the mouth of the gorge, which soon narrows. After 150m you will pass a small bridge – continue up the riverbed. At 380m you pass beneath the main road bridge and continue on up the now constantly narrowing streambed, hopping between boulders. After 40m ignore the path left to Oitylo but continue up the streambed, sometimes on the path just to the right of it and sometimes actually in it. After about 300m there is a cliff on your right hand side – if you hack through the undergrowth to reach it, you can see an ancient inscription on the stone slabs (look out for a cairn to guide you). Finally after another 2.5 km you will reach a junction with another streambed coming down from the left. Keep to the right hand streambed and follow a beautiful grassy path to the right hand side of it up and down for around 200m, and then bearing further to the right, climb steeply up the path which zig-zags up a rocky outcrop on your left. The monastery is directly above you now, though it is invisible until you reach the top. Keep your eyes peeled for way-marks as it is not very clear. You will arrive in a grassy parking area below the church and go to right-hand side of buildings to find the entrance. In a small room on the right you can sign the visitors' book, eat some *loukoumi* and even make yourself a coffee! Return by retracing your steps.

After the Spiliotissa diversion, the main road passes a number of small agricultural villages clinging to the edge of the basin that drops down into the gorge. The right fork to **Karea** can be taken as an additional detour as it rejoins the main road later. If you didn't go the cave church, it is visible on the crown of a small hill down in the gorge down on your left. Before reaching Oitylo, below a sharp right hand bend, is a good example of an old kalderimi bridge with the path itself meandering up the hillside. Shortly after this, a track leads off to your right and follows the eastern side of a wide gorge. It starts off paved but soon deteriorates into a track which is really only suitable for a 4x4. If you follow this track you eventually reach the **Monastery of Tsigou**, perched on an overhanging rock on the mountain slopes. A defensive wall with many *doufekotrypes* (firing loops) encloses the church and buildings and a square tower protects the eastern corner of the complex. A track takes you to the main entrance gate, which is locked, but the adjacent wall has collapsed allowing entry. A very unusual feature is the remains of a round tower that protected this gateway. The templon in the church has some damaged frescoes while bits of others are visible where the plaster/whitewash covering has flaked away. The tower has been restored and looks as though it is sometimes occupied but the other monastic buildings are derelict. The view south from here is quite stunning and you can see right down the gorge and across Kelefa to the mountains above Areopolis.

Inner Mani -"The Mani Loop"

The most obvious way to explore the area once known as *Kakavou-lia* ('evil counsel') is to follow the road that runs down one coast and then loops round to come back up the other side, starting and finishing at **Areopolis**. The total driving time to do this is just under 2 hours with no stops, so doing it in one day is perfectly possible if an early start is taken. The landscape is very different from the outer Mani – much more barren and windswept. It is such a dry area that a French traveller in the 18th century recorded,

"When a Kakavoulian gets married, his first job is to measure how much water is in the cistern because it is one of the most important dowry gifts. Whoever lavishes a lot of water on the wedding is considered rich. This extravagance makes an impression and all the region learns about how much water the in-laws drank."

Driving on each of the coasts is also very different. On the west side the road enjoys a relatively straight course on a wide plateau whereas the mountains come dramatically down to sea level on the east coast, causing the road to bend and twist. This is not their only difference. The west coast is all about tower villages and churches; the east offers a greater number of swimming opportunities in a series of small, fairly secluded pebbly coves, many of which have beach-side tavernas. Whatever your chosen itinerary, it is a "must do" experience – the combination of the harsh landscape and rugged coastline, the austere tower houses and their violent history and the religious fervour intrinsic to every one of the numerous churches, gives the area a unique, mystical quality, appropriate for an area right on the fringes of Europe.

For a really full day out, or to stay overnight to enjoy a couple of days in the area, you could combine the Loop with the Mini Circuit and/or a visit to Tainaron.

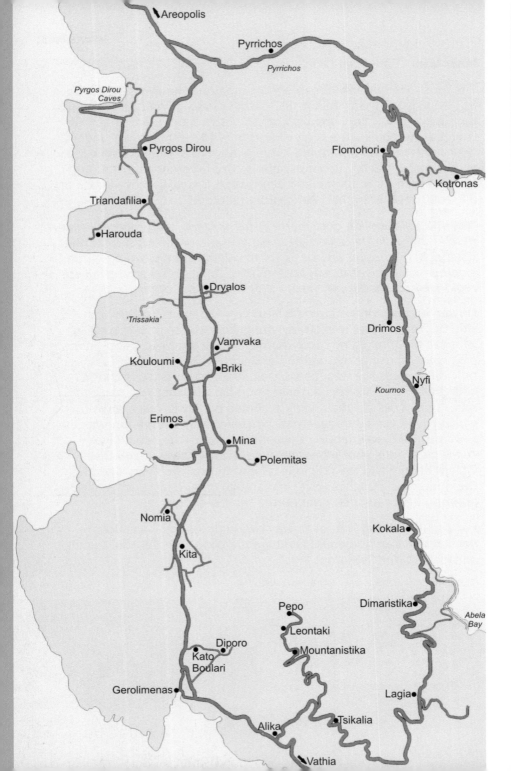

Areopolis

"The first is Tsimova (Areopolis), a handsome town and large, governed by a Captain named Mavromichali. The Tsimovites only are worthy men, their manners and good customs show it – in appearance merchants but secretly pirates"

Nikitas Nifakos circa. 1800

The town is of great historic importance to Greece as it was here that the war for independence against 350 years of Turkish occupation began. On 17th March 1821, a banner was raised and allegiance sworn under the motto "Victory or Death" by the various Maniat clan leaders assembled. They then marched to Kardamyli and on to Kalamata. The seven-year struggle had begun. In recognition of this role, the town was renamed Areopolis after Ares, the god of war, in 1836. Previously it had been known by its Slavic name, Tsimova.

In the last decade Areopolis has seen something of a boom. The central square, dominated by a statue of Petrobey Mavromichalis, has been repaved, a new police station and town hall built, a number of new bars and cafes have opened, along with hotels to accommodate visitors and on the outskirts of the town are a number of recently built, huge stone shops and supply yards. However it has by no means lost its quality of an atmospheric gateway into Mesa Mani and no tour of the Mani is complete without stopping here. At the very least it warrants a coffee stop or lunch. The main square is the centre of life in the town and is a great place to 'people watch'. There is a market every Saturday, mainly selling fruit and vegetables, turning the square into a hive of activity. However, Areopolis deserves a little more time. Its narrow alleys and cobbled streets are a photographer's dream and, being a historic town, there are a number of places worth visiting.

Areopolis –   the statue of Mavromichalis,

the main square on 'Oxi Day'

a cobbled alley

old doorway

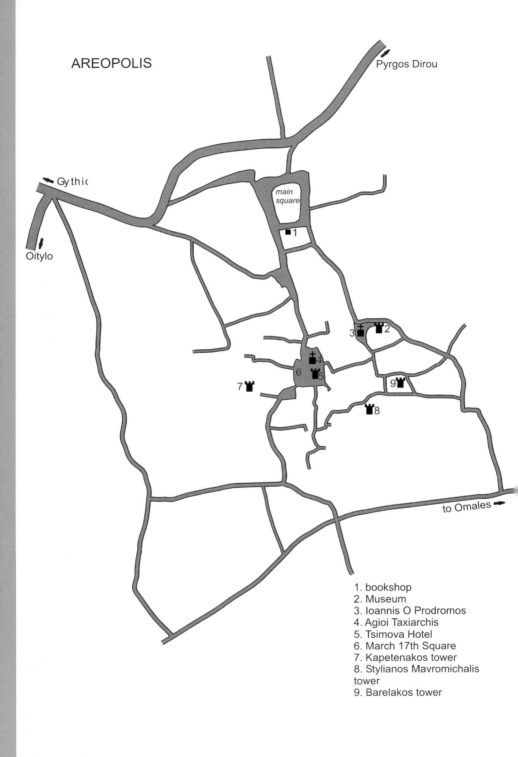

AREOPOLIS

Pyrgos Dirou

Gythio

Oitylo

main square

■1

3 ✝■ 🏰2

✝■4

6 🏰5

7 🏰

9🏰

🏰8

to Omales ➤

1. bookshop
2. Museum
3. Ioannis O Prodromos
4. Agioi Taxiarchis
5. Tsimova Hotel
6. March 17th Square
7. Kapetenakos tower
8. Stylianos Mavromichalis tower
9. Barelakos tower

To the west of the main square lies the old town with its narrow, winding alleys, fortified houses and smattering of churches set amongst which is the 17th March Square flanked by old houses and overlooked by the tall bell tower of the Taxiarchis Church. The marble relief on one of the walls of the square commemorates the time and place where "Petrobey" plunged the Greek flag into the ground (a hole in the centre of the square represents the actual spot) with the cry of "Victory or Death". The rest of the country's war cry was "Freedom or Death"– the Maniats considered themselves to be free anyway. Petrobey's full name was Petros Mavromichalis and he came from the most dominant family in the area. The suffix 'Bey' meant local ruler – a system imposed late on during the Turkish rule in an attempt to control the area. The appointed Bey, who was always from a powerful Maniat family, was in theory subject to the Ottomans. However, in reality the Beys were working towards the common goal of liberating Greece. The Mavromichalis family had steadily gained control over the region. In 1690 they were listed among the "notable" families based at Kelefa, near the fortress across the gorge from Oitylo and from here moved to Areopolis, which grew into a powerful base fortified by various towers and financed by trade and piracy. They also annexed the small harbour just below Areopolis at Limeni to challenge the supremacy of Oitylo. Petrobey's palatial tower house still dominates the harbour.

The family distinguished itself in the battles that marked the long War of Independence. However, once victory was achieved they soon became disenchanted with the new state. They, like many of those who fought, expected their contribution to be recognised and to be rewarded by political power and position. This was given mainly to intellectuals and others returning from exile who had played no part in the war. Furthermore, the idea of central government and taxa-

Areopolis Map –

4 – carving from the Taxiarches church

5 – the museum's latest exhibit

8 – the Stylianos Tower

9 – the Barelakos Tower

tion didn't sit well with the Maniats who valued their freedom and independence. Revolt fermented in the Mani and the first president of Greece, Ioannis Kapodistrias, held Petrobey under house arrest as a hostage in Nafplio. He managed to evade the guards once but was retaken before reaching the Mani. Had he reached Areopolis, there is a strong possibility that an uprising would have ensued. The situation though continued to be insufferable to the clan and on 9th October 1831, Giorgios and Konstantinos Mavromichalis took matters into their own hands and assassinated Kapodistrias outside a church in Nafplio. Petrobey was not implicated in the killing and was eventually released.

The Taxiarchis Church on the March 17th Square was built in 1798 and dedicated to St. Michael and all the "warrior" saints. It is often locked and the frescoes inside are modern. Externally, at the top of the curved apse are carvings of the Zodiac and there are more above the main door.

Next to the church is the restored tower of the Hotel Tsimova. A real character, Giorgios, runs it and on the ground floor he has assembled his own collection of weapons. Displayed in 2 cabinets the museum includes guns from the War of Independence and from both world wars and some replicas. There used to be an unexploded bomb outside the door but this has been removed. There is no entrance fee but a donation is always welcome.

If you visit one church in Areopolis, Agios Ioannis O Prodromos (John the Baptist) is probably the one as the frescoes are still in good condition, making their content easily decipherable. Painted in 1859 by Papa- Ioan-

nis Fragakis from nearby Pyrgos Dirou, the frescoes to the right of the altar are a kind of picture-book story for the illiterate, showing in sequence the Last Supper, the Betrayal, Jesus before Kaiafas and then Pilate 'washing his hands' followed by Jesus mocked and then scourged. Beneath this sequence, by the altar is the image of John the Baptist, depicted in the usual way of appearing scruffy and dishevelled, with wings. Around the entrance door is another standard in Byzantine painting – at the top is the Crucifixion and under is The Last Judgment, with unfortunate souls plunging down into hell.

Fragakis died before the paintings were finished but one wonders if it was he who got the proportions slightly wrong in the image of Christ in the fresco showing Pilate washing his hands, as by shortening his torso, his feet appear to be off the ground. In fact the figure seems to be floating like a helium-filled balloon anchored only by the rope in the hands of one of the soldiers.

Areopolis has a number of towers, most of which were built by the Mavromichalis clan. The Kyriakoulis tower has smaller dwellings around it that formed a small, fortified settlement. The Kapetanakos tower has been converted into an hotel where as a guest, you could wage war with the neighbouring Londas tower hotel. The original tower built by Stylianos Mavromichalis in 1760 was added to in the 19th century when the tower was raised and the house converted to what amounted to a mansion. It has an extremely high curtain wall and again the objective was to impress.

There is a great bookshop on the square, next to the cake shop. Its owner, Giorgios, is a real Mani enthusiast and has a good stock of maps, books and recently a DVD as well as his own Mani magazine (in Greek).

A Byzantine museum is due to open in the spring of 2006, located in the restored tower next to the church of Ioannis O Prodromos. It promises to ensure that local treasures housed in locked churches will now be on permanent display beyond the grasp of unscrupulous thieves.

By following the map out of Areopolis on the road to **Omales**, it is possible to walk down to the pebbly beach of Pyrgos and then on the caves of Pyrgos Dirou. Once you come to the T–junction marked on the map of Areopolis, simply turn left and follow the road all the way down to the beach. The concrete gives way to a dirt road and as you near the sea, it swings right. To get to the beach you have to hop over the wall by the house and walk down some steps to get on to the rocks. You will see steps ahead of you on the other side of a very small beach that bring you out onto the tarmac road to the beach. It should take just over an hour to here from town. There is no cafe on the beach so you will need to take plenty of water. It is also possible to cut across the small headland at the far end of the beach to get to the caves of Pyrgos Dirou. An earth path runs around the back of the concrete hut – simply follow it for 5 minutes to get to the caves. The ticket office is 100m up the road.

Pyrgos Dirou

Pyrgos Dirou is 10 km south on the main road from Areopolis. The modern village is spread out along the main road and you turn right in the middle of the village to get to the famous Vlyhada Caves. This junction is well signed – 5km to the caves. The small market square on the right before this turn has a statue of 'The Amazon of Pyrgos' commemorating the women who repulsed a large force of Turkish troops using only knives, rocks and sick-

Areopolis Map –   7 – Ioannis O Prodromos

7 – 'floating Jesus', Ioannis O Prodromos

2 – the mesuem

walking to the beach at Pyrgos Dirou via Omales

les. The battle took place in June 1826 against the forces of Ibrahim Pasha. The Maniat men had left to defend the wall at Verga (outside Kalamata) where the Pasha's main army, having swept across the Peloponnese after the fall of Mesalongi, was attacking the Maniat defences. A force of 1,500 Egyptian soldiers landed in the bay at Pyrgos Dirou with the objective of seizing Tsimova (Areopolis), trapping the main Maniat forces to the north and opening the road to Gythio. Ibrahim Pasha was an extremely able general and this would have been a brilliant tactic to outflank and entrap the Maniat force but he underestimated the Maniat women. When the alarm was raised, they were harvesting their crops and attacked the force in fierce 'hand to hand' combat. They were armed only with their sickles, sticks and stones but forced the Ottomans into a defensive position until reinforcements of men and more women arrived to drive them out. Only one third of the landing force escaped to their ships and the rest were destroyed.

The road to the caves takes you past the old village. After the supermarket and bakery, a sign on the left indicates a "Fortified Settlement" Follow this road to a large church, fork left and you soon come to the 25m high tower and buildings of the Sklavounakos clan, which is an impressive example of a fortified stronghold.

the Vlyhada Caves, Pyrgos Dirou

Back on the main road, you pass a couple of tavernas on your way to the caves and on a sweeping left bend a concrete road drops down to the beach of Pyrgos Dirou. If you go to the beach, don't be tempted to take the dirt road back to Areopolis as a short cut – it won't save any time at all.

The Vlyhada Caves are the area's number one tourist attraction. A large network of hugely impressive stalactite-studded caves can be explored- from a punt with the final few hundred metres now done on foot. The opening times are JUN–SEP: 8.30–17.30 and OCT–MAY: 8.30–15.00 (closed Mondays) and admission is 12 euros (7 for children). Tel: 27330 52222.

The caves were discovered in 1895 and full exploration began in 1949. They were finally open to the public in the 1960s. The museum exhibits bones, pottery fragments, amphorae, needles etc dating from the Bronze Age families who lived there before the entrance was blocked by an earthquake around 3000 BC. It is cool inside even in summer and in places the passages get quite narrow. The caves are well lit and when you exit you will be given the chance to buy a photo of your party in the punt. If possible, it is advisable to get there early to avoid the tourist buses arriving from mid-morning onwards. There is another Amazon of Pyrgos statue before the entrance and below there is a small pebbly beach for a swim. A short 5-minute walk, over the small headland, to the main beach of Pyrgos Dirou starts at the first bend in the road on leaving the caves. Up to your left is a rusty gate with a couple of concrete steps. The path starts here.

South of Pyrgos Dirou the road takes

you deep into Kakavoulia where the plain is littered with numerous tower villages. Equal in significance to the area's history of feuding to gain control of limited resources, resulting in the phenomenon of the tower house, is the prolific and sustained programme of church building (which still continues today). Even if churches are not your thing, they are an intrinsic part of Deep Mani and their tiled domed roofs appear at every twist and turn. They vary greatly in age and due to the threat of theft are often, frustratingly, kept locked. But taking the time to visit one or two, referring to the section on church frescoes when access inside is possible, should be part of any day out in the area. Heading south from Pyrgos Dirou along the main road, here is a summary of where to find the most interesting examples.

the beach at Pyrgos Dirou

the Taxiarches church, Glezos

Just as you leave Pirgos Dirou an unsigned concrete road takes you to **Glezos**. Wiggle your way through the village and at the T-junction at the top end, turn right. After 250m you'll come to the Church of the Taxiarches (the Warrior Angels) on the right. This 11th century cruciform church has stone buttresses and a few re-used bits of marble to support the walls. Inside there are only fragments of frescoes left exposed and one of these appears to be the Archangel Michael after whom the church is named. New aluminium doors and windows show that after 1000 years the church is still being used because of the neighbouring graveyard (the key to the church is usually in the door). Returning to the main road and after 2km there is a right turn signed to **Triandafilia** and **Harouda**. Pass through Triandafilia and **Nikandrio**. Keep right at a junction with the locked, barrel vaulted church of St Michael and carry on to Harouda. Ignore the first right turn as you enter the village and as you drive through you'll see one or two ruined megalithic houses and, on a bend, a ruined megalithic church. Continue to the outskirts of the village and you will reach the beautiful 11th century

cemetery, Nikandrio

St Michael, Harouda

church, dedicated again to St. Michael, partially hidden behind a high wall with a gate that gives access to the courtyard. The church has a tall, marble campanile, which contains several pieces of old marble, but like most of the churches, this is a more recent addition. The octagonal dome has arched facets with intricate brickwork decorations. The door of the church has a wonderful carved lintel. Walking round the outside of the church, you cannot fail to notice the massive rectangular blocks of marble, interspersed with sandstone blocks, with which the walls have been constructed. The intricate cloisonne brickwork decorations are also exceptional. On the north side of the church is what appears to be the square base of a tower on top of which is an unusually large bell. The church contains some wonderful frescoes but many have been damaged by smoke and by water seepage. The whole of the narthex has been whitewashed and the key holder explains that this was because it made the women who stood there uncomfortable to turn their backs on the saints who adorned the rear walls! The marble tie beams and decorations on the templon are fantastic but most remarkable of all is the ring of decorated marble which runs round the base of the dome. The demand to see this church is very high and the key holder keeps a low profile in summer or else she would spend all her time unlocking and locking the church. The best time to catch her is in the late afternoon or early evening when she goes to the church to clean it, light candles etc. In fact, in looking at the high security front door, she should really be called the 'keys' holder. Returning to the main road it is quicker to take the right fork at the barrel vaulted St Michael you passed earlier.

A short distance further south (approx 2 kilometres) on the main road, there is a road that goes off to your left that connects a series of villages that run parallel to the main road. Refer to the map to decide where you want to turn up. Again, in a southerly direction, the villages run as follows:

Fragoulias – a tiny hamlet of no particular note – nor is there a signpost there telling you its name.

Next is **Dryalos** (again, no signpost) but there is a fine tower on your right as you enter the village, which will help you identify it. Most of the village is above the road to the east so take the first turn on your left and drive up the hill. It is an old village with many old houses, some of which have been restored, and some old towers that are mainly derelict. Another road leads off to your right and takes you into a small square where there is a large church with a very impressive bell tower built alongside it. The icons inside indicate that the church is dedicated once again to Agioi Taxiarchis, the Archangels Michael and Gabriel, and there is also a fine fresco of this pair just to the left of the iconostasis. St Michael is carrying his sword and wearing armour decorated with fierce faces on his breastplate, epaulettes and greaves. There are no frescoes on the ceiling, just faded powder-blue paint, but both sides have frescoes as you near the plain, modern iconostasis. These include Agios Konstantinos and Agia Eleni, (both wearing the crowns and the rich robes of Byzantine Emperors), Agios Petros, Agios Andreas. The road turns to the right and brings you back to the main road at the far end of the village and the twin chapel church dedicated to St. George.

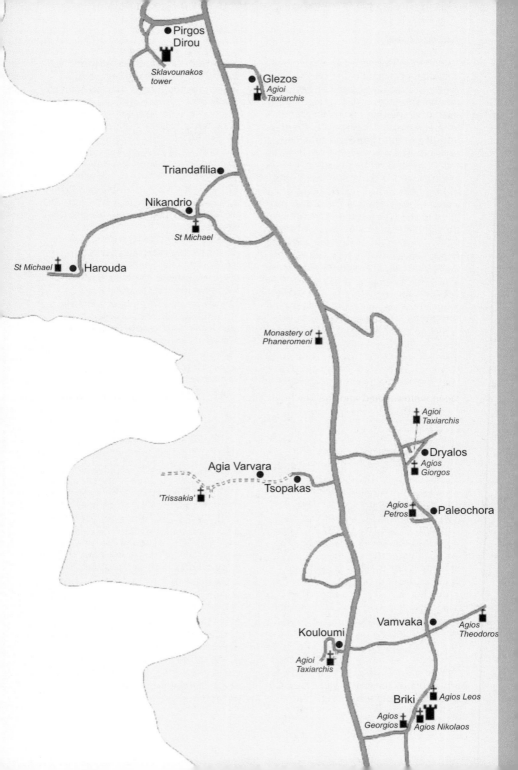

Paleohora – one of many such named villages in Greece ('old village'). To the right is a fine tower house that has been restored and appears to be lived in. As you leave the hamlet, on your right you will see a graveyard and then a concrete road that leads down to it. Go down here and stop at the graveyard where an old kalderimi leads down from the hamlet. A gate in the modern wall leads you to a derelict church, Agios Petros, on your left with a second, older, derelict megalithic church alongside it to the south, both with single apses. There is not much left of either church but Agios Petros still has some faint frescoes even though it has no roof. Two marble columns support a crude lintel in the doorway of the templon but the remains of arches on either side of the church show that there was an older templon here at one time. Below the conch of the sanctuary is a fresco of St John Chrysostomos – the best-preserved fresco in the church.

Driving through the village of **Vamvaka,** you'll come to a crossroads where right takes you down to the main road. Left will take you in a matter of metres to Agios Theodoros, a beautiful yet decaying 11th century church. The key holder lives close by – down from the church and to the right are a cluster of houses. Locate a grey gate and shout "kleethee parakalo" (a hard 'th' as in *tha*t). There is a striking fresco of the Virgin Mary behind the templon in the conch of the apse but this is the only fresco that has survived and is said to be post-Byzantine. However, on this occasion wall paintings bow in importance to some of the stonework inside. One of the marble tie beams below the dome has an inscription that reads as

"Remember, O Lord, Thy servant Leo and his wife and children. His great devotion having provided these
adornments, let those who sing here pray for him. Amen. They were accomplished by the hand of Nikitas the Marbler, August 6583."

This not only tells us a precise date for the church (the Byzantine calendar date of 6583 translates into 1075 AD) but given the lack of other examples of craftsmen dating their work, Theodoros' example has been used as a useful yardstick for experts to date other churches in the area. Nikitas' work is also visible on the templon and his workshop seems to have had a number of clients commissioning work in other nearby projects. Even if you fail to get inside the church, it is still worth a visit. There are ancient marble grave slabs embedded in the walls (one has an inscription that reads "Farewell Diophantes, Farewell Dawn, Farewell Fortuna") and obvious comparisons in cloisonne work to the similarly dated Taxiarches churches at Glezos and Charouda, though sadly, Theodoros has not aged as well as the former.

The next village on is **Briki**. Briki has a number of churches. As you approach the village you will see a large derelict tower dwelling and a tower beyond it. When you are about 50 metres from the tower dwelling, there is a sign nailed to an olive tree on the left side of the road. Stop here and if you look through the trees to the left you will see the pile of stones that is the ruin of the church of Agios Leon. The age of this church is uncertain but it is thought to have been built in the late 10th century. A tiny door in the south wall gives you access to the church, the most noticeable feature of which is the gaping hole in the middle where the roof used to be. This is, however, of special interest to students of Byzantine architecture because it is the only church in the Mani and one of the very few in Greece that had a 'tetra-conch'. After passing a handsome tower on the left you will come to the 13th century church of Agios Nikolaos on your left with its cupola sitting elegantly on top of the solid block of the church. Inside the church, the frescoes are mostly faded and damaged and many are covered by a greenish mould. This is both sad and frustrating because Rogan points out that there are variations in some of the frescoes that represent a Maniat break with traditional classic Byzantine iconography. For example, the crucifixion shows Christ with his eyes open – a feature rejected by Byzantine artists in the 11th century. Similarly, the depiction of one of the Magi turning back while the other two continue their journey. Rogan also says that Salome is depicted wearing earrings and the apron of a Maniat peasant girl and that "*The impact made by this 'contradiction' is tremendous.*" Unfortunately, these references are now difficult to see well because of damage. There is, however, evidence of one blatant break with tradition still visible above the conch of the apse. The 'Holy Veil' of Christ is displayed being held in the hands of St Veronica whereas Byzantine tradition demanded that the Holy Veil and the Holy Tile be depicted on their own, which Rogan describes as "*a highly dogmatic character and demanding the maximum of abstract rendering.*" The photographs in Nikolaos Drandakis's book were only taken a few years ago but the state of the frescoes today shows a serious and rapid deterioration. A little further on a road leads down to the main road and on this corner is the ruined Byzantine Church of Agios Giorgios. It was a single–apse, vaulted church but the roof has completely fallen in, now offering a much easier way in (the door is very low and overgrown). A massive marble lintel, which once ran the width of the church on top of the templon, is lying on the ground. It is blackened and stained by the elements but beautifully carved and an inscription on it once again proves it to be the work of

Agioi Theodoros, Vamvaka

Tower–house, Briki

Agios Nikolaos, Briki

Agios Giorgios, Briki

Nikitas. Here and there are the faded remnants of frescoes but in the conch of the apse, you can still see the Virgin Mary with a truly remarkable face – but you'll have to fight your way through the undergrowth to get a glimpse.

Mina has many fine old towers and defensive houses, as well as a number of new buildings. But to keep going for a little while longer on the 'church trail', the following hamlet of **Polemitas** has more to offer. If approaching Mina from Briki, take the first turn on the left through the village and straight across at the crossroads. Ignore the next left turn and on the far side of the tiny hamlet of Polemitas, park on a bend by a small breeze-block water cistern. On the other side of the road a worn path leads to the Church of Archangel Michael, looking more like a goat pen than a church – once you realise that it is not just a pile of stones! The door in the north wall is tiny and it is pitch black inside so if you visit this church remember to take a torch. Above the door on the inside is a lengthy inscription that Drandakis has translated and it confirms the church dedication and dates the frescoes to 1278. It also names the painter as Giorgos Konstantinianos from an unidentified village called Agia Thekla. The frescoes are patchy to say the least. A few metres further up the road another path leads to Agios Nikolaos, a single-apse, barrel-vaulted church. The low doorway at the west end is set in walls about

'the Virgin of Briki'

four feet thick but once inside, you will be surprised by how tall the church is. On either side of the naos there are three arches set in the walls and, at the east end, these are plastered and painted with some very fine frescoes. There is also an arch spanning the middle of the naos and the whole effect is wonderful. The frescoes, according to Nikolaos Drandakis, are from the second half of the 14th century but no date is given for the church. The frescoes are mostly in very good condition and feature many female saints, including Sts Barbara, Nonna, Kyriaki, Kalliniki, Thekla and Anastasia. The portraits of saints Barbara and Kyriaki are almost identical, right down to their earrings and headdress, and the only difference being the patterns of their clothing. On the south wall in the arch nearest the templon is a fresco known as the "*Deisis*" or 'entreaty'. It is a set piece which always shows Christ 'Pantocrator' with Mary on his right and John the Baptist on his left, both in attitudes of supplication. The Virgin stands on Christ's right in keeping with the words of Psalm 45:9, "upon thy right hand did stand the queen". On the opposite wall are St George and St Kyriaki.

If you choose not to take the diversion to these villages and instead continue on the main Areopolis road, about 200 metres after the turn to Dryalos you will pass a modern building on your right with a sign indicating this is the Monastery of Phaneromeni. There is a high wall at the far end of which you can park and follow the steps down into a large courtyard where an inscription on a piece of carved marble dates this church to 1079. The church is usually open and the remaining frescoes are badly damaged by chipping which was done to apply another coat of plaster before repainting. There is a very crude 'Deisis' which probably dates to the building of the church. The monastery is still used by nuns. A little further south on the main road you will see a small sign on your right which points to Tsopakas and St. Barbara. Turn here and follow the road into the village. By a modern church on the right stop the car and approach the low stone wall. What it encloses will take your breath away.....

A sadly unfruitful attempt to preserve one of the many decaying churches in the Mani lies beyond the village. Keep straight, passing Agios Varvara on the right as the road bends and continue on to 'Trissakia' (a contraction of 3 small churches in Greek – *tria ekklesakia*). The dirt road is fine to drive on carefully. The real name of the church is Agios Theodoros and is actually three barrel-vaulted churches lying side by side. From the outside it does not compare to Glezos or Harouda and presumably this church qualified for help as there are two large holes in the roof of the larger, central vault but unfortunately the steel structure built to give protection from the elements has itself fallen prey to strong winds and the corrugated roof panels now lie all around. Though now even more unim-pressive from the outside, surprising treasures lie within. Inside the main vault is a wonderful, carved marble templon. It is still intact and close examination shows that the marble has been worked by exceptional craftsmen. The fate of what is left of the frescoes is inevitable given their exposure to sun and rain. The main body of the church was once covered in fres-coes but among the only really discernible ones remaining are of the 'Mesopentikos-to', the Last Supper and the seizing of Christ in the Garden of Gethsemane. It is easy to identify Judas at the Last Supper because he has been painted smaller than the rest and without a halo and looks like a naughty boy, while the disciples appear to regard him with contempt. The large crack running through this fresco heralds its ultimate fate. The scene in Gethse-

Tower-house, Mina

The church of Archangel Michael, Polemitas

'Deisis' – Agios Nikolaos, Polemitas

'Trissakia'

mane shows Christ with a rope around his neck and the soldiers in Frankish rather than Byzantine uniform. The depiction of a rope in this picture is unique but intended by the artist to remind you that this betrayal was followed by Christ before Pilate and of Christ 'Elkomenos' – 'being dragged'. In the bottom left corner is Peter cutting off the ear of one of the attendants. Nikolaos Drandakis doesn't give a date for the church but suggests the frescoes are late 13th century while Rogan states they are 14th century. Return to the main road by the same route.

If you feel a little downhearted about the plight of Trissakia, better news awaits further south where three churches have enjoyed having their exteriors restored, ensuring a prolonged life. Pass the KMOIL garage back on the main road and opposite a left turn up to Vamvaka turn right down an unsigned, narrow concrete road into **Kouloumi**. You quickly come to a right-hand bend with a dirt road off to the left and the church lies a few hundred metres down this lane. Drandakis calls this Church Asomati (All Saints) and Rogan calls it Taxiarchis while Greenhalgh calls it St. Michael's! It seems also that All Saints and Archangel Michael are closely tied so all three names are probably applicable. To add to the confusion, Drandakis dates the church to the late 12th century while Rogan lists it as Post-Byzantine. Greenhalgh agrees with Drandakis. The church recently underwent a massive restoration and is looking very pristine is its attractive setting with a backdrop of cypress trees and towers on the ridge behind it. It has three semi-circular apses and an octagonal drum. All in all, very photogenic though unfortunately there is no sign of a keyholder.

Travelling on the main road south from here, you will pass through Lakkos and a small church on the left houses two marble panels in its wall that are thought again to be the work of Nikitas. 400m further on, a sign on the right directs you to **Erimos** and Agia Barbara down a road to your right. Follow this road down through the olives and you pass a ruined megalithic church with a single marble column still visible inside among the jumble of stones. Continuing along the road you reach Erimos and on the other side of the village you come to the 12th century church of St. Barbara, circa 1150 according to Rogan. It is a beautifully proportioned, triple-apse church with an octagonal dome and some wonderful cloisonne decoration that has been restored to its former glory with the original decorative ceramic bowls set into the brickwork. The marble arches on the drum are new and shiny but will look better once they have weathered, as will the water spouts with gargoyle faces, which are also new and very bright. The marble panels set in the windows are mostly original and finely carved. The interior of the church is disappointing. There are a few bits of frescoes and lots of little squares cut in the new plaster – presumably to see if there are any frescoes underneath. The templon is new and partially covers a fresco of John the Baptist and another unidentified Saint and the conch of the apse has a Virgin 'Platytera' plus saints etc but is not remarkable. It is usually locked but if you are determined to get in, hang around for a while and if you are lucky, the key holder will spot you and come to let you in. But again it is worth visiting just to appreciate the restoration.

The final restored church to consider visiting is on an unsigned left turn just before a sign on the right adver-

tising the 'SUPERMARKET NIARXOS'. The
beautiful l2th century church of Tourloti is
on your right along a paved road. It is
actually the church of Saints Sergius and
Bacchus as inscribed above the door –
military saints from Asia Minor and rarely
included in the Mani pantheon – but is
usually referred to by the local name of
the 'domed one'. The church is locked,
the key holder once again being Dimitris
Kolokouris. However there is not much of
interest inside the church as most of the
interior walls are bare and remaining frescoes badly faded or damaged.

The detour to the Mini Circuit starts with
the right turn to Mezapos, see page 121.

Kita and Kaloni

Back on the main road, the next village is
Kita, once the most powerful village in the
Niklianiko and the site of the last great
inter-family feud in 1870 that was eventually suppressed by a battalion of 400
regular soldiers with artillery support. The
Earl of Carnarvon recorded a feud that
had raged in the town prior to his arrival.

"For thirty years previously to 1839, the
best blood of Kita had been drained in a
deadly and embittered strife which arose
out of an imaginary insult to a young girl
whose scarf was held too long by her
partner in the dance of some village festival. For thirty years the two factions
exterminated each other; murder was not
disguised, it was the avowed profession of
every clansman and the recognised mode
of warfare."

The towers and fortified houses of Kita
are fascinating and worth a wander round.
Many of the windows and walls of the
buildings have relief carvings on them so
keep a watch for these as you make your
way round. In modern times, local rivalry
is limited to the competition for business
between the two mini-markets on the
main road.

A narrow road leads from behind Kita to

the Last Supper, Trissakia

Kaloumi

'Tourloti'

Kita towers

the village of Kaloni, higher up the mountain slope, where there are more towers and fortified houses.

Nomia

Opposite Kita, on the other side of the road, is Nomia. Inevitably a rival village to Kita, this too is a fascinating village to walk round. Normally, tower houses were built with the house and tower as separate components alongside each other but in Nomia there is a good example of a tower house built as a single unit by the powerful Messisklis family. The tower is five stories high and dominates the eastern side of the village, although the crack in the stonework suggests that it might not do so for much longer. The family could man the tower from within the house while a second entrance allowed clan members access from outside. The house was originally two stories high with a marble roof. In the yard of a small derelict house nearby is a rusty, six-foot cannon cemented into the floor. If you follow the road that takes you right behind the village you will see a large, ugly, unfinished church at the end of a short road. There are several old marble columns lying around outside and above the west door is a rather crude old tombstone embedded in the wall on its side. Next to this is a beautiful fragment of carved marble, presumably from another church. It is quite badly damaged and shows a griffin attacking what looks like a cow or bull as well as some other intricate designs. Damaged though it is, it shows how skilful some of the stonemasons were in days gone by.

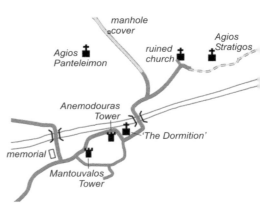

Boulari – Lower and Upper

Driving south from Kita for about 5 kilometres, shortly before you reach Gerolimenas, there are two turnings on your left to Boulari, neither of which are signposted. There are effectively two villages, Kato & Ano or Upper and Lower Boulari and the upper village in particular is an interesting place to wander around and from where you can take a circular walk up into the hills to the remote villages of **Pepo** and **Leontaki**. The main street of the upper village, below the large modern church, is dominated by a tower once defended by the mighty Mantouvalos clan in direct opposition to the Mavromichalis'. A little further on is the much older Anemodouras Tower that may be early 17th century, when the village was recorded as having a population of 40 families (compared to nowadays when you will be aware of only a handful of houses still being inhabited). This tower was built with huge stones without mortar and rises from walls two metres thick at the base tapering to 80 cms thick at the top. Access to the tower was from the house that 'leans' on one of the outer walls and both the house and tower originally had marble roof tiles. A second house has been added to the first at a later date. Agios Panteleimon is one of the earliest surviving churches in the Mani with some frescoes over 1,000 years old. To reach it, drive past the large modern church of 'The Dormition' and take the next left turn; (on some maps this area is marked as Diporo).You pass some houses and derelict houses and towers and the road turns to track. Approximately 100 metres further on, you will see a manhole cover protruding from the dirt road. Directly below this you will see the slate roof of the church. It is an easy scramble down to the church, which is not locked. The frescoes are dated by an inscription to 991 and although somewhat crude, are very striking – especially the portraits of the martyrs Panteleimon and Niketas in the double conch set in the apse behind the strangely shaped templon. The whole effect gives the sanctuary a cave-like quality. Other images include the Ascension, Baptism, washing of the new-born Christ, various Saints and a later (possibly 13th century) portrait of Agia Kyriaki.

At the top end of the village, where the road effectively finishes, a short walk continuing upwards brings you to the beautiful 11th century church of Agios Stratigos. It is famous for the frescoes inside but unfortunately, like Episcopi, contacting the key holder in Pyrgos Dirou is necessary to get inside– as with Episcopi, Dimitris Kolokouris holds the key and so needs to be contacted in advance to arrange a viewing (phone 27330 52953). The graveyard has some old graves covered with "tikles"(slate tiles). It used to be customary to use the *tikles* from church roofs to cover graves and this accounts for the damage and destruction of many frescoes which then suffered from rain seeping through the damaged roofs. If you do get hold of the key, the effort will soon be rewarded as the church hosts very fine 12th– 14th century paintings in good condition (be sure to have a strong torch with you). Greenhalgh provides a very detailed plan in his book that identifies each scene, saint and martyr. With the two towers of Leontaki perched on the hill behind, this is a very photogenic spot and

Boulari – Anemodouras Tower

Mantouvalos Tower

Agios Panteleimon

Agios Stratigos

encapsulates the history of medieval Mesa Mani. In getting to the church you will have passed the beginning of the walk up to Leontaki on your right– way–marks clearly reveal the beginning of this walk– see walk 182.

If you have visited just a few of the churches mentioned in the last few pages and possibly detoured into the Mini Circuit, then you are probably in need of refuelling. The picturesque seaside village of Gerolimenas awaits with several cafes and tavernas over-looking the sea. There are three roads entering the village so if you miss the first, don't worry.

Gerolimenas

The tiny harbour at Gerolimenas was only established in the 1870s. An outsider from Syros brought his mer-cantile wealth here to establish a jetty and warehousing and so the village was born. Prior to this period a smaller cove was used a little further to the south of Gerolimenas at Giali. An insight into how the village was fifty years ago is given by Kevin Andrews, an American archaeologist, who spent four years in Greece right in the middle of the vicious civil war and wrote up his experiences in "The Flight of Ikaros". He came to the Mani from his studies in Athens by ship (in those days this would have been the quickest way down from the capital), docking at Gerolimenas and was clearly affected by his initial impres-sions;

"Someone helped me out on to the pebbly beach of a port just big enough for a few fishing boats. Peo-ple thronged around me in total silence, with swarthy faces close to mine, faces the colour of earth with eye-sockets like black holes under the vertical sun. Here there was no gabble of tongues, none of the glis-tening, mercurial web of glances avid of perception: all eyes looked straight ahead. Everybody was armed; round the port and up and down the street shot-guns and rifles pointed behind each man's back, with cartridge-belts slung one upon the other across chests and shoulders, holsters stick-ing out of trouser pockets, while the swarm of intent and speechless men moved like troops in a village behind the lines."

Nowadays, the village is much more welcoming and indeed is experienc-ing something of a boom compared with the rest of Mesa Mani. The quality of the accommodation has been improved dramatically, spurred on by the conversion of one of the original warehouses into the Kyrimai Hotel, thus enticing Athenians down for a weekend break. There are a number of tavernas and cafes on the water's edge with fresh fish inevitably available. As Andrews stated, the beach is pebbly, flanked on one side by sheer dramatic cliffs– so it is a great stopping off point for a quick swim and a bite to eat before head-ing off elsewhere or to use as a base for more detailed exploration. In the

the beach at Gerolimenas

main square there is a bust to Major Panayiotis Mantouvalos of nearby Boulari, who was a hero of the victorious Albanian campaign of 1940–41 against the Italians.

From Gerolimenas the road continues south towards Alika on a flat, coastal road. On your right you will see the ruins of a couple of windmills and a tower which used to protect the small anchorage of **Giali**. This was the harbour controlled by the Mantouvali clan of Boulari before the development of Gerolimenas as a port. The clan offended the Mavromichalis clan by boarding one of their ships and removing part of the cargo as 'harbour dues' and they retaliated with an attack on the Mantouvali tower at Boulari. The dispute ended when one of the Mavromichalis men fell for the charms of one of the Mantavouli women who had been ferrying powder and shot to her brothers defending the tower. A truce was called, a marriage arranged and the dispute settled by a wedding feast of legendary duration and magnificence. The anchorage looks very insignificant from the main road but if you walk to the large tower by the waters edge, you will see that it is quite large and well sheltered and that the tower affords good protection to any ship moored here. It was for the protection of shipping from pirates and Turks that the "harbour dues" were charged. There is about 6 square metres of sandy beach at the harbour so it would not be too difficult to make it exclusively yours. A concrete road runs down the side of an old house to the windmills and harbour.

From here you will reach **Alika** after 2km and this is where you fork left to stay on the Mani Loop or turn right down to Tainaron. Before deciding which way to turn, Alika is worth wandering around to get an idea of how building methods developed as the village has examples of older 'megalithic' houses, characterised by their massive stone foundations and walls, as well as a good example of an

Gerolimenas

fresh octopus, Gerolimenas

Giali

Alika

older war tower, the Philipakos Tower up to your left as well as several more recent tower houses and tower dwellings.

The right turn to Tainaron begins on page 135.

Continuing on the Loop the left turn is actually a fork – the left branch takes you up into the village, the right fork is a continuation of the main road that now starts to loop across to the east coast, often referred to as the 'sunny' side of the Mani (though this is hardly true in the late afternoon when the sinking sun casts the whole area into shadow).

The road starts to climb and great views open up down to Kyparissos and Vathia. If you enjoy narrow roads with vertiginous sheer drops, the first turning you come to is a must. By a large eucalyptus tree on your right, a sharp left turn is signed to **Mountanistika**. The 4km road was mercifully asphalted in 2002 and it really is quite a driving experience. Ignore the turnings to Marathos and then Kotrafi and keep climbing up, hoping that you don't meet another vehicle coming the other way (which, when you get to the village and see how depopulated it is, you'll realise is very unlikely). As you ascend you (not the driver) will notice an astonishing level of terracing formed into the side of the hills – every inch of land was used to feed a much larger population.

After the dramatic approach, to wander around the village, park to the right of the road by the church. The village runs in a line along the ridge and most of the houses and towers were built surprisingly late, between 1880 and 1910. The views to the south are stunning as you are at an altitude of 600m. The road continues through the village and on to **Leontaki** with an even greater abundance of terracing all around. You will pass a plaque on the wall that declares a community-spirited gesture;

"In memory of Glykeria Dritsakou. Family and friends contributed money instead of a wreath in order to cement the section of the pathway from Kampitiko to Trikaino. Ever in the thoughts of her husband and children."

Leontaki has a resident population of three at the time of going to print and it is not difficult to understand why most have left. The same is true of **Pepo**, hidden in the valley beneath, whose outskirts are dominated by prickly pear trees. A stone path runs along the dry riverbed from Pepo back down to Boulari, so to embark on any journey in the old days would first have required this longish walk. Quite an effort if you have run out of sugar. The detour to Mountanistika, Leontaki and Pepo is an incredible experience.

Back on the main road the next village you pass through is **Tsikkalia**

Mountanistika

where a cannon pointing directly at you greets your arrival. Like Mountanistika, Tsikkalia is also set along a ridge. More marble spoilia are visible in the church – possibly from Kyparissos below? Above the main door of the church and below the campanile there is a curious piece of marble embedded in the wall. It appears to be part of an ancient marble carving and depicts a bull's head, yoked with a garland of fruit and flowers to another bull's head, most of which is missing. Above the garland is what appears to be a pair of 'flip-flop' style sandals. A short distance beyond Tsikkalia as you continue your journey eastwards, you look down on the legendary village of Vathia with its many towers crowded on the peak of a hill. The road now takes you across to the eastern side of the mountains and you start to travel north again. On your right you will see a roadside shrine and a gravel road leading off to your right. If you follow this you will see a village on your left, which is Korogonianika and then the road climbs higher until you reach another village which is Kainourgia. It is possible to get down to Porto Kaiyo from here though the road down is not completely asphalted.

Just before the road gets to Lagia, a right turn goes down to **Piontes** and its tower complex.

Lagia

Lagia is 5 or 6 kilometres from Tsikkalia and in a way deserves a greater reputation than Vathia as a feuding tower village, where four families lived in independently sited settlements, each with its own church. Many of the towers here were built in the older style of sloping, tapering walls while elsewhere, towers were being built with vertical walls and could consequently be built much higher. Some reached up to 20 metres with 7 floors. One of the towers in Lagia (it is claimed locally) was built overnight by 400 men of one clan to gain an advantage by sunrise. Lagia was the

Leontaki

Pepo

bull's head relief, Tsikkalia

Lagia

home of the Mani's famous doctor, Papadakis, who kept records of all the casualties of war and feuds that he treated in the middle 18th century. He travelled throughout the region and his records include many priests that he treated for bullet, knife, sword and rock wounds. He drew crude illustrations in the margin of his records showing the people he treated and the location and type of wound that he treated them for. Altogether he lists 700 wounded patients from 42 villages during the 53 years from 1715 to 1768. In some disputes there were more than 50 wounded in each village.

As you enter the village you first pass a smart new cafe on the left and then comes the old village Kafenion – the walls of which are a hotchpotch of murals and photographs with bits of sculpture and bric-a-brac lying around on shelves, fridges etc. According to one old newspaper cutting on the wall, it was a rendezvous for local artists and it is an interesting place to stop for a cold drink or a coffee. The centre is a little further on where a large new church dominates the square. There is a taverna too if you are hungry. The statue is another commemoration of Maniat military service. He was a helicopter pilot who was killed in a helicopter crash in 1996 in the confrontation with Turkey over the rock island of Imia, between Kos and the Turkish mainland. The square is the obvious place to park if you want to explore.

The first of a number of fairly secluded pebbly coves lies at the end of a right turn after Lagia. Another fairly vertiginous road (asphalt) snakes down to the coastal village of **Agios Kiprianos**. On entering the village turn left to the village beach or right along a dirt road to the even more isolated Abelo Beach, which has plenty of natural shade but no cafe or taverna. There is another road to these beaches further along, after **Dimaristika** that has a much gentler gradient, following the coast.

Shortly after Lagia, across a small gorge around which the road follows the contours, you will see Dimaristika perched among the rocks, scrub-bushes and cacti. A sturdy tower and integrated houses dominate the craggy hilltop with defensive houses scattered below. **Kokala** is 9 kilometres from Lagia and also has a small harbour with cafes and a burst of greenery, compared to the barren, baked rock and prickly pear cacti that characterise the 'sunny' side of Mesa Mani. There is a small beach and

Abelo Beach

Agios Giorgios

The first possible turning into the Mini Circuit comes once you have passed the turn to Erimos and come to a 'crossroads' with Mina to your left and Agios Giorgios and Mezapos to your right. Agios Giorgios is a microcosm of a typical Mesa Mani settlement – a small group of defensively built houses surround a taller war tower for additional protection with the church outside on the road towards Mezapos. The ruined, single–apse megalithic church with a *tikles* roof is on your left as you leave the village. This is the Byzantine church of Agios Giorgios and must have given its name to the hamlet. It is thought to be 13th century and is looking its age: there is a big hole in the ceiling and not much left inside. The only fresco worthy of the name is on the left templon wall inside the sanctuary. This shows St. Michael dressed like a Byzantine soldier and an unidentified female saint.

defensive settlement, Agios Giorgios

Agios Giorgios, Agios Giorgios

Mezapos

Having passed through Agios Giorgios, the final bend leading into Mezapos sees the road forking – left takes you into the heart of the village where there is a taverna, right drops steeply down and bends round to a small pebbly cove. As you face the sea at the cove, up to your left in the rocks are several graves that are probably Homeric. Indeed, Tim Severin, in reconstructing the route Odysseus took from Troy back to Ithaca, identified Mezapos as the possible home of the Laestrygonians, unpleasant giants who pelted Odysseus' fleet with rocks, sinking eleven ships. It is also thought to be the location of Homer's *Messe* which according to the Iliad sent ships to Troy. The deep harbour was used in later times by pirates and the infamous Sassaris clan from Mezapos were a constant thorn in the Mavromichalis domination of the area. Later the harbour served as a weekly stopping-off point for the ferry from Piraeus.

Mezapos

Cove at Mezapos

The road through the village is now a metal road all the way up to Stavri. If you are prepared to walk on such surfaces (and dodge the dogs who always seem to congregate there) there is a pleasant circular walk from Mezapos up to the renowned Episkopi church (pictured on the front cover) and back to Mezapos on paths running through the olives. See the walking section.

Heading towards Stavri by car you will get a view of Episkopi up on your left once you have passed another 12th century church down on your right.

Vlacherna

To get down to the church and ruined tower it is best to leave the car on the main road and walk the short distance. Named after the Virgin of Vlachernae in Constantinople, this 12th century church is always open – a piece of string keeps the door closed tight – though there is now little left in terms of internal paintings. What is just about discernible is a John the Baptist on the templon and there is a raising of Lazarus. Greehhalgh refers to it as the poets' church – it's easy to see why from its location if you give it a brief visit.

Continuing along the main road to **Stavri** another church appears on the hill to your left.

'Vlacherna'

Episkopi

This beautiful 12th century church was restored in the 1980s and houses some of the best wall paintings in Mesa Mani. However, to get inside requires some effort – the key holder, Dimitris Kolokouris lives in Pyrgos Dirou and so needs to be contacted in advance to arrange a viewing (phone 27330 52953). Dimitris does not speak English and in any case his role is to keep the church secure, not to act as a guide. If you do use his services, a tip of some kind would be appropriate. If this seems too difficult, the church's location is wonderful anyway. It sits in a peaceful spot with great views over Tigani and so is worth visiting even if you do not get inside. It is possible to get there by car by heading through another village called **Agios Giorgios** or *Agiorgis* and on to the tiny hamlet of **Katagiorgis**. Turn left between two tower houses, park the car and follow the stone path for 5 minutes. If you do manage to get inside there are a few things to watch out for.

The tall octagonal cupola is supported inside by buttresses behind the templon and two columns with old Ionic capitals in the nave. There is some fine carved marble on the tie beams, the lip of the dome and the small arch above the doorway leading into the bema. The frescoes of the Virgin and Christ which flank this doorway are 18th century, as is the Virgin Platytera in the apse above the altar, but the remaining frescoes adorning all the walls are 12th century and in the main, reasonably well preserved. They include: the Mandilion and Holy Tile, – Christ's face imprinted on the scarf on his way to the crucifixion and then transferred to the tile – which were used to rebut the arguments of iconoclasm; excerpts from the life and martyrdom of St George; excerpts from the life of Christ and hosts of Saints and Archangels. The west door of the church leads into the narthex where the congregation was sharply reminded of the fate that awaits those who fall by the wayside with graphic depictions of snakes writhing around the naked bodies of two red-headed 'fallen' women, hideous grinning faces gnashing their teeth, heads being consumed by worms and other scenes from the Last Judgement.

After Episkopi, back on the Mezapos–Stavri road where the road bears left, a much older church in a bad state of collapse appears, again on the left. Agios Procopios very probably dates from the 9th century as the inside of the church has no discernible wall paintings but rather faint symbols where the frescoes should be– this tells us the church was influenced by the iconoclastic period, 711– 843, which banned the portrayal of human figures in wall paintings and so internal decoration was limited merely to geometric shapes. Continuing along the road will bring you to a T-junction – left into Stavri and right down to the Tigani peninsula.

Gardenitsa

The second turning off the main road into the Mini Circuit brings you to the village of Gardenitsa where there are two more churches worth seeing. Ignore the sign for Pano Gardenitsa and continue a little further and turn right at the sign for **Kato Gardenitsa**, less than a kilometre before you come to Kita. A concrete road takes you into the village where you reach a T-junction. Look to your right and you will see the 11th Century church of Agios Sotiras (St. Saviour) on your right, with a ruined tower nearby. It is a domed cruciform church with three apses – the one in the centre is a pentagon and the other two are semi-hexagonal. The drum of the cupola has ornate arches on each facet and inscribed columns on the angles of

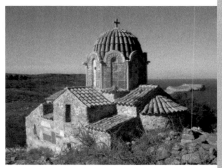

Episkopi

Agios Procopios

cross symbol, Agios Procopios

Agios Sotiras, Gardenitsa

the octagon. It has a domed outer narthex or entrance porch supported on arches, which are in turn supported by marble pillars. This feature is thought to be a 12th century addition. The arches of the outer narthex are decorated with dentil-course brick bands, as are other parts of the exterior of the church. The doorway has some rather crude carved marble crosses and designs which were painted at one time. The family who live across the road in a modern, flat-roofed house holds the key to this church and they are usually quite willing to come across and let you in. The interior is disappointing because much of it has been whitewashed. There are however some frescoes and fragments remaining, especially in the prothesis and diakonikon.

The other notable church in Gardenitsa is Agios Petros and to reach it drive past the T-junction and continue on the concrete road until you reach another T-junction. Turn left here and follow the track until it peters out by a restored tower with a large stone wall enclosing a courtyard. You have to park here and continue along the somewhat thorny track running due south: you can see the *tikles* (slate tiles) of the roof of the church just above the olive trees about three hundred metres away. Agios Petros is a single-apse, barrel-vaulted church that has not been positively dated but is thought to be 12th century. The outside is very plain except for a bricked-up doorway in the south wall with a marble lintel inscribed with a crudely carved cross – above which is a tympanum that shelters a very large mud-built wasp nest. The plain exterior of the church conceals a wonderful collection of frescoes that are thought to be 13th century. Some are damaged or destroyed but the remainder are well worth the thorny walk to see. As

you enter the church, an arch supporting the vaulted roof delineates a small narthex. A second arch separates the naos from the sanctuary and you can plainly see that a templon used to be erected here but has been totally destroyed and in fact, the broken fragments of carved marble are stacked against the walls. An additional feature of the church is that the single apse has two recesses with conches depicting Agia Paraskevi on the left and the Archangel Michael on the right. Below the conches are full-length portraits of saints, a theme carried forward to the pillar between the recesses where St Zacharias is portrayed. A splendid Archangel Michael is painted on the south wall, in the Naos section between the two arches. On his left are Agia Eleni and Agios Konstantinos supporting a large cross between them and wearing crowns and equally lavish robes. On the curve of the ceiling on the opposite wall is the Nativity. A semi-circular medallion shows the right hand of God blessing the baby Jesus wrapped in swaddling clothes below, with the star of Bethlehem between them. The manger is attended by angels while the head of a goat and a mule or horse are peering into the cradle. The Virgin Mary is to the right of the scene, enclosed in a 'lozenge' while Joseph is shown directly below the manger. The two men on Joseph's right are the shepherds looking after the sheep or goats that are scattered around in the scene.

Inside the door on the north wall, just above three medallions of Saints, is a very ugly, naked figure lying on the ground with his hands tied behind his back and a couple of feet planted on top him. This is all that remains of the scene which depicted Christ's descent into hell. It is His feet which are shown standing on Satan. Another rather confusing scene is the triumphal entry into Jerusalem combined with the raising of Lazarus shown as one continuous painting. Christ is shown riding a white horse or mule with garments and branches strewn in his path and a small boy in a tree waving a branch and apparently holding a cross. Immediately to the right of this is Christ standing at the entrance to a tomb with two men unwrapping the shroud in which Lazarus has been wrapped.

Agios Petros, Gardenitsa

Stavri

A typical Mani village, full of atmosphere but with not a lot happening in it except that it is home to the Tsitsiris Castle hotel which you will have seen signposted back on the main road. This would be a great base for exploration if you are staying in Mesa Mani. The main part of the building was originally a war tower and the terrace on top of the newer rooms has great views across to the mountains. If you have entered Stavri from the main road and not Mezapos then the hotel appears on your right. To get down to the Tigani peninsula continue past the hotel, maybe having stopped for a cup of mountain tea and keep straight, ignoring all turnings left and right. You will soon pass the road on your right that leads down to Mezapos – keep going straight, past the hamlet of Agia Kyriaki perched above on the right and head on to what is now a dirt road (which may have a gate across it with a sign telling you please to keep it closed to keep the cows in). Park the car where the road ends to begin the walk down to Tigani.

Inside Agios Petros, Gardenitsa

the 'Frying Pan'

walking across Tigani

Tigani

Literally translated as 'frying pan', it is very obvious how this causeway got its name. As is typical of the Mani, it is unclear exactly *what* was built or by *whom* up on the raised escarpment at the far end. The old battlements surrounding the 'pan' part of the frying pan clearly

suggest a defensive building was placed above, but the common assertion that it was the site of the 13th century Frankish Grand Maina castle of the Villhardouins is by no means irrefutable (see the introduction on castles). Despite this uncertainty it is still worth walking to the site if only to become an expert archaeologist for an hour or so in a fantastic location. What is clear are the foundations of an early Christian basilica – a style of building that died out in the 8th century and during the excavation work that took place in the 1970s, grave offerings were found dating from the 6th century. This substantial building measured 22m x 15m. Greenhalgh believes that its grand size indicates that it was the cathedral for the Byzantine bishopric of the Mani recorded from the time of Emperor Leo the Wise (AD 866–912).

It may simply be the case that Tigani has a much older history than was originally thought and that neither the Franks nor the Venetians ever fortified it themselves. The evidence of 'Cyclopean' masonry at the south-western corner could date as far back as the 13th century BC and though no pottery has been found to confirm this, it seems likely that the Mezapos area was a power centre during the Greek Bronze Age. Regarding its medieval history, the controversy continues. Greenhalgh was uncommitted, referring to the debate as *"tantalising mystery"*,

amateur archaeology!

although like him, if you walk up there and consider its position with the harbour of Mezapos close by and the natural defence of the cliffs around the site, it becomes difficult not to imagine it being used defensively over the centuries;

"But whether William's (Villhardouin) great castle was here or not, it is likely that the two-headed eagle of the house of the Palaeologus fluttered over Tigani and its great church in the thirteenth century, and when the last great era of Byzantium had passed and the Peloponnese became a battleground for Turks and Venetians, it is no less likely that the Lion of St Mark claimed this Maniat Monemvasia for the Republic more than once in the fifteenth century."

A clear dirt path takes you down on to the 'handle'. A series of cairns mark the easiest route across the pebbles and rocks up to the site. Set amongst the rocks are a series of stone salt pans. It was here that Leigh Fermor met a mother and daughter collecting sea salt on his travels in the 50s. It is incredible to think that on this stark, barren land, a meagre living was being made (they told him that on a good day they made 6 pence – a clear indication of how poor the area was and indeed, to a certain extent, still is). Once you near the battlement walls the path veers upwards and to the right as you approach them. Watch out for a 'hoof print' in the steps as you enter the site – supposedly from when a defeated princess leapt on horseback into the sea to escape capture. From the car to this point will take a leisurely 40 minutes. Once up on the site, the basilica foundations are straight in front of you. The entrance to the church is at the far end as you first approach the curved wall of the apse at the altar end of the building.

Good boots are needed for the rocky terrain and be sure to take plenty of water as
it always seems a few degrees hotter
down on the exposed causeway. Naturally, the walk back is a little tougher!

"Agitria"

If, once you are back at the car, you feel
like walking a little further, there is another interesting detour. About 50m before
the gate across the road you will see a
cairn on your right and the beginning of a
path dropping down to a stone water
trough. The path is well marked and last
year was well cleared by the local council.
As it reaches the cliff edge, it winds down
and is slightly vertiginous at this point.
Before heading down, the game here is to
try and spot the purpose of this detour –
a 13th century Byzantine church set in a
mind-befuddling location. If you fail to
locate it, keep going down the path and
looking ahead should soon bring the
church into view. Again the walk back up
to the road is harder going than coming
down. It should take around 45 minutes
each way. So, if you are planning to visit
both Tigani and Agitria you should allow
about 4 hours.

The church of Odigitraea – 'Our Lady who
shows the way' – abbreviated locally to
"Agitria", is set in an amazing position.
Perched on the edge of a sheer drop
down to the sea and under steep cliffs
behind, it is perhaps the greatest example
in the Mani of Byzantine religious fervour.
You cannot help but wonder how materials were brought here and why it was
located in such an isolated spot. It is fairly
certain that hermit monks lived in the
caves behind the church at one time (as
did the salt-collectors Leigh Fermor met).
The church is never locked and is well
worth a look inside. The church is 'cruciform' with a dome from about 1200 AD
and a narthex added at a later date possibly in the 13th century or slightly earlier.
Inside are wonderful carved marble decorations on the column capitals, around the

'Agitria'

walking to Agitria

Archangel Michael

red, plastic chairs

doorways and above the door that separates the naos from the narthex. This door was the original entrance to the church before the narthex was added. The badly damaged frescoes are from the 13th and 18th centuries and the most striking is the 13th century depiction of the Archangel Michael in his Byzantine 'laminar' armour

"...but what this one (painting) lacks in elegance of feature he more than makes up for in the lively expressiveness of his wide face with its bent nose and big eyes. For this is no heavenly bureaucrat or armchair general but a real leader of the Host who has fought manfully against the powers of evil in a harsh world." Deep into the Mani, Peter Greenhalgh.

When Greenhalgh visited the church, we can be fairly sure that the rather inappropriate red plastic picnic table and chairs outside were not there.

Coming back into Stavri from Tigani, take the right turn just before the hotel if you want to continue on to Kipoula and Cavo Grosso. You will immediately pass a modern church on your right. The dirt road snakes downwards and then steeply upwards, through the tiny hamlets of Agios Athanasios and Pori and on to Kipoula. Just before you hit the 'centre' of Kipoula you will see a track running off to your left. Follow this as it curves to the right behind the village and then you will see a church on your right with a *tikles* roof. It has

a single apse and what was probably an ossuary built onto the north wall, and although it looks very plain from the outside, the interior is a completely different story. The first thing you notice as you enter is that it has two arched recesses, one on either side of the naos. They are not very high but they are a most unusual feature and still have frescoes inside and around them. Above the archway on the south wall is an inscription and from this we know that the church was built in 1265 and is dedicated to the Agioi Anargyroi though it mainly deals with the financing of the project;

"The most venerable church was founded for fourteen and a half coins. (They offered) the priest Michael one coin, his brother, Leon, one coin, Kalarchos one coin, Michael one fourth, Kolarchos half a coin. It was finished by my hand, I who am Nikolaos the painter from the village Retzitza, together with my brother and pupil Theodore, in the month of June, on the sixth day, 6773 (1265)."

Rekitza is on the border of Messinia and Arcadia.

Kipoula and ancient Ippola

Even the origins of the name of the modern day village of Kipoula is open to conjecture – the diminutive of *'kipos'* ('garden' in Greek) or a continuation of the name of the ancient settlement of Ippola? If the latter, this could be taken even further as part of

Cavo Grosso

this settlement was Ano ('*apano*' or 'upper') Poula up on Cavo Grosso, thus the lower part could be "*kato*" Poula which when contracted gives the modern day Kipoula.. As you pass through the village, stop to muse over the extraordinary 'church within a church' on your right. The story here is that a local in an act of religious fervour decided to build a new church around the already existing family church. The patron died before completion and the project was left unfinished. The modern building is unusual in design and the inner church, though locked, has some interesting marble fragments embedded in its outer walls, presumably pilfered from much earlier buildings. Heading out of the hamlet you soon come to a sign taking you off on a wide dirt track to your right to ancient Ippola. Or does it? Once again the exact location of this site is unknown – not surprising when you consider that as early as the 3rd century AD the 'city'was in ruins according to the travel writer Pausanias. The most common opinion is that Ippola was split, with the Ano Poula providing an acropolis. Pausanias refers to a shrine to Athena which some maps mark as being up on Cavo Grosso which makes sense if, as Leake asserted in 1805, the ancient site did indeed make use of the height of the escarpment as an impressive sight for a temple.

Cavo Grosso

If you fancy your chances of locating the shrine to Athena or have a penchant for walking along very rocky paths or indeed would like to meet some local cows, then a visit up to Cavo Grosso is a must. The views are fantastic – to the north Tigani, Mezapos and beyond to Areopolis, east across the plain to the mountains (and in particular the two towers of Leontaki, nestling in the hills like Bugs Bunny's teeth) and south all the way down to Tainaron. Cavo Grosso was known as the '*Thyrides*' (windows) in ancient times due to a number of sea-caves lining its base. Nowadays, the plateau is a labyrinth of

inside Anargyroi, Kipoula

churches perched on the edge of Carvo Grosso

ruins on Cavo Grosso

view from Cavo Grosso

ruins and stone walls, all partially hidden by low growing scrub. Heading along the dirt road from Kipoula, the first path zig-zags up past two easily visible churches, nestling in the side of the escarpment. If you park here and walk up, there are two choices once on top – heading north to two derelict churches and then back again or heading south, coming down another path near the village of Dri and then along the dirt road back to the car. The walk to the churches will take around 45 minutes each way. Once you have hopped over the walls that run the length of the eastern side of the plateau, it is not difficult to pick up the rocky path that fairly immediately passes the first ruin and after this, red way-marks help you to keep to the easiest route. The two churches, perched right on the cliff edge above Kipoula, are not completely derelict and Agios Theodoros, the northern one of the two, contains fluted marble columns and column bases. The other also has some carved marbles which have obviously come from an earlier temple or building, presumably from ancient Ippola. The very faint wall paintings have surprising significance to Byzantine art historians (surprising because if you look down to watch where you are putting your feet, this 1000 year old relic has now clearly been reduced to being used as a cow shed...) as there are remains of frescoes from three distinct periods: can you make out the 11th century Descent into Hell and the Entry into Jerusalem on the curve of the south wall or the 13th century Ascension scene painted on the ceiling just inside the sanctuary?

See page 181 for the circular walk.

Heading eastwards from Cavo Grosso back into the plain and the confusing network of roads, the chances of getting a little lost are further increased by a profusion of Niklian villages all beginning with 'K'. Karavas, Kounos, Keria, Kechrianika, Kita and Kaloni form a kind of ring around the southern end of the mini circuit. Each could simply be driven through en route elsewhere or if you want to stop for a little exploration and to clear your mind to work out exactly where you are, there are a few things that could be pointed out. Kita and Kaloni are back on the main road, so if you want to visit them and rejoin the main road at Gerolimenas, you'll have to backtrack up the main road.

Karavas

Whichever direction you approach from you need to turn into a narrow, signed lane into the village and turn right, past two derelict churches on your left and park where the road bends sharply to the left by a tall tower built onto the corner of a house. There is a narrow path running due west into the olive groves – follow this for about 100 metres and you come to the church of Agios Nikitas. All the frescoes are fairly damaged and faded but have been dated by N. Gioles, a lecturer on Byzantine Archaeology, to a period between 1270 and 1290 in the main body of the church and in the narthex to the second decade of the 14th century when the narthex was built. The former include a barely visible Virgin in the conch of the apse, flanked by the Archangel Gabriel, 'The Harrowing of Hell', the Nativity, fragments of the Presentation in the Temple and a small section (back end of donkey) from the Triumphal Entry. There are various saints including Agios Nikitas wearing a coronet and mounted on a white horse. All that remains of the crucifixion on the west wall is a group of soldiers, one of whom is carrying a long tapering

'Norman' style shield. In the narthex, above the door which leads into the nave, is a fresco of the Panagia 'Kecharitomeni' which means 'The Charming'. Other depictions include Michael and Gabriel flanking the Panagia, the Baptism, Saints Nikolaos and possibly Damian to the left of the door, other Saints on the north wall and a very faded 'Assumption' of the Virgin on the south wall.

Kounos

As you approach Kounos from Karavas, about 50 metres before the junction from Kipoula, there is a white concrete house on your left and immediately before it, a concrete road running off to the left. Take this road and keep bearing left until you reach a 'car park' outside the walls and gate of a graveyard. This is known locally as 'Pentakia' (the five churches) and there are two churches here that you could visit if you are in the mood. There are a further two churches in ruins and among the bushes is probably a fifth; hence the name.

The larger of the two churches is called Agios Giorgios. Inside the church, there are some wonderful frescoes although many are damaged or faded, including St George with a very strange looking horse's head with what appears to be St George's shield behind it, a badly faded Last Supper and numerous armed saints. A fairly barren apse does have the gem of a fairly severe looking St Simeon the Stylite – and rightly so for an ascetic who spent 40 years perched 60 feet in the air on a pillar.

The similar but smaller (and longer: could it originally have been 2 churches to make up the 5?) Agios Nikolaos next door has the usual Hodegetria and Christ Enthroned on the templon with John the Baptist flanking them on one wall and on the opposing wall the 'Dormition of the Virgin Mary' – the 'Koimesis' which means literally the 'falling asleep' or death of the

churches on Cavo Grosso

Agioi Theodoros, Cavo Grosso

Agios Nikitas, Karavas

Simeon the Stylite, Agios Giorgios, Kounos

Virgin. The Virgin is shown lying on a bed surrounded by the Apostles and Christ holding her soul represented by a child wrapped in swaddling clothes. If you look carefully at the edge of the bier in which the Virgin is lying, you will see a pair of disembodied hands and, to the left of this, an angel holding a sword. This is not always depicted in Dormition icons but refers to a legend recorded in 4th century texts and Byzantine writings that say that a Jew, Jephonias, touched the bier and an angel immediately cut off his hands. In the 'Painters' Manual' of Dionysius of Fourna, he describes the scene to include *"a Hebrew is before the bed with his hands cut off and hanging from the bed and an angel with a naked sword."*

Keria

Another detour to another church can be found at Keria. Once you have turned into the village the 13th century Agios Ioannis is on your right. It has recycled a great variety of carved marble in the outer walls in a seemingly random manner. Two ancient columns are set in the concrete of the courtyard and you can see two or three Ionic column capitals embedded in the west wall as well as other fragments of old marble which must have come from an early temple – perhaps at Ippola. There are also elaborately carved Byzantine marble pieces that must have come from an older church templon. Unfortunately, some of these 'borrowed' pieces have been stolen themselves, the most glaring example of which was an ancient tombstone that was laid horizontally to the right of the door, showing two women and two men holding hands as though saying a fond farewell. This was recorded and sketched by the Italian Anconitano Ciriaco who travelled through this area in 1447. Someone hacked this antique out of the church wall in the spring of 1999.

Ochia

Heading back to the main road from Keria, the village of Ochia off to your right, offers a circular detour and a chance to take in a few more churches and towers, some of which have folkloric carvings and sculptures in their walls. The 12th century church of Agios Nikolaos is set just outside the village and is recognisable by a large, three-tier bell tower – a rarity in Mesa Mani whereas there are many in the Exo Mani. This domed church is set back from the road on the other side of the village and is architecturally interesting, sporting a number of gargoyle-like waterspouts around the dome. As you pass through Ochia you will see a couple of ruined towers and another twin church, dedicated to Agios Petros (St. Peter) and Panagia (Virgin Mary). They are both barrel-vaulted, built of megalithic stones. Their templons have the remains of some frescoes inside and in one, the doorway of the templon is made of two large pillars with a large lintel perched precariously above them.

From Ochia the road continues down to the little fishing village of Gerolimenas and the main Areopolis road.

Agios Ioannis, Keria

Tainaron

The final tip of the Mani, like the Mini Circuit, requires you to turn off the main 'Loop' road – this time at Alika, some 3kms east of Gerolimenas. The predominance of churches declines in this final stretch of land. But there is no shortage of alternative attractions: the most renowned tower village of the Mani, Vathia, a great sandy beach at Marmaris, lunch at Porto Kagio, a visit to ancient Tainaron and a walk out to the lighthouse right at the end of the peninsula.

Porto Kagio

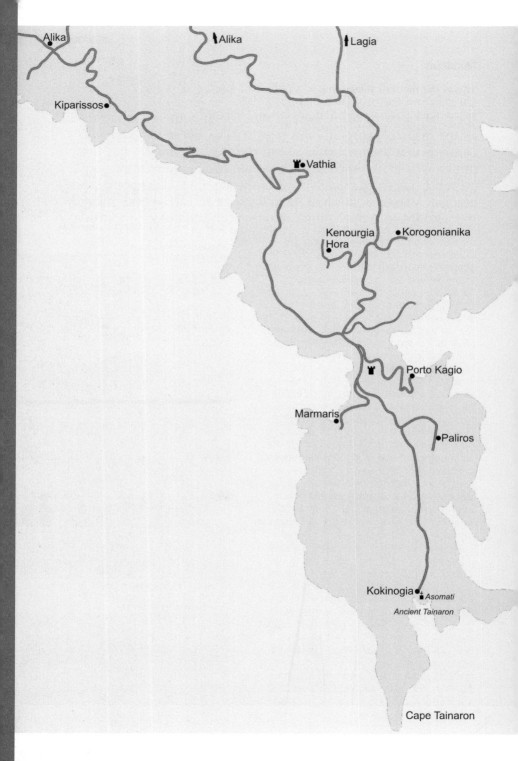

Kiparissos

This is the modern village that was once the site of the ancient town Pausanias called "Kainopolis whose name was formerly Tainaron", a member of the Union of Free Lakonians and the most important port south of Mezapos. It rose to prominence during the Roman Period and it was here in 468 AD that Genseric's Vandals tried to land from North Africa in an attempt to conquer the Peloponnese. They were defeated and gave up the attempt. Pausanias recorded a sanctuary of Demeter and a shrine of Aphrodite "on the seashore with a standing stone statue". Simple speculation leads to the conclusion that it served as a resettlement from Tainaron – hence the name is a contraction of "new town". There is still ample evidence of ancient times and by parking the car and wandering around it is impossible *not* to spot ancient spoilia embedded in walls throughout the village. Kiparissos spreads along an unusually straight part of the main road – the entrance and exit to it are un-missable as the road becomes extremely narrow in both cases and extra care in driving is needed. Once in the village a brown sign on the right encouragingly declares "the archaeological site of ancient Kainopolis". Unfortunately no museum or fenced in area awaits. Instead, a short walk along a track towards a pleasant pebbly beach begins to reveal an ancient past. Firstly, on your right, you will pass a well that can be accessed both from above ground or by dropping down a flight of steps (certainly not a modern way of drawing water). A little further on, the church of Agias Paraskavi, again to your right, has marble pieces in its walls that must have been borrowed from much earlier buildings. The best 'exhibit' lies at the back of the beach. Hiding amongst the stone walls there is a marble statue base that has a fairly clear inscription – as with the base at Thalames, it seems that Marcus Aurelius (Emperor 121-180AD) was the subject of the missing statue. His name is

recycling of building materials, Kiparissos

statue-base, Kiparissos

close-up of inscription

the harbour at Kiparissos

mentioned twice, once as being an *epimeletes* (one in charge) and once probably in reference to the commissioning of the work, which came "through the *ephorship* (officials) of those around M Aurelios". There are two indentations on the top of the base where the statue's feet would have been placed.

The tower that crowns the headland has marble foundations embedded there that suggests that something much older once stood there. The climb up to it is not easy as there is no clearly defined path and the unusually high stone walls make finding a sensible route a little tricky. Looking down from the tower towards the modern village, the ruins of the basilica of St. Peter are clearly visible and more marble columns are scattered around. More inscribed statue bases can be found at the basilica, one of which is more readable than its compatriot back on the beach. It literally translates as:

The City   (honours?.....) Julia Domna, revered wife of the emperor, Caesar Lucius SEPTIMIUS SEVERUS Pius Pertinax Augustus Arabicus Adiabenicus Parthicus, the Great and Garlanded, and mother of the emperor Caesar Marcus Aurelius Antoninus Augustus."

Julia Domna (170-217 A.D.) was born in Syria and was an educated, forceful woman who accompanied her husband and son (better known as Caracalla) on military campaigns. In fact she was so involved in her son's life that she starved herself to death when Caracalla was assassinated. The text goes on to list the minor officials who were in charge of setting up the statue, ending with "the Quaestor Rufus" - presumably the highest-ranking official. Two inscribed *stelai* were used to make the west door. St. Peter is dated

to the early 6th century and cited by some as evidence of the earliest Christian conversion of the Mani and is very close in size to the basilica on Tigani. To find the beginning of the path up to the basilica, retrace your steps about half way back to the road from the beach

Returning to the main road, evidence of antiquity continues. On your left you will pass a derelict house that has a marble Ionic capital set in the wall above the door. A little further on a concrete road runs off to the right (signed "the monastery Panagias"). Following the road/ path to its end brings you to a lovely spot – a church shaded by eucalyptus trees with views over the small harbour of Kiparissos. The small square in front of the church has several columns forming a boundary wall and more chunks of marble and more recently engraved stonework are visible in the church walls. To get to the harbour (which surprisingly has no cafe) return to the main road, turn right and turn right again just before the road narrows. This road curves back to the harbour. As you reach the sea, another church on your right has more marble in its walls including a block with a Latin inscription. Inside the church, a marble slab, which serves as the altar, is inscribed to the "City of Tainaron".

Vathia

If you continue along the main road you soon pass a pebbly cove for a more private swim and after this the road starts climbing up to Vathia, which is the towered village that features in most of the travel brochures and other advertisements for the Mani. The first glimpse of the village perched high on a hill is impressive to say the least and the cluster of slender towers are reminiscent of the hill towns of Tuscany. They were certainly not built merely for show as Vathia seems to have been the scene of some of the most intense internal feuding in the area. In 1805 Colonel Leake and his party decided to give it a wide berth:

"At 8.30 the sea is near us on the right hand and the village (Vathia) half a mile on our left. We halt five minutes to allow time to Gika and Poliko to answer the inquiries of a party of armed men from Vathia, who meet us on the road. This village, my guides say, has been divided into two parties for the last forty years, in which time they reckon that about 100 men have been killed".

In Leigh Fermor's time of writing some of the towers were still occupied but these days Vathia has almost totally submitted to the trend of depopulation, ironically, without much of a fight. There have been efforts to inject life into this historic village: the Greek Ministry of Tourism, EOT, half-heartedly opened a hotel in the late 1990s where guests stayed in their own tower. But unfortunately this venture was badly run and soon closed. Instead the only sign of life you are likely to meet are the packs of dogs which hang around the entrance to the village. The net result of these factors, increased further by a fire that burnt all the surrounding hillsides in the late 1990s, is that there is a strong, eerie atmosphere about the place. Simply by wandering about the village, it is easy to imagine the harshness of life in a tower village.

Beyond Vathia, the road meanders above the rocky coastline, passing isolated houses and towers and some wonderful scenery. After about 4 kilometres you come to a tarmac road on your left with a signpost to **Lagia**. This road forks within 100 metres – left and up to Lagia, the right fork takes you round the north side of the bay of **Porto Kagio** to a former monastery and a castle. A large church marks the site of the monastery and

the basilica of St. Peter. Kiparissos

columns outside Panagia Monastery, Kiparissos

more ancient remains behind the church

Vathia

beyond this the road passes a fertile gully fed by a mountain spring which emerges from the rock by the roadside. This gully used to provide a dramatic splash of greenery but much of the flora was destroyed by a fire which swept the hillsides in the summer of 1997. The road follows the contour round the side of the slope until you reach the high curtain walls of the castle. There are new and restored houses here but it is still clear that the castle was a formidable bastion built by the Turks in 1570 to protect the anchorage from use by pirates and as a base for naval operations against the Venetian lines of supply to Cyprus. In succeeding years it became a focus of conflict between the Turks and Maniats. To get to the picturesque bay of Porto Kagio below, return to the main road, turn left and take the next left fork.

Porto Kagio

The road winds down to the beach of Porto Kagio. The name translates from the Italian as the Bay of Quails and in times gone by this migratory bird was caught here in great numbers. Local author Kyriakos Kassis, whose family dominate the graveyard at nearby Paliros, describes the technique employed – the birds were trapped in nets suspended between two poles or by a solo hunter holding up a large butterfly net. The birds were then salted and cured. Nowadays, though it is possible to sight the odd flock on their travels, their numbers have significantly diminished. The sound of shotguns going off during the hunting season is very common throughout the Mani and unfortunately birds fall into the category of 'let's shoot anything that moves'.

The bay holds obvious strategic importance for the area and has a long history. It is almost certain that Porto Kagio is ancient Psamathus which Pausanias and other writers referred to but of which there is little trace now. There are some twenty tombs cut into the rock high on a ridge to the southwest of the port. They date from the Hellenistic period and are thought to be those of mercenaries, many of whom congregated in this area in classical times and much later, to offer their services to passing ships. A short walk to the mouth of the bay brings you to a monument to Lambros Katsonis. He held a commission from the Russian Imperial Court and operated against Turkish shipping under the Russian flag. The bay saw warfare again in the Second World War when during the evacuation of Allied troops in April 1941, Porto Kagio was one of the locations where British destroyers took off stragglers. There is even an exciting story of Luftwaffe Stuka dive bombers nearly hitting an allied warship in the bay – it escaped by going full steam ahead and frantically making smoke. In modern day Porto Kagio the only sailing vessels you are likely to see are yachts, moored up in the harbour to make use of the couple of fish tavernas and cafes that front the beach, which is a mixture of coarse sand and pebbles. A very pleasant setting for lunch and a swim. It is possible to extend the walk to the lighthouse by starting and finishing here. To join the walk on page 186 follow the sign in the middle of the beach to the mini-market. Pass the mini-market on your right and where the road turns into a path turn left at a rusty gate, heading towards a 2-story apartment block. The path up the hill begins behind this and will add an extra half hour or so to the main walk (each way). Once the path brings you out on tarmac (making a mental note of this spot for the return leg), turn right and follow the road to the next junction, turning left to the "Death Oracle". The dirt road up to Mianes is on your right.

To reach Marmaris, retrace the road back to the road junction and turn left.

Marmaris

As you approach Marmaris, a road leads off to your left. This is the main route down to ancient Tainaron. Marmaris is probably ancient Achilleus, a small harbour in classical times which was mentioned by Pausanias and other historians but can have had little significance since they give no detail other than the name. The first building you reach is a taverna which has recently added rooms to let that look straight down onto the beach. The path leading down to the golden sandy beach passes by the side of the taverna. Even in the height of summer it is not too crowded. The main part of the village sits on the cliffs where it could have been more easily defended and another path leads down the steep slopes from the village to the second sandy bay where the ancient harbour used to be. An astonishing sight at Marmaris, as in many other places in the Mani, are the old terraces on the steep hillsides high above the village. The effort needed to build these for the cultivation of wheat or corn is mind-blowing and illustrates the lengths people had to go to in order to survive in this harsh environment.

To continue south, return to the junction you passed as you approached Marmaris. The road takes you past an astonishingly large, recently redecorated church to a junction. The road to the left goes to **Paliros** and the road to the right takes you further south, signed rather scarily to the Death Oracle.

Paliros is an old village with an amazing number of houses being restored or already completed. Continuing your journey south, you come to a track on your

the monastery and castle, Porto Kagio

lunch at Porto Kagio

the two beaches at Marmaris

beach 1, Marmaris

right with a signpost pointing to
Mianes. On the other side of the road
is a sensible place to park if you want
to follow the track up into the hills to
walk down to the lighthouse in a
slightly more dramatic way than simply following the dirt path from
Tainaron (see page 186).

The road continues south and on
your left you catch glimpses of
secluded inlets and small bays with
shingle beaches and scattered, ruined
buildings. You finally reach a few
scattered houses, some new buildings offering rooms and a taverna.
Below you are the Bay of Asomati and
the ancient city of Tainaron.

Ancient Tainaron

Parking below the taverna, it is hard
to believe that the area was once a
thriving ancient town well-recorded
by Pausanias. The barren hills and
isolated buildings give no hint that
the bay was ever inhabited on a large
scale. But a closer inspection starts to
reveal enough to allow the imagination to start putting the site together
– and whatever work is put into
exploring it there are 3 pebbly coves
to cool down in after your efforts.
The first clue lies directly in front.
Standing on the small promontory
which juts out into the sea between
two small coves is the ruined church
of Asomati, from which the bay is

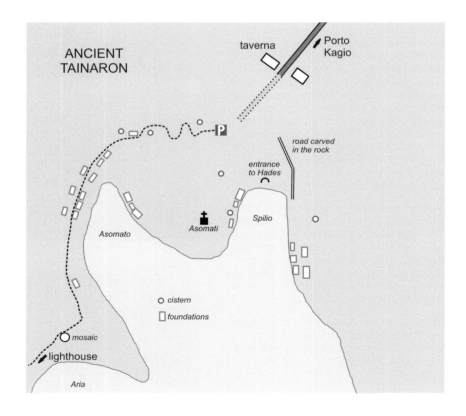

ANCIENT
TAINARON

taverna

Porto
Kagio

road carved
in the rock

entrance
to Hades

Spilio

Asomato

Asomati

o cistern

☐ foundations

mosaic

lighthouse

Aria

named, and which may have been the site of the Temple of Poseidon. This has never been proved, but a temple to Poseidon stood here for over a thousand years and was known throughout the ancient world as a sanctuary. Parts of this ruined church are constructed with massive stone blocks that could be ancient masonry. Col. Leake visited this site and, examining the outside of the building, he noted

Mianes

"This altar end is formed in part of Hellenic masonry, not quite regular; the stones, though very large, being not all quadrangular. At the end of this piece of Hellenic wall, near the altar, a narrow ancient door remains, which is not apparent from within, having been immured in converting the temple into a church. Several other parts of the church walls are formed of ancient wrought blocks, but that which is to the right of the altar only is original in its construction and site."

Tainaron

He also noted that the church was not aligned to the east. His description is still valid today and the point he was making is that the church was built using parts of the temple, or of another ancient building which was still in situ and not just by using stones that were scattered around the general area. The doorway he refers to is still visible on the outside of the church but, exactly as he noted, it does not give access to the inside.

The entrance to hell or Hades was also reputed to be at this ancient site. However, if you are hoping to find a cave system to parallel those at Pyrgos Dirou, you are going to be disappointed, as indeed Pausanias was;

Asomati

The entrance to Hades

"Some of the Greek poets have written that at this place Herakles brought up the hound of Hades, yet no road leads underground through the cave nor is it credible that the gods should have an underground house where they collected the souls of the dead."

Maybe he had taken Strabo a little too seriously before arriving there, as he previously had written,

"In the bend of the seaboard one comes, first, to a headland that projects into the sea, Taenarum, with its temple of Poseidon situated in a grove; and secondly, near by, to the cavern through which, according to the myth-writers, Cerberus was brought up from Hades by Herakles."

The cave itself is situated at the back of the cove to the left of the church as you face the sea, screened by shrubs and trees and used now to store the paraphernalia of the local fishing boats. Just beyond it are the oblong foundations of a building that could be another contender for the location of the temple.

Pausanias also mentions *"...on the cape itself a shrine, shaped like a cave, with a statue of Poseidon in front of it."* This shrine was probably the site of the Death Oracle. Peter Levi suggests that the 'cutting' in the rock on the other side of the promontory is all that is left of the "cave-like" shrine and records that in 1856, seventy bronze statuettes were

found here. Pausanias also referred to other aspects of the site he found interesting;

"Among other dedications at Tainaron is Arion the musician in bronze on a dolphin. Herodotus told the story of Arion and the dolphin from hearsay in his records of Lydia; and I have seen the dolphin at Poroselene showing its gratitude to a boy who cured it when it was wounded by fishermen; I saw it come when he called it and carry him when he wanted to ride on it. There was also a water spring at Tainaron which works no miracles these days, but once (so they say) if you looked into the water it would show you the harbours and ships. A woman stopped the water from ever showing such sights again by washing dirty clothes in it."

Herodotus does indeed tell the story of how, on his way back to Corinth, Arion's life was saved by a friendly dolphin after scheming sailors had forced him overboard. Herodotus suggests it was Arion himself who commissioned the statue at Tainaron.

With further exploration it is not difficult to discern the outlines of the

foundations at ancient Tainaron

foundations of what must have been a substantial town at Tainaron along with numerous cisterns for collecting water. These are clearly visible both north and south of the promontory of the church and it is possible to make out small streets, houses and steps cut into the rocks and some large, rectangular blocks of masonry. Among the jumble of foundations on the other side of the promontory from the cave, a clearly worn path heads off to the lighthouse at the end of the peninsula. Just beyond the first small cove lies the remains of a mosaic floor, exposed to the elements, whose wave pattern helps confirm the existence of the sanctuary to Poseidon. The growth of the town was not solely due to the religious sanctity and refuge offered but also due to its strategic location in terms of both war and commerce. It was here that in the 3rd century B.C the Greeks from Tarentum, a well established satellite city on the heel of mainland Italy, came to buy 5000 mercenaries to help in their ultimately futile attempt to defeat the emerging power of the Romans. Soon after it must have become the unofficial centre of the anti-Spartan Union of Free Laconians – an organisation not officially recognised until 21BC by the emperor Augustus. Kainopolis further north eventually succeeded Tainaron as head of this fiercely defended union and once the Romans had 'liberated' Sparta in 67BC, it must have reverted to a place of pilgrimage and peace.

The walk out to the lighthouse from the taverna takes a leisurely 50 minutes one way and the path gets a little rocky in places. It is well worth the effort as it is a wonderfully tranquil spot and a great place to do some serious 'ship spotting'. In 1941 the British fleet would have been visible attacking the Italian navy in the Battle of Matapan as part of the Allied retreat from Greece. It was such an overwhelming victory that the Italian fleet never showed its face again. Today you can see all kinds of ships plying their route to other Mediterranean ports.

water cistern, Tainaron

mosaic, Tainaron

pebbly cove, Tainaron

walking back from the lighthouse

Gythio

This section of the Mani offers the only passage through the Taygetos mountains from east to west. The main road running from Areopolis to Gythio follows a fertile, river valley and takes around 40 minutes to complete by car. This is the quickest route to get to Sparti/Mystras from Stoupa/Kardamyli with the picturesque waterfront town of Gythio providing an obvious break en route. Spending more time in the area could involve visiting Passava castle and one of a number of excellent sandy beaches (most of which are a far cry from the crowded sands of Stoupa) which could then turn a full day out into another 'loop', returning from Gythio via Skoutari and Kotronas.

Five minutes out of Areopolis, having passed the right turns to Sotiras and Skala you can take a short detour off the main road. Opposite the left turn to Kelefa village and castle, a right turn takes you through **Vachos**, **Drosospigi** and **Neohori**, rejoining the main road at **Karioupoli**. The route gently winds through the hills above the plain and gives an impression of life off the beaten track. Both Vachos, with its fanciful street lighting that suggests an improvement since Leake's visit, when he described it as a collection *"of about thirty miserable huts"* and Drosospigi have kafenia in their main squares in which you can relax in and observe village life from. Once out of the latter, great views open up down to the Bay of Skoutari, Gythio and the Malean peninsula. After passing a rather Bavarian looking modern tower house, you'll come to a junction– right takes you down to Skoutari, left to the tiny hamlet of **Elea** and on to Neohori which also has a cafe by its main church. Just out of Neohori by a small church, the road continues by heading left and down– keeping straight takes you up to **Kafki** and its solitary tower.

Karioupoli

Just before you reach the main road to Gythio, there is a tarmac road doubling back sharply on your right which climbs up to Karioupoli. First you pass a small ruined tower then turn left past the splendid Kosanakos tower into the small square with the restored church of St. Peter.

Karioupoli was the fortified complex of the Phokas–Kavalierakis family. The family moved from Kelefa after Thomas Phokas was made a Knight of St. Mark by the Venetians for his efforts on their behalf and the 'Kavalierakis' (Cavalier) part of the name commemorates this title. The tower has a substantial house attached and immediately behind it are the gates to another fortified section of the complex, bounded by an imposing fortified wall. The gate is flanked by pillars which support a slightly 'pointed' arch above which is a coat of arms with a double–headed eagle motif. The Phokas family claimed descent from the Byzantine Emperor Nikephoros Phokas so incorporated the double–headed eagle into their coat of arms. A small alley to the right of the gate leads behind the complex where there

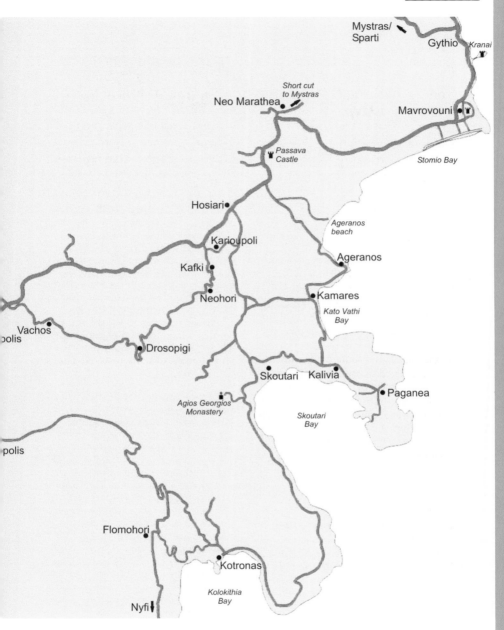

is another small church with some badly defaced and faded frescoes on the templon. To get back to the main road, retrace your way in past the tower but keep straight (not left) to continue down to the next junction where left will take you back to the main Gythio road at **Hosiari**.

The main road passes the 'Spider Pub' and then a right turn signed Belle Hellene Hotel (see page 152). Shortly after these two landmarks, where the road bends left, you get your first glimpse of Passava castle, perched on the crown of the hill directly ahead.

Passava Castle

Passava Castle dominates the southern cliff where the road to Gythio passes through a narrow gorge. It is not easy to see from the ground, but a substantial part of the castle, especially the curtain walls, still survive– remnants of a very long history.

Passava has been identified as ancient Las, which according to the Iliad sent a contingent to Troy under the command of Menelaos and which was later a Free Lakonian City according to Pausanias. The hill on which the castle stands was known as Asia and this part of the city was already in ruins when Pausanias visited here – *"The present city is built over the land between three mountains, Ilion, Asia and Knakadion, though it used to stand on the crest of Asia and there are still ruins of the ancient city to this day, with a statue of Herakles in front of the walls and a battle trophy for a victory against Macedonia: the battle was with a detachment of Philip's army when he invaded Lakonia, which had left the main army to devastate the coast. In the ruins is a Temple of Asian Athene."*

Philip V of Macedonia looted Lakonia in 218 BC and the description "Asian

Athene" is because of the name of the hill. He goes on to say,

"At a place called Arainon is the grave of Las, with a statue standing on the tumulus. The people here say this Las was their founder and that he was killed by Achilles."

Arainon may be the modern village of Ageranos on Cape Vathy. Pausanias went on to describe several temples and sanctuaries in the new city and the archaeologist E.S. Forster published a report for the British School at Athens in which he identified the plain south of Passava as the site of the city. This is now agricultural land but several statues were found here as well as Hellenic and Doric masonry. Strabo tells us that the Dioscouri once captured Las after a siege which is why they had the appellation 'Lapersae' – 'Sackers of Las'. He also says that the Spartans "used Las as a naval station because of its good harbour." Clearly Passava is nowhere near the sea but it is thought that the harbour of Las was at modern Ageranos.

The castle itself was built after 1220 by Jean of Nully who had been given the fiefdom of Passava by the French Marshal of Achaia. The name is thought to derive from "pas avant" (no further) or "passe avant" (go ahead) and although the castle dominates the pass giving access to the Mani, the name suggests that the Mani itself was outside their control. After the Franks were defeated at Pelagonia in 1259, the Baroness of Passava was taken to Constantinople as a hostage to make sure William of Villehardouin kept the treaty he had signed with the emperor Michael VIII Palaiologos. William broke the treaty and so the Baroness was held at Constantinople until 1275. She returned to Passava on her release but found her castle occupied by Maniats who continued to occupy it until 1481 when it was taken by the Turks. They rebuilt the castle and garrisoned it so that it formed part of the defensive chain they established along with Kelefa and Zarnata castles to try and control the Mani. When the Venetians defeated the Turks in 1684, they were allies of the Maniats and had no need of this castle so they destroyed it but when the Turks in turn defeated the Venetians, they rebuilt the castle and held it from 1715 until 1780. They evacuated the castle during the Orlov uprising in 1770 but soon reoccupied it after this disastrous campaign. In 1780, the Maniats slaughtered the entire garrison and their families after the arrest and execution of Exarchos Grigorakis who was the head of the powerful clan, which was then based at Ageranos and Skoutari. Zanetos Grigorakis took over the leadership of the clan and expanded his power in the area and built a complex at Mavrovouni and a tower on the island of Kranai at Gythio. He was made Bey of the Mani in 1782 so the man behind the massacre of the Turkish Garrison became the Governor on behalf of Turkey a mere two years later.

To reach the castle, park in an open area where there is a brown archaeological sign by the main road. A path (of sorts) snakes up the right side of the hill– you need to get to the entrance on the other side of the hill as you face it. The path soon runs out and you then have to find your own route to the summit. It is a harder climb than it looks from the ground; wear stout boots and trousers because the going is rough and thorny in places. When you reach the summit, you will see the remains of massive walls and will have to find a gap to enter the grounds of the castle. The walls that remain are impressive. They stand about 12 meters high with a parapet running behind the battlements along which you can walk in various places. The grounds of the castle are heavily overgrown and there are mounds of rubble where buildings used to stand. The remains of a large building in the centre of the area might once have been a mosque. On the

Vachos

Kosanakos Tower, Karioupoli

Passava Castle

Passava Castle

wall which overlooks the gorge there are two towers and from the circular tower on the west side, a fantastic panoramic view clearly shows why this site was chosen as a castle.

Back towards Gythio there is a possible short cut to Mystras if you are pushed for time, which bypasses Gythio completely. Take the left turn signed Nea Marathea at a low building painted with the Nissan logo and follow the road, initially keeping right, all the way to Agios Vassilios and on to the Sparti road.

As Gythio nears you will come to stretch of road hosting a plethora of petrol stations and campsites. Getting to the long sandy beach of Stomia Bay is not as easy as it should be as many of the campsites that lie between the road and the beach control access. The easiest way is to turn right at the end of this stretch of road just after the KMOIL garage on the left. The beach has a number of bars/tavernas/apartments and will get quite busy in the summer due to its close proximity to Gythio. However it is over a km long so it should not be difficult to walk a little way to get away from the crowds.

The road heads away from the beach across a headland that hosts the village of **Mavrovouni**. To take a quick look at the castle that crowns the village and enjoy its narrow winding streets, take the second turning into it opposite a sign on the left advertising the "TAVERNA KHPOS". Once you have passed a restored tower on the right

you'll come to a pretty square on your left. Getting to the castle by car is tricky as the roads are very narrow and in any case there is nowhere to park, so the best option is to park on the square and walk up the road to the left of the square as you look at it. Mavrovouni literally means Black Mountain and it was here that Zanetbey Grigorakis built a fortified stronghold called the Goulades or Beanika. It was constructed on the summit in the shape of a trapezium with a strong curtain wall approx 4 meters high. On the SE and SW corners were two round towers between which was an arched gateway and guardhouse. The other two corners were protected by buildings – the NE corner was reinforced with a two storey "palace" which had a parapet around the flat roof and turrets on the corners and the NW corner had a two storey fortified building. This had a double-vaulted ground floor for animals and "official" rooms above it. The palace has completely disappeared and only one of the two vaulted rooms that supported the other building remains. The south wall with the corner towers still stands but the gateway is ruined and the guardhouse destroyed: the complex suffered damage during a Turkish attack in 1803. The Turks had deposed Zanetbey but he was still causing them many problems, so they launched a heavy attack on Gythio and Mavrovouni. The attack failed to defeat Zanetbey although the Turks did destroy some towers. The stronghold was abandoned after 1821. The other tower dwellings at Mavrovouni

Stomia Bay, Mavrovouni

belonged to the extended Grigorakis family and several remain inhabited to this day.

Heading back from the square to the main road, Gythio is only a few minutes away.

Gythio

Modern day Gythio is the eastern gateway into the Mani, and mainly consists of pho-togenic, neo-classical buildings as it only developed into a town in the mid 19th century. Prior to this, it was little more than a village. The port sees a few cruise ships come and go and there is a weekly ferry to Kythira and Crete. At the far end of the town as you approach are numerous banks, the bus station and tourist information office. It is a very pleasant place to stop for lunch, to stay in overnight or just to have a revitalising coffee en route to Mystras. Its late recent development hides a long and varied history.

As you descend into the town the first thing you'll see is the island of Kranai (now called Marathonisi– 'fennel island') linked by a causeway. This was the scene of the first recorded "visitors" to Gythio. It was here that Paris, prince of Troy, apparently spent his first night with Helen, having whisked her away from Sparta and her husband, Menelaos. Such was the impact of that night that ten years later, according to Homer, Paris was moved to remind Helen of its delights (Iliad, 3). On the island is the tower of Zanetbey Grigorakis which has been restored and turned into a Mani Museum and there is also a small church which has been built on the foundations of an earlier temple. The museum does not contain "artefacts" from the Mani or a great deal about its history but has an excellent display about the various travellers who visited and wrote about the Mani over the centuries and some architectural details on various towers and buildings.

We know from Pausanias that it boasted temples to Demeter and Athene and that statues of Hermes and Apollo, the mythical

Mavrovouni Castle

Grigorakis Tower, Kranai, Gythio

Gythio

Gythio

founders of the city, graced the square. Like every self-respecting Greek city, Gythio had a story behind it. Mythology claims that it was founded to mark the end of a quarrel between Heracles and Apollo over the sacred tripod at Delphi. Heracles had gone to Delphi, we are told, in the hope that the oracle would provide a cure for the fits of violent rage which possessed him from time to time. The oracle refused to reply. So Heracles, incensed, seized the tripod from the temple in order to found an oracle of his own. Apollo, patron god of Delphi, confronted Heracles and it needed intervention from Zeus himself to separate them by hurling a thunderbolt. Gythio was apparently the visible proof that they were reconciled. Pausanias also mentions a large bronze statue of Asclepios and one of Poseidon. Gythio, from early times, had become Sparta's port and therefore was the chief target for Athenian attack in the Peloponnesian War (431- 404 B.C.). In the lead-up to war Thucydides tells us that the Athenian general, Tolmides ,bringing fifty warships and four thousand men, set fire to the dockyards at Gythio. The ultimate Spartan victory in the war must have lead to Gythio enjoying some of the spoils.

Things only got better during the later Roman conquest as the town was initially given the position of head of the Union of Free Laconians, officially recognised by Augustus in 21 B.C. It caused a golden age in its fortunes not least fuelled by the Roman demand for the purple dye made from murex found in abundance in the seas between Gythio and Kithera.

Sadly little remains of its ancient history, most of it being swallowed by the sea. The Roman theatre was apparently not impressive enough for Pausanias to mention it. Its remains are most easily reached by following the main road through the town, ignoring left turns to

Sparta. Once you reach a traffic island by a basketball court turn sharp left and then first right. The theatre is one block up, next to army barracks.

The Union of Free Laconia lasted well into the last years of the third century A.D. and was finally destroyed in the fourth century Alaric's Visigoths. The town then fell into decline and was never to recover its status and grandeur from Roman times. In 1805 Leake commented that it consisted of "a hundred wretched houses in the midst of which stands a large church". The best house he saw, he tells us, had floors of trodden earth. Its only recent significance is in being part of the area controlled by the Gregorakis clan- hence the tower on Marathonisi.

Ageranos

To reach Ageranos, return towards Areopolis for approximately 10 kilometers and, just past Passava, turn left where signs indicate the Belle Helene Hotel and Ageranos Camping. Where the road forks, the left fork heads to the campsite and brings you out in the middle of a long sandy beach. The camp site run a cantina on the beach for sandwiches and drinks as well as a full taverna within their site. Being a little further from Gythio is does not get as busy as the beach at Stomia Bay. To get to Agenaros village, which looks over the beach, take the left fork which passes through fields of cane.

Pausanias recorded a temple of Artemis Diktynna by the sea on a cape, to the left of which a river flowed into the sea, and this is thought to be this headland. In front of the church to your left as you enter Agenaros there used to be a large column which may have come from this temple. Ageranos is also the possible site of the tomb of Las (see Passava Castle).

The village was the stronghold of Antonbey Grigorakis, who was Bey of the Mani from 1803 to 1808, and his nephews also had small strongholds here. The main fortification is just behind the large family church. The tower has an unusual feature in that it is reinforced by a two storey semi-cylindrical buttress and the large building on the other side of the courtyard, facing the sea, has a similar projection. The curtain walls are reinforced by the buildings of the complex and by two circular turrets on the N.W. corner of the wall.

the Roman theatre, Gythio

Ageranos Beach

On the opposite side of the road, the smaller walled complexes of the Bey's nephews parade up the hill in mutually supportive positions which would make any attack on this headland a very formidable task. The topmost complex has an impressive tower which dominates the skyline.

In Leake's time, this village was called Vathy and it was here that the "feud" between two priests took place that Leake recorded. The son of a priest had accidentally killed a boy who was related to another priest.

"The latter papas declared war against the former, which is done in Mani in a formal manner, by crying out in the streets. The first papas went to his church to say mass with pistols in his girdle; such being a common custom in Mani; but as usual in such cases, he laid them behind the altar, on assuming the robe in which the priest performs divine service. The other papas entered the church with some of his party, and the instant the office was concluded, walked up to his enemy, who was still in his robes, and fired a pistol at him, which flashed in the pan (failed to fire properly): the latter, then running behind the altar, seized his arms, shot his enemy and one of his adherents, and drove all the rest from the church. The affair was then settled by the interposition of the Bey himself, in whose village it had happened."

Ageranos Beach

Grigorakis Tower, Ageranos

Two more sandy beaches lie in Kato Vathi Bay, a little further on from Agenaros. As you drop down to the bay, ignore the right turn and keep straight to an old stone bridge. The first beach lies in the hamlet of **Kamares**, at the end of the road to the left and has a taverna at one end. The second beach and the road on to Skoutari requires crossing the ford at the bridge (which will be dry in summer). The marshland behind the second beach is a haven for migratory birds in the spring and a haven for camper vans in the summer. Leaving Kato Vathi Bay behind, the next junction you reach takes you left to **Kalivia** and right to **Skoutari.** The detour to Kalivia does not offer much. There are some more unusual modern interpretations of the tower house (pinky red and cream!) and a very small sand/pebble beach at **Paghanea,** though the road down to it is in poor condition.

Skoutari

Turning right at the T–junction, takes you to Skoutari, about 3 kilometers to the west. As you approach Skoutari you will see the village spread out on the side of a hill running down to a beach. On your right, before reaching the village is what was once a small post-Byzantine monastery of the Zoodokos Pigi with a re-pointed church (locked) and evidence of out buildings that once must have had a defensive role.

There is a small circular route through Skoutari which takes you past many ruined houses and towers– scene of the last vendetta as late as 1931. The most direct route is left as you enter

the village. You soon come to a square with a war memorial and a ruined tower, which locals believe to have been that of Katsanos, a local kapetan, related to the Grigorakis clan. If that is accurate, then it is the tower which Leake described as harbouring many fleas etc when he stayed there. Also on the square is a small, barrel vaulted church, Agios Ioannis o Chrisostomos (St John Chrisostomos – one of the leading early theologians and writers of the Orthodox Liturgy). The vault is covered with frescoes, identifiable from both the New and Old Testament, varying in quality of condition. Luckily access is guaranteed as the key is kept under a stone on the sill of the window to the left of the door – well worth a look inside. Inscriptions inside date the paintings to 1750 and were the work of Anagnostes of Langada and Nikolaos of Nomitsi, who were employed in similar projects elsewhere in the Mani-comparisons can easily be made with Agios Theodoros at Kambos for example in the treatment of the Ainoi (Last Psalms).

The beach is well-signed and requires a left turn at the junction to Kotronas. The beach is a wonderful, sandy stretch with a pleasant taverna at one end and a small harbour at the other; beyond the taverna is another smaller sandy beach. Right on the edge of the beach is a small, 15th century domed church dedicated to St. Barbara with a few remaining late 18th century frescoes inside. The archaeologist E.S. Forster argues that Skoutari is the probable site of ancient Asine which was

Skoutari Beach

besieged by Philip V of Macedonia (although he failed to capture it). He states, *"There are distinct traces of Roman buildings near the sea and a number of ancient blocks and columns built into the modern village".* Pausanias didn't come this way so we cannot rely on him for an identification and not all archaeologists agree with Forster. Parking on the beach is difficult as the road is very narrow– much easier to park in a natural 'lay by' about 100m before the beach.

Progress on to Kotronas is rapid as this stretch of road is probably the widest in the whole Mani.

Kotronas

Kotronas is a delightful fishing port with a couple of towers, seafront tavernas and a small beach. It provides the opportunity to cool off with a refreshing dip. It has been identified as the ancient town of Teuthrone which Pausanias visited and where he recorded *"the god they worship most is Issorian Artemis and they have a spring called Naia."* It was also one of the Free Lakonian Cities.

The main part of Teuthrone seems to have been the small island of Skopa, now linked by a causeway to the mainland. Here there is evidence of mediaeval masonry suggesting a sizeable castle. There is a restored church on the island with old marble built into it. Although there is little to see by way of ruins, it is a very tranquil spot, reached by driving through the village, parking when you get near the Areopolis sign and following a track that starts by painted white millstone.

The quickest way back to Areopolis is on the Areopolis/Lagia road, through the plain of Pyrrichos (see page 190).

Kamares Beach

Paghanea Beach

Skoutari Beach

Halikia Beach, Kotronas

Vardounia

The area of **Vardounia** is north of the Areopolis to Gythio road on the eastern side of the Taygetos Mountains and as far north as Arna. The name comes from a castle which was built near the village of Agios Nikolaos. Vardounia has a different feeling from the rest of the Mani. The landscape is not as mountainous and the villages are more modern architecturally as the Turkish occupation of nearby Mystras and the Lakonian plain meant that much of the area was sparsely occupied by the Greeks. More than this, several sources refer to a dominant Albanian presence in the area - a domination that only ended with the outbreak of war in 1821 when many of the Peloponnesian Albanians retreated to Tripolis, only to be besieged by Kolokotronis and his forces.

If you are based on the west coast at Stoupa/Kardamyli, the most dramatic way of getting there is 'over the top', which could be extended into a more adventurous way of getting to Mystras/Sparti. A road runs across the mountains from either Exohori or Saidona, past the space-age looking **Panagia Yiatrissa** monastery and down to Gythio. The drive is fantastic on a clear day but definitely requires the hiring of a jeep (or a vehicle with a high wheel base) as the road is not yet concreted all the way - and even in a jeep it will take over an hour to get to Yiatrissa. The alternative is to drive to Areopolis, turn left to Gythio and turn off up into the wooded foothills of Taygetos . It is possible to explore this area in yet another loop as will now be described - so if you drive over the top, the decision remains whether to continue in a clockwise or anti-clockwise direction from Agios Nikolaos down to Gythio.

Note: If you are driving over the top, once out of Saidona or Exohori, there is only one road. Once up on the ridge, you will pass a stone spring on your left. A little after this point you will reach a junction, left to Agios Dimitrios and into the Vassiliki Forest, right to Yiatrissa. It's worth stopping here and climbing the bank on the far side of the road to get a great view of Profitas Ilias, the highest peak in Taygetos.

The turning needed to begin the loop is past Gythio. To bypass Gythio, if you are coming from Areopolis, turn left where there is a clear 'NISSAN' sign painted on a stone wall, signed 'Nea Marathea' and follow the road, initially keeping right, all the way to Agios Vassilios and on to the Sparti road. At the time of going to print,

there was evidence of what must be a larger Gythio bypass under construction. At the Sparti road turn left and you will soon see a left turn signed 'Arna 22km'. Take this road, ignore the left turn to Agios Nikolaos a short distance along and follow the signs to Arna. The road starts to cross a series of low wooded hills and valleys

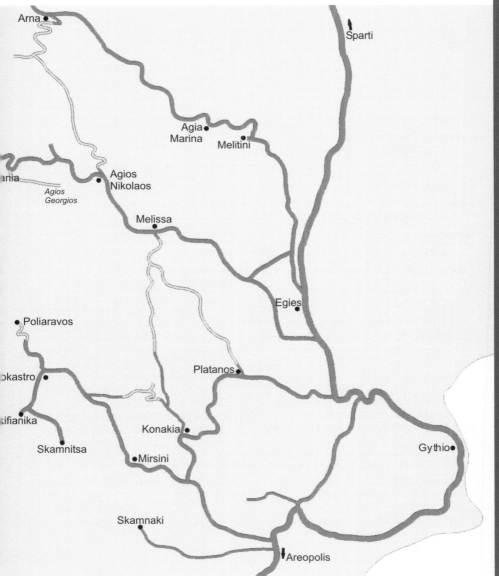

'OVER THE TOP'

Vasiliki Forest

Exohori

Kitriniaris Tower

Saidona

Kastania

Kariovouni

Panagia Yiatrissa

Stoupa

Gythio

Platsa

Milea

that are very beautiful and very different from other parts of the Mani. Modern **Petrina** is the first example of how relatively new the villages are in this area. Once you have crossed the Kolopanos River, fork right at **Lemonia**, pass through **Melitini** and on to **Agia Marina** (also known as Tseria). The church from which the latter takes its name is perched on top of a hill to the left and is one of the few Byzantine churches in the area and was recently restored (but is now permanently locked). Eventually, the mountains that have seemed fairly distant, come closer as the road climbs up to **Arna**. Leake, though he

never actually visited the area, listed a number of villages as being Turkish and at Arna noted that there were 5 *pyrgoi* (towers) and 90 Turkish houses in 1805, living side by side with a smaller Greek population of one *pyrgos* and 30 houses. As you enter the square of this friendly village you cannot help but be impressed by the enormous plane tree that dwarfs the surrounding houses and the kafenion.

From Arna it is possible to get across to **Agios Nikolaos** in a normal car as the dirt road is in good enough condition at the time of writing. Head back from the square but take the road on the right that starts to drop down immediately. The road winds its way down to the valley floor and is a beautiful drive. At an unsigned T-junction, turn left and the road eventually crosses a bridge. Ignore an unsigned right turn and soon the little white church of the cemetery at Agios Nikolaos comes into view above you. As you approach the outskirts of the village, the rocky outcrop to your left has some clearly visible remains on top but this is not the site of Vardounia Castle. Once in the village square, straight across takes you back down to Gythio. The road on up to **Mikri Kastania** is found by doubling back on yourself and taking the left fork. As you leave the village, you are level with the small white church off to your right and beyond this is the rocky crag with the ruins of Vardounia Castle.

Vardounia Castle

Again there has been some debate as to the exact origins of this fortification. Initially thought to have been Venetian, then possibly Frankish, more recent research has at least confirmed that the castle was given to Korkodilos Kladas in the 1470s by the Ottomans in what was ultimately to be a failed gesture to reconcile the two parties. In fact at this time the Venetians were involved and, as part of their peace with the Turks in 1479, they snubbed the Kladas clan by giving the castle back to the Turks. This outraged Kladas and caused war to break out again. How long the castle had been in existence prior to this known event is not so clear but many feel that its location could easily fit within the Frankish policy of building to defend against the Melingi up in the mountains. Its strategic position is as obvious as Tigani, guarding the fertile plains below and access over the mountains. The climb up is very steep and once on top, overgrown, hidden cisterns make exploration a little hazardous.

5 km further on lies **Mikri Kastania** (as

plane tree, Arna

the River Arna

the Arna Valley

Vardounia Castle, crowning the second hill-top

opposed to Kastania on the other side of the mountains above Stoupa) which has more the appearance of a typical Mani village with fortified houses and a couple of towers. Before you reach the village a dirt road runs off to the left on a sharp right hand bend that leads to the stunningly positioned church of Agios Giorgios. (In the winter of 2005/2006, this was closed by a large landslide but may again be open). The large Byzantine church, possibly 13th or 14th century, stands in a dominating position overlooking a valley and the mountains beyond. The interior has been extensively whitewashed but some frescoes remain which suggest a date of the same period as the church itself. Ruined buildings nearby may show that at some later stage there was a monastery here. It's a beautiful site and a great place for a picnic lunch.

Mikri Kastania

Approaching from Agios Nikolaos, the first thing you cannot help but notice is an extraordinary memorial on the outskirts of the village. A carved marble facade shows the "sortie" described below with the Maniat families, including women, children and a priest, charging the Turkish troops who are depicted wearing their "turned up" shoes or slippers. You will also see a couple of the cannonballs of which Kolokotronis is so disparaging. The story behind the memorial stems from the fact that Theodoros Kolokotronis' father, Konstantinos, was fatally wounded defending one of the towers of Panayotaros Venetsanakis. He and Panayotaros were defending one tower while Panayotaros' eighty-year old father held another. They were called upon to surrender and give up one of their sons each to be held as hostages, whereupon they would be allowed to go free, but they refused. Theodoros, a young teenager at the time, was with his father and later recorded,

"The Turkish army then prepared to besiege them vigorously; they brought up cannon and bombs and poured upon them an unceasing fire both by night and day. Their bombs and their cannons however, did not inspire the besieged with any dread and for twelve nights and for twelve days they stood out nobly and bravely."

They were hoping for help from elsewhere in the Mani but when none came, they decided to sortie from the tower and escape. Kostantes Kolokotronis and two of his brothers, Apostoles and Giorgos were killed; his other brother, Anagnostes escaped with Theodoros. Some children, including two of Theodoros's little brothers were captured along with Panayotaros. But, while the children were spared, Panayotaros was executed. His father stayed defending his tower but was eventually captured alive and hanged after his hands and feet were cut off.

Konstantinos' headless body was later found at Arna and interred at Garbelia near Milia. These two towers can still be seen in the village. One of them stands high above the village on the south side and the other is on the north side, just beyond and above the small square. The latter was in fact two fortified houses, one of two storeys and the other three, enclosed in a defensive wall and connected by a stone bridge which ran between them on the second floor. So it was more like a small castle than a tower. This "castle" is being restored and will be used as a museum and accommodation for visitors sometime in the future.....

From the small square, which has a delightful taverna , the road continues towards the monastery of **Panagia Yiatrissa**. ('The Healing Virgin'). The monastery sits on the watershed of the Taygetos and you can see both east and west of the mountain range; the village far below you to the west is Milia (see Exo Mani). The monastery itself is a sprawling, concrete maze of rooms and the main church is modern inside with some earlier, carved door surrounds. There is also a large Gynaikonitis or women's gallery. In general the buildings are not particularly inspiring but on August 15th the faithful congregate for an impressively large *panagiri* (religious festival), enjoying the stunning views from a vantage point, 1000m above sea level.

From here, you must return to Agios Niko- laos – do not be tempted to follow the track which leads north from here along the ridge unless you are in a 4x4.

Once back in Agios Nikolaos, head straight across the square and on to **Kokina Louria**. As you enter the village, don't be tempted to turn right into the village as the streets become very narrow and you may not get out again. The next village is **Melissa**. A right turn just before the main church, signed Krini, offers a continuation of the 4x4 trip. The dirt road snakes through the hills (and for a while is actually part of the E4 pan-european walking route). Ignore the left turn up to **Krini** and head up round the base of a prominent hill – perched on top of this hill are the remains of a castle which won't be visible until you have driven a way up the track. Soon you will pass another more visible fort on your left. Both of these buildings were built by Kapetan Zaharias, a renowned *Klepht* who fought constantly against the Turks. Although he was not a Maniat, Zaharias became dedicated to the cause and was linked to the Maniats in that his father was godfather to Kolokotronis. As a young man he saw both his father and older brother killed by the Turks and so set about trying to unite the clans into one force to repel the enemy. He built fortress-

Agios Giorgios, near Mikri Kastania

Mikri Kastania

Panagia Yiatrissa

Zaharias Castle

es in his own village of Varvitsa (near the peak of Mount Parnon) first and then saw the need to have a stronghold in the Mani. He therefore built these castles along with a church (next to the second castle) and hospital just outside the modern village of **Ligereas**. He corresponded with Napoleon Bonaparte to solicit foreign help and in 1803 Napoleon sent the Stephanopoli brothers (see 'Oitylo') to meet Zaharias at Kitries to assess how likely a Greek revolution was. His assassination in the same year put pay to his plans. He was betrayed in Tseria, above Kardamyli, by Maniats – he was shot and then beheaded. Another letter from Napoleon was found in his pocket, detailing the plans for revolution – plans which due to his death were never carried out. The motivation for his assassination is unclear but one theory is that Mourtzinos from Kardamyli was responsible due to concern that Zaharias would challenge his autonomy.

The dirt road carries on past Ligereas, turns surprisingly into tarmac and then reaches a junction. The 4x4 excursion can be further extended by turning right and heading up into the hills once more past Tombra and on to Sidirokastro and back down through Mersini, or turning left to Konakia.

In a regular car the potential 'loop route' continues back in Melissa. Follow the road through the village and down into the fertile Lakonian plain. Cross over the small bridge that spans the River Sminos and continue to the main Gythio-Sparti road. The route can end here or can continue by heading back into the area a few kilometres along the main road towards Gythio. Turn off at the sign to Platanos/Konakia. Pass through **Platanos**, taking the left fork at the end of the village and carry on to **Konakia**. At the far end of Konakia there is a choice: to keep

straight to **Pilala** (the Xatzakos Tower dominating this hamlet is visible ahead from this junction) and then on to the Zaharias Castle at Ligereas (from this end it can be reached with a minimum of dirt road) or to turn left to get to **Mersini** and **Sidirokastro**. The Xatzakos tower is a substantial building and has a plaque dating it to 1776. Despite the addition of a concrete balcony, concrete battlements and a metal chimney protruding from a wall at a jaunty angle, it is still an impressive building. Below one wall is an old cannon which has been mounted on wheels made from the old grindstones of an olive press.

Heading down the narrow and slightly pot-holed road to the Mersini junction you soon pass the monastery of Agios Giorgios on your left, beneath road level. Steps take you down to the church, which is not usually locked. The original Byzantine cross-in-square church has been extended to the west at some later stage with a narthex almost as large in floor space as the main naos area. Much of the inside has been plastered but a few frescoes still remain. The Last Judgement is visible in the narthex and in the naos there are Post-Byzantine paintings dated to 1832.Turning right at the next T-junction takes you to Mersini, left takes you back down to the main Areopolis-Gythio road. Mersini has a church that hosts another good example of the Ainoi frescoes – Agios Giorgios is to the north west of the village in a small dip below the centre. It is unfortunately locked and the key holder can be found on the other side of the main square, just the other side of the taverna. The road up to Sidirokastro is good asphalt all the way. It climbs up a long valley in a northwesterly direction through the tiny village of **Profitis Ilias** with **Ano Tombra** clinging to a hillside to the right. As the road swings to a more westerly direction the scenery becomes more rugged as you hairpin up a pass before arriving at a T-junction. To the north are more valleys leading deep into the Taygetos overlooked by the peak of Zizali at nearly 1500 metres. **Sidirokastro** ('iron castle'), is spread along the road which has a turnoff signposted to **Poliaravos** and **Misochori** and another junction further on to **Skifianika** and **Skamnitsa**. The road to Poliaravos deteriorates quite badly and should not be attempted in a regular car. The village is significant as it was site of Ibrahim Pasha's final attempt to invade the Mani in August 1826 – after his failures in Verga and Pyrgos Dirou in June of that year. The Egyptian army would have been seen approaching from a long way off and it was no wonder that the Maniats selected this site to oppose it. The invading force was defeated and withdrew back to the plains of Lakonia and abandoned any further ideas of subduing the Maniats. At the bottom end of Skifianika, Agios Athanasios is tucked between buildings and shaded by a tree – a tiny cross on top of a small metal gate is the best indicator of its location. Inside the wall paintings are dated to 1762 and 1775 and are quite typical of their period in the Mani. Though damaged in places by damp, they are clear enough to interpret. Around the base of the walls are depictions of "the damned" who are naked and being subjected to various rather painful tortures by devils.

Back on the main road, 200m towards Areopolis, is one final turning to **Skamnaki** – 5 kms off to the right. The road starts reasonably but becomes a rough track in some places. The village is still typically Maniat, with a few towers and defensive houses and a number of newer buildings. Leake reported, *"At Skamnaki, ancient coins and sepulchres are said to be found."* It may be possible that the area around here was the site of ancient Hypsi where Pausanias described *"a sanctuary of Asklepios and Artemis of the Bay Tree"* but there has not been a positive identification.

Xatsakos Tower, Pilala

The monastery of Agios Giorgios, Konakia

Sidirokastro

Poliaravos

Circular Walks

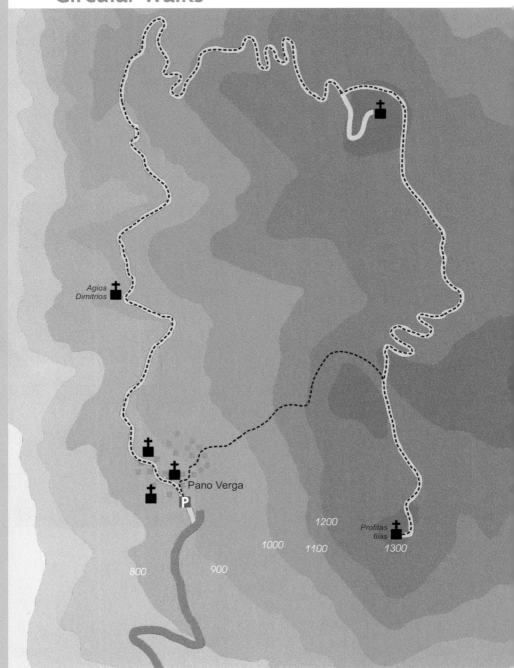

Agios
Dimitrios

Pano Verga

P

1200

Profitas
Ilias

1300

1000

1100

800

900

metal sign, this time reading:
ΦΑΡΑΓΓΙ ΚΟΣΚΑΡΑΓΑΣ
ΩΡΕΣ
ΕΟΣ ΚΑΛΑΜΑΤΑΣ

From here there is a stony path, which passes through a wall to the right, then descends rocky terraces, crossing a gully to the left before reaching a dirt road. Follow the road left until it peters out and becomes a footpath through fields, eventually becoming a narrow, gravelly path, which zig-zags down to the river bed of the Koskarakas Gorge. The path is faint in places so keep a keen eye out for the red and yellow paint markings.

the Biliovas path

towards Altomira

The final section of the path down deteriorates into a scree slope which has to be slithered down to reach the gorge bed. Here you turn right (downstream) for a 2 hour gorge walk. In places the riverbed is quite even and you can admire the sheer walls and rock formations. At other times there are massive boulders to be negotiated. Look out for painted arrows directing the way to easier routes, sometimes facilitated by metal handholds cemented into the rock. From late autumn until early summer there may be running water in the gorge and care should be taken after heavy rainfall.

As the walls of the gorge start to reduce in size you will reach a stone footbridge across the riverbed. Exit the gorge to the left and turn right onto the bridge. This is part of a cobbled path that will lead you up to the church of Agios Nikolaos, from where a dirt road leads you back to Sotirianika, turning right at the end of the track from the church. Rejoin your car at the water cisterns seen at the beginning of the walk.

deep into the gorge

bridge over the Koskaraka Gorge

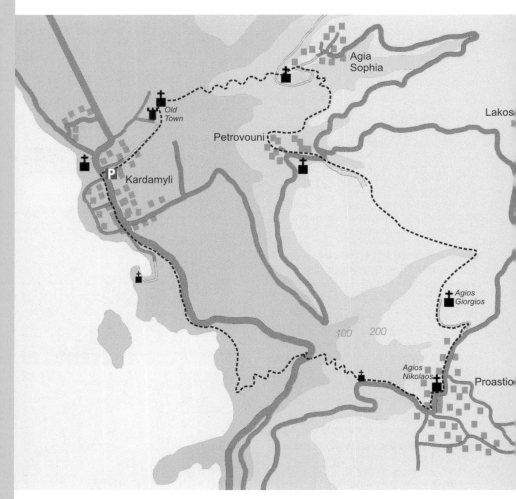

Kardamyli Kalderimi

Kardamyli – Agia Sophia – Petrovouni – Proastio – Kardamyli

Timings

Around **3 hours** in total

Kardamyli-Petrovouni: 1 hour 15 mins

Petrovouni-Proastio: 1 hour

Proastio– Kardamyli: 40 mins

Nature of Walk

A real classic of the area, passing historic Old Kardamyli before climbing to around 200m above sea level to enjoy great views down to the coast. Initially, a steep kalderimi heads up to Agia Sophia, a small village perched above Kardamyli, with views down into the Viros Gorge. The path then immediately drops back down again into a shady gully before gently rising again to Petrovouni. From here to Proastio the path crosses a plateau covered in superb olive groves. The descent from Proastio is fast and ends up with the option of a cooling swim at Kalamitsi before the short walk back to Kardamyli.

Places of Interest

See page 62 for Old Kardamyli. A little further up the kalderimi lie the supposed Tombs of the Dioscouri. The tiny village of Petrovouni is interesting to walk around and you could spend a few hours in Proastio, looking at a few churches and having a *meze* in one the 3 kafenia.

from Kardamyli to Agia Sophia

the Italian Orchid

The walk begins at the northern end of Kardamyli at the village square where there is plenty of room for parking. Head up the lane by the war memorial and keep following it once you have passed the last houses. Where the recently restored stone path crosses a small bridge, you need to head up a small way-marked path, past a small church (with a couple of ossuaries, which you can peek into if you feel inclined), following it round into the square of the Troupakis Fortified Settlement and its museum,

Exit the square through the arch by the church and pick up the path ahead of you (clearly marked with black and yellow marks). This path takes you all the way up to Agia Sophia - you can see the priests' house perched above you. After 100m you'll pass the Dioscouri Tombs on your right. Carry on up the kalderimi with a gorge initially on your right and then the Viros Gorge on your left. After around 25 minutes a stone arch that fronts a dried-up spring appears on your right - turn right and up to reach the church of Agia Sophia.

Agios Giorgios, Proastio

aloni, Proastrio

From the church, head past the cemetery and 40m after, turn right down a track taking you down into the gully below. The path narrows and is a little difficult in

places before reaching the stream bed. Cross the stream and the path continues to the right. After 500m you will come to another stone cistern, this time with water in, and troughs to hand for washing clothes. A green walkers' sign (Kardamyli) indicates a right turn. Follow the path below a low cliff on which Petrovouni is perched. The path takes you to the beginning of a wonderful kalderimi and the view here is stunning. To cut the walk short, simply head down the kalderimi to the main road and turn right to get back to Kardamyli.

To carry on to Proastio, follow the marked path round the outskirts of Petrovouni, enjoying the views down to the sea. Cross the little square to which the path brings you and turn left on the road. Pass a church on the right and then a little further on, turn right up a concrete track. Where the track divides take the left fork, following the wire fence. Once past the tiny chapel, pick up the way-marked path through the olives. Proastio is now visible ahead and the next landmark is the Monastery of Agios Giorgios, set in a clump of cypress trees. To get there the path heads inland as you have to skirt around a gully. At a crossroads of tracks, bear left, following the marks on trees – the path is now heading gently downwards and is also way-marked on rocks. Ignore the right turn at a stone wall, keeping straight with a rock face on the left. You are now in 'Orchid Alley' – in May you could see Giant Orchids, the pink Italian orchid and Bee Orchids in this area. Follow the path right and it soon starts to climb gently. Once you reach a clearing with olive trees, the path heads left and up over way-marked rocks. The church of Agios Giorgios is unlocked and worth a look inside. From the church follow the track towards the village. Where the track bends left, head down over a rocky area as a short cut, bringing you to the road ahead. On the other side of the road is evidence of an old stone quarry and a small Mycenean tomb.

Follow the road into the village, past the church of Agios Nikolaos on the right and then the mini market with a kafenion opposite. You are now heading out of the village. Turn off the road at a walkers' sign on the right by a small chapel – this kalderimi drops down to the main road. Cross the road, turn right and then almost immediately left down a concrete track to Kalamitsi Beach. Just before the beach, locate a path on the right opposite a long black gate. Take this path through the olives all the way to the main road on the other side of the bay. Continue along the main road to Kardamyli.

Agia Sophia

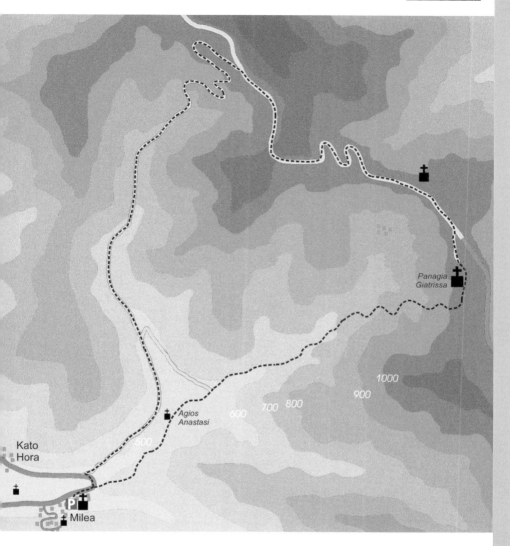

Kato
Hora

Agios
Anastasi

Panagia
Giatrissa

600

700 800

900

1000

600

Milea

Space Station Number 5

Milea – Yiatrissa – Milea

Timings
Around **4 hours** in total – a 12km walk.
Allow 2.5 hours up to the monastery and slightly less to get back down.

Nature of walk

Coming out of Milea, you pass through beautiful olive groves before the path follows a dry riverbed upstream. The last half of the ascent sees the path leaving the valley floor to reach the ridge above. A total climb of 500m in altitude – tough, but worth it for the views. The walk down is much easier on a wide dirt track.

Places of interest

The villages of Milea are interesting to explore and Panagia Yiatrissa is extraordinary in design and location.

The drive to Milea from Stoupa takes around 30 minutes. It is possible to use the local bus which, at the time of going to print, leaves Kardamyli at 6am, passes through Stoupa and then carries on to Milea (please check these times). Whether you drive or take the bus, the easiest place to start is in the main square of Milea. Retrace your route in to the village until you get to a brown shrine on the right with a green walkers' sign next to it, directing you up a concrete track. About 150m later, two faint blue arrows on the road point to a dirt rack on the left. The track soon narrows as you pass through wonderful olive groves. Ignore two successive left turns and follow more blue way–marks and metal arrows.

Once you have passed a small stone bridge (over the streambed you will be following up the valley) and a white chapel, the path becomes wooded and eventually widens back into a dirt road. Another dirt road joins from the left where there are more way–marks – turn right and head towards the cowshed. Pass to the left of the shed. From this point the monastery comes into view more and more, perched on the ridge above you. To get there simply follow the way–marked path all the way. It crosses the streambed 4 times and expect to pass through, or around, at least one makeshift gate.

An hour or so after leaving Milea, the path leaves the valley floor and starts to become steeper, leaving the olives behind to be replaced by shade–providing pine. Across the valley you can see the dirt road that will bring you back down.

Once on the ridge and away from the trees, a dirt path takes you right up to the buttressed walls of the monastery. From here, follow the gravel road for 2.5 km until you reach a dirt road dropping down to your left. It is around 5km back to Milea. Ignore all turnings off it. At the bottom, turn left at the main road for the short walk back to the car.

Panagia Yiatrissa high on the ridge above Milea

Three Grassy Meadows

Thalames–Langada–Thalames

Timings
Around **5 hours** in total including a
stop for a packed lunch
To first meadow: 1hr 45mins
To second meadow: 30mins
To third meadow: 1 hr
To Thalames: 1hr 15 mins

Nature of walk

A real escape into the mountains
giving an insight into what happens
up there. Walnut and apple orchards,
shepherds' huts, water cisterns and
feeding troughs suggest how the
land is used though it is very unlikely you will actually meet a living soul:
you are far more likely to come
across livestock of varying kinds.
The views are stunning and the walk
isutterly peaceful.

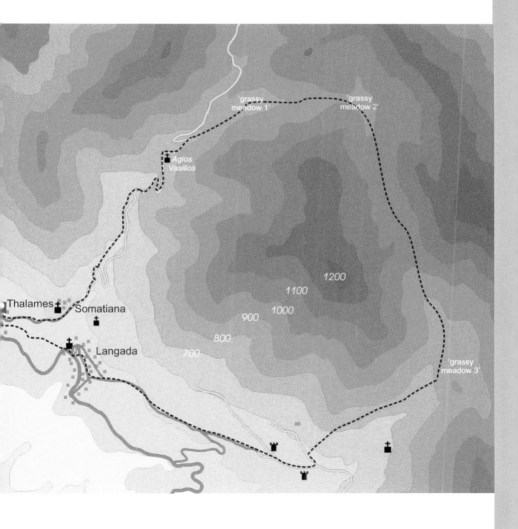

Long trousers and good boots are recommended as the predominantly rocky paths are overgrown in places.

It is quite a tough, long walk, climbing from 400m to over 1000m above sea level. A packed lunch is required and plenty of water.

Places of interest

See the section on Thalames and Langada (pages 84–86)

The walk begins in Thalames. If you have driven from Stoupa, this takes about 20 mins or half an hour in the bus. From the main square with the 'Platanos' taverna, head south on the main road and turn left by the traffic mirror up an unsigned concrete road to the hamlet of Somatiana. The road becomes a dirt track, drops down a little and then starts to climb. 10 minutes after the hamlet, at a sharp right hand bend, head off the road, up the left side of a clearly definable streambed. The path soon becomes a kalderimi. The hill to your right is what you are walking around.

Keep to the left side of this small gulley. After you have passed a dry stone wall running parallel to the path, the path drops down into the

apples in Grassy Meadow 3

streambed and steeply up the other side. Soon you pass a stone enclosure used for keeping livestock and you may notice a lot of engravings on rocks around here– bored shepherds, entertaining themselves. The path becomes a little clearer as you come to another stone hut and reach the dirt track. Keep beneath the road following the path round, passing a large animal enclosure with feeding troughs. Where the path forks, keep right as the left fork heads back down. There are a number of goat paths on this right hand bank – choose any, keeping approximately half way up the bank between the streambed and the road, aiming for a solitary tree ahead of you. Rejoin the dirt road at the tree and snake your way upwards. A small church, Agios Vasilios is the next landmark (not very interesting– built in 1959 with no wall paintings inside). 150m after the church, the road bends sharply left– you need to keep going in the same direction you approached the bend by finding a path on the left side of another streambed, ignoring the fork that drops immediately across it.

20 minutes along the path you will emerge into Grassy Meadow One. Head straight across towards a group of walnut trees. The path begins again by the largest tree (there are more feeding troughs here and a large underground water cistern). The path heads up and after another 20 minutes or so you will come to the much larger Grassy Meadow Two. Once on the plateau, bear right and head towards the hut at the far end, which makes a perfect place to stop for lunch. From the hut keep going in the same direction locating the path that takes you up to the saddle which is the highest point of the walk. Pass to the right of a rocky outcrop and then another

group of walnut trees. Keep to the left of the next outcrop and head towards a circular stone animal enclosure. Just beyond this the descent begins, initially down the right side of the valley– Grassy Meadow Three is soon visible below you and to get your bearings, from the centre of the meadow you will turn right down the final valley. The path, which is a little overgrown here, winds down to the apple orchard below, keeping to the right of the trees. Once past the orchard, identify the circular concrete lid of another cavernous water cistern (and take a peek inside). To the right of this is a low wall in a break in the tree line. Hop over this and the path down starts on the left and then swings over to the right.

lunch, Grassy Meadow 2

apple orchard, Grassy Meadow 3

This path takes about 45 minutes to get onto a dirt road on the outskirts of Langada. The dirt road across the valley stops at the church of Panagia Yiatrissa where a celebration is held every September. Once you reach the dirt road, turn left and then almost immediately right to pass the ruined tower. At the T–junction turn right onto what is now a concrete road and follow it all the way into the village. As you enter the village, ignore the right turn by the house with the green door and carry on down. At the next junction with blue doors turn right and after 20m, left down some steps, turning right at the bottom down an alley. Soon you will come to some steps that take you down to the main road. Turn right into the village square, pass the church and follow the green walkers sign along a great (though overgrown) kalderimi all the way to Thalames, passing Agia Sophia en route.

Grassy Meadow 3

heading down to Langada

Churches and Frying Pans

Mezapos-Episcopi-Gardenitsa-Mezapos

Timings

Around 2 hours in total
Mezpos to Episcopi: 40 mins
Episcopi to Gardenitsa: 1hr
Gardenitsa to Mezapos: 15 mins

Nature of walk

I included this relatively short walk as it offers the chance to walk in the heart of 'Niklianiko' and get a real feeling for Mesa Mani. The sea and Tigani (the frying pan peninsula) form a dramatic backdrop to towers and churches. I personally cut back the unattended path to Agios Petros in the spring of 2006 but since then it may have become overgrown a little in which case long trousers are recommended. There is unavoidable asphalt before and after Episcopi which, if you have already done a lot of kalderimi walking, may come as a welcome

relief. If you are after a fuller day's walking it could be extended by including the walk out to Tigani (page 127) instead of turning left up to Episkopi but continuing staight towards Stavri, turning right at the t-junction and on to Tigani. The return leg offers the choice of retracing back to Episcopi or continuing into Stavri to pick up the walk at Agios Giorgios i.e. taking the main road out of Stavri as far as the turning to Agios Petros.

Places of interest

Three important Mani churches- at Vlacherna, Episcopi and Agios Petros near Gardenitsa.

The walk begins in **Mezapos**. As you approach the village by car the walk begins on the other side of it on the road up to **Stravri**. The best place to leave the car therefore is in the centre of the village in the parking area near the main church. There is no convenient place to park once through the

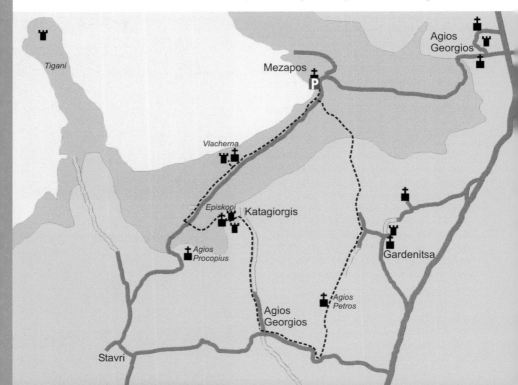

village. Wherever you chose to park, leave the village to the south where the road briefly climbs steeply.

After 20 minutes a track runs off to your right down to the ruins of a tower and the 12th century church of Vlacherna (page 124)- a 5 minute detour.

Continuing on the main road for another 15-20 minutes brings you to the small hamlet of **Fokaloto** on the right. At this point look up to the hill on your left to identify another Byzantine church- head towards it from the main road across an area of flat, clear land. To get to Episkopi (page124), aim to the right of the church to find the easiest route up following the stone walls that run up to the small grave-yard that lies beneath the church.

Having stopped to admire this renowned church, follow the stone path upwards. Keep straight when the path becomes asphalt and at the two towers of **Katagior-gis** turn right. Follow the road to Agios Giorgios and turn left at the main road.

After 15 minutes the road starts to descend. On the third sharp bend, a low concrete building behind large gates on the left is the landmark to turn off left down a walled path. This path takes you all the way to **Gardenitsa**. Several times along the path the wall has collapsed, but don't be tempted to follow the tracks that have been formed by livestock at these points- keep straight.

To stop to look at Agios Petros (page126) en route you'll have to hop over the wall as you pass it on your left. Hop back over the wall and continue along the path. Keep straight where the path becomes a wider track and ignore the right turn into the heart of Gardenitsa. The road bends left and at the T-junction turn right. A path develops where the asphalt finishes.

Keep straight on this path, past two hous-es on your right, all the way down to the main Mezapos-Stavri road. Turn right to collect your car in Mezapos.

Episcopi

Tigani as a permanent backdrop

Agios Petros

Mezapos in view

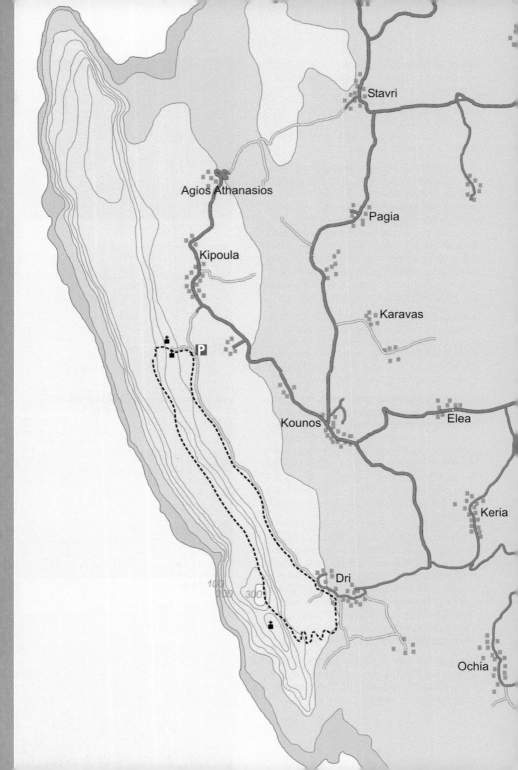

Big, Bad Cavo Grosso

Timings
Around **2 3/4 hours** in total
Up on Cavo Grosso: 2 hrs
Dri back to the car: 45 mins

Nature of walk

This walk comes with a health warning. It is not easy to keep to the path as the scrub is thick and prickly. Trousers will get ripped, blood will be drawn and tempers will fray. So why include it in the book? Partly to put out a warning as it is shown on the Anavasi walking map and partly as it may appeal to those who enjoy finding a route through such a terrain. The views help soften the experience, especially at the southern end of the escarpment.

Thick, long trousers and good boots essential.

Places of interest

There are ruined buildings and walls scattered all over Cavo Grosso. As you walk south, it is believed that the castle 'Kastro tis Oraias' was located on the conical hill at the far end.

The walk begins along the dirt road south of Kipoula. Park where you come to two clearly visible churches tucked into the side of the escarpment. The path up zig-zags up past them and once at the top, turn left and do your best to follow the path that is way-marked in places. The path generally cuts a route close to the cliff edge. If you do lose it, you can not get lost as the hill is visible ahead. About half way you will pass a ruined church. The path back down starts after you have walked over the second, smaller hump- a clearly defined path takes you down as you enjoy great views to the south, all the way to the light house at Tainaron.

Once on the dirt road, head north, taking the left fork at Dri. At the tarmac, turn left and up - this road will take you back to your car.

location of 'Kastro tis Orias'?

ruins on Cavo Grosso

ruined church

view from southern end of Grosso

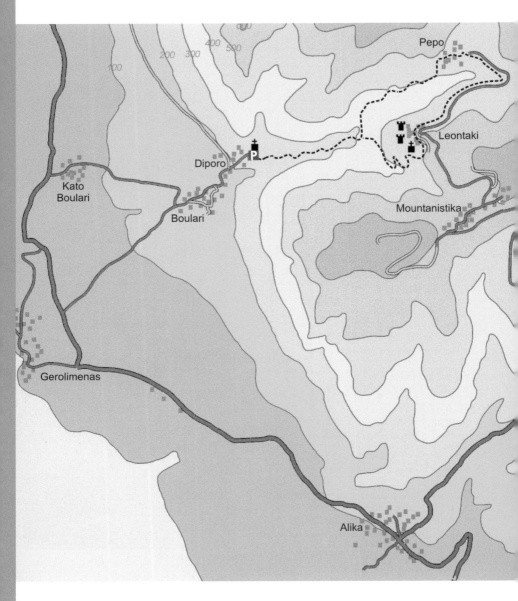

A Population of 3

Boulari (Diporo) – Pepo – Leontaki – Boulari

Timings
Around **2 1/2 hours** in total
Boulari to Pepo: 1 hr
Pepo to Leontaki: 30 mins
Leontaki to Boulari: 1 hr

Nature of walk

A real step back in time as the walk follows the old path that at one time linked the hill villages of **Pepo** and **Leontaki** to Boulari and the coast at Gerolimenas. The path is rocky but clear of vegetation and follows the course of the dry riverbed below, climbing steadily from 200m to 500m. The views back down get increasingly more dramatic. Both Pepo and Leontaki are seriously depopulated (the latter now has 3 full time residents) and the imagination kicks into overdrive getting a feel for what life must have been like here in days gone by. You can't help but marvel at the effort that went into creating such an extensive amount of terracing. The beginning of the walk, with the landmark 'twin towers' of Leontaki crowning the hill in front of you, may suggest that it is hard going. This is not really the case as the path *gradually* skirts around the hill, coming up the other side. The descent is initially much steeper and more direct.

towards Pepo

towards Pepo

Long trousers are not required, water is.

If you have a co-driver not interested in walking then you could meet in the dramatically set Mountanistika, a little further on along the concrete road from Leontaki (see page 116)

Places of interest

See page 112 for Boulari. The church of Agios Stratigos- Dimitris Kolokouris holds the key and so needs to be contacted in advance to arrange a viewing (phone 27330 52953).

concrete road up to Leontaki

Leontaki

The walk begins at the top end of Upper Boulari often referred to as Diporo.

Leave your car where the road finishes and continue uphill along a wide track for 20m and identify red way marks on your right (the detour to Agios Stratigos is a couple of minutes further up the track). The path immediately drops into

the streambed and continues on the other side where it heads steadily up the south bank of the valley.

After 30 mins you'll pass an open cistern at a point where another gully joins the riverbed from the right (this is where you will rejoin the path on the return leg). The path for now dips into this gully but continues following the original riverbed, initially zigzagging to create a short cut.

Another 20 mins further on and the path crosses the riverbed (which may be a little overgrown) and continues on the other side. Keep following the blue way marks and don't be tempted to head off on another path heading up the hillside.

As the buildings of Pepo slowly come into view, a stone wall runs across the path in a partially collapsed state. Hop over it, turn left and follow the way marks up to a house with a balcony and then right to take you down through the village. You will emerge in a wide clear space with a church. The concrete track up to Leontaki begins here and runs behind the church. It's a gentle 30 mins up to Leontaki.

If you take the first entrance into the village, turn left down an alley (passing one of the few houses still inhabited) to bring you into an open area. Equally, the second entrance brings you directly to this point. From here you will see the large church that is the next landmark though you may want to have a brief exploration of the village.

Follow the track past the church and where it becomes concrete take the walled path dropping away to your right. You will soon pass another smaller church as the path begins to zig zag down into the gully below.

After 20 mins you'll emerge on the path that brought you up. Turn left to get back to the car.

heading up from Boulari

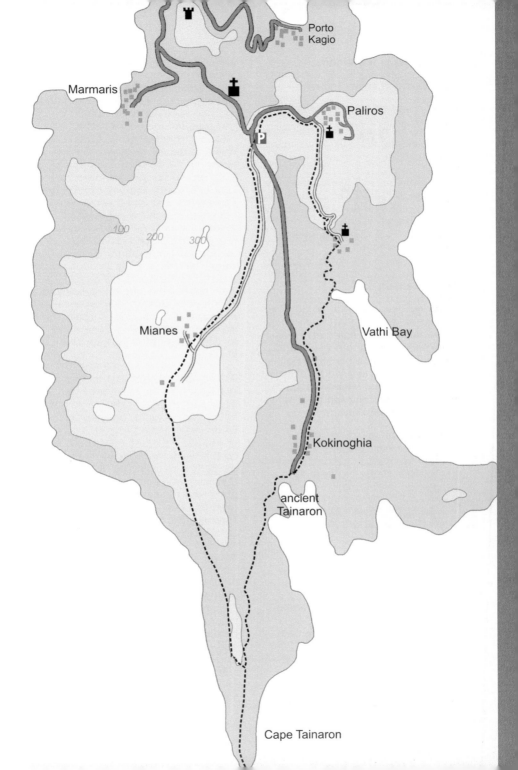

Porto
Kagio

Marmaris

Paliros

P

100 200 300

Mianes

Vathi Bay

Kokinoghia

ancient
Tainaron

Cape Tainaron

To the End of the World

Mianes -Lighthouse -Tainaron – Paliros

Timings
Just under **4 hours** in total (see page 140 to extend the walk by an hour)
The car to the lighthouse: I hr 45 mins
The lighthouse to Tainaron: 50 mins
Tainaron to Paliros: 1hr 15mins (this could be cut short by simply following the asphalt road from Tainaron back to the car, therefore totally bypassing Paliros).

Nature of Walk

Stunning views over the Ionian and Aegean seas to the west and east respectively as the lighthouse is approached A wide dirt road up to Mianes. Off-piste across spine of hills, picking up well-worn dirt path to lighthouse and back to Tainaron. Rocky path and then dirt track to Paliros. Tarmac to finish.

Chance for a cooling dip and a drink/something to eat at Tainaron, another swim stop later at the pebbly beach at Vathy. No need for long trousers.

Not advisable to walk from Mianes when there is a strong wind.

Places of Interest

The ancient site of Tainaron (page 142).

Once you have passed the **Marmaris** junction and turned right to the Death Oracle at Tainaron, the best place to leave your car is just after the turning up to **Mianes** where there is a clear area on your left. Retrace your steps and start heading up to Mianes.

After 20–25 minutes you will approach the tiny hamlet. When you arrive in Mianes, turn left at the major junction of paths between the walls and houses, wiggle round to the right and then once in the meadow, continue at the same level round to the left of the windowless house on the horizon. Once at the walls on the skyline look down to your left (south) and you can see the spine stretching away over various humps and even the lighthouse is visible. Having orientated yourself in this way the direction is obvious – there is no clear path to follow so simply pick out a route through the low shrubs and rocks. As a rule I keep to the right side of the spine as a path does develop later on so keep an eye open for it. Once spotted, make use of it as by this stage you may be tiring of finding your own way.

As you approach the last rocky crag switch over to the left side of the ridge and the main Tainaron / lighthouse path is visible beneath you. Drop down to join this path whenever you like – the last opportunity to do this will become clear! When on the path, turn right and follow it all the way to the lighthouse. This is a great spot to take a rest, gaze out towards Crete and do a little ship spotting. The lighthouse is now fully automated.

Return all the way to **Tainaron** on the same dirt path where you may pass other lighthouse-seekers coming the other way. As you approach **Tainaron**, now the modern day hamlet of **Kokkinogia**, you will soon become aware of an older history. The wave mosaic just lying exposed to the elements is the most obvious indicator though, by stopping to look a little closer, foundations hewn into the rocks are all around you as well as a number of cisterns. Having passed the last of three pebbly coves, the path heads up to the church of **Agii Asomati** and the welcome site of a taverna just above.

Continue on the main road past the taverna through the village until you pass the last house on the right (a white-washed bungalow with brown shutters). Keep going for another 200m until you come to a plot of land totally enclosed by a dry stone wall, again on your right. At the furthest end of this walled field head right off the road, over some boulders and start heading down to the cove now in view (to check you have turned off at the right place look behind you at one of the boulders lying by the road– one should have a blue arrow painted on). As you descend the terracing keep to the right of the gully where a rocky path of sorts will take you to the isolated beach

The path continues on the far end of the beach and winds upwards, once you have passed some umbrella pines offering some welcome shade. The path soon becomes walled-in and the first houses you pass make up tiny **Koureli**. At the telegraph pole, turn left and follow the path, keeping straight when it becomes a wider track. Soon the main part of the fortified village of **Paliros** appears on your right. After the track passes to the left of a church it becomes asphalt. Keep straight, ignore the sharp right turn and soon you will come once again to the 'Death Oracle' junction. Turn left and rejoin your car.

on the ridge above Tainaron

lighthouse in sight

to the end of the world....

back to Tainaron

GUIDED WALKS IN THE MANI

If you would prefer to explore the wilds of the Mani without having to think of following directions or consulting a map, Anna Butcher guides walks throughout the Mani year-round.

There are opportunities for day walks, weekends or even trips of two weeks, graded for various levels of fitness. In the longer trips, accommodation is in unusual, unique and characterful guest-houses, and there is the chance to sample unusual Greek cuisine which is often prepared specially, accompanied by some fine wines. Abundant picnic lunches are always a highlight and are usually followed by a siesta!

All trips have been carefully researched to combine spectacular walking, some unusual historical gems and any places of cultural interest en route, with opportunities to learn about the huge variety of flowers and herbs on the peninsula, many of which are endemic. Trips can also be tailored to suit individual interests.

Anna has worked as a freelance mountain guide in Greece for nearly a decade. Fluent in Greek, having studied and worked in Athens before deciding on a more alternative lifestyle, she has dedicated every spare moment to researching walks in places that are off the beaten track and have brought her into contact with people who share her love of nature. She has recently restored an old stone house in the Mani, from where she organises her walks.

For more information, please contact Anna:

In the UK +44 207 733 9980
In Greece +30 27330 52611 or +30 6937 772 996
Email: asimi.ab@virgin.net

Or for a package from the UK:
www.sunvil.co.uk/sunvil/home/destinations/Greece/Walking_in_Greece.asp

towards Areopolis

on Tigani

a 5-star picnic...

...followed by a siesta

The Kastro is a family run hotel, located near the old part of the village. Ritsa Beach is a 10 minute walk and Kardamyli High St is only 2 minutes away for bars and tavernas. There are 2 supermarkets directly opposite the hotel.

The hotel has 15 rooms, divided between the 'tower' and the 'castle'. There are 10 studios (sleeping 2–3 people) and 5 apartments (2 sleeping 3 people, 3 sleeping 4 people). The ground floor apartment has been altered to accommodate wheelchair-users. All of the rooms are furnished in a traditional style and each have a kitchenette, en suite, TV, AC, telephone, and balcony.

Breakfast is available if required in the communal dining room and there is a shady area at the front of the hotel to enjoy an evening drink before dinner.

Limited car parking is available.

The family also run a taverna with the same name just outside Kardamyli, past the school. A large, airy veranda looks out over Ritsa Bay and they use their own meat, vegetables and organic olive oil in the kitchen. They have vegetarian dishes every day.

Tel: (+30) 27210 73226
Fax: (+30) 27210 73685
Taverna: 27210 73951
Email: info@kastro-mani.gr
www.kastro-mani.gr

Kastro Bedroom

Shady terrace

Views to the sea

Kitchinette

Vardia Hotel
Kardamyli

The **'Vardia' Hotel** (*lit. "change of guard"*) is so named because the hotel is located right next to the famous old guard tower on the high hill just behind Kardamyli. Here, 400 years ago, Kardamyliot soldiers used to stand watch over the old village and, from this unique vantage point, they would protect the inhabitants against invasion from pirates and renegades. Nowadays, the view is more important than defence. Below everything is visible – the old village, the new village, the bay, southern Mani, and right across the Messinian Gulf to the western peninsula of the Peloponnese.

Front terrace

Studio

Vardia came to life in 1995. The Dimitreas family wanted to build a hotel whose facade would blend harmoniously with the natural beauty of the surrounding countryside, and so they adopted traditional designs for the architecture and used local stone (extracted during the excavation process) to create a structure which is natural and extremely pleasing to the eye. Vardia is comprised of **18** independent hotel-style apartments and studios, giving an overall appearance of a very large villa but feeling like a house. There is one 2-bed apartment (sleeps 4-5) and six 1-bed apartments (sleeps 2-4), all with en suite, fully equipped kitchen, living area, private balcony with uninterrupted views, air conditioning, TV and telephone. The eleven studios (ideal for couples and singles) have the same amenities in one spacious area.

All rooms are serviced on a daily basis, with change of sheets and towels every other day. The hotel has a large forecourt with ample parking space, a reception area, a cosy dining room and a very lush and spacious garden with paved terraces where you can relax in peace and enjoy the surrounding views. Breakfast is set out each morning in our dining room, and we serve hot coffee and tea, with fresh eggs from our own chickens, bread, honey and yoghurt.

The hotel is a favoured resort for summer holiday-makers, but it is steadfastly also becoming an all-year-round destination for visitors who return time and time again from all over the world to enjoy the beauty and peace of the other seasons in the Mani.

The view!

Sitting room

Fotini Dimitreas
Tel +30 27210 73777   Fax +30 27210 73156
info@vardia-hotel.gr www.vardia-hotel.gr
Off season: Tel +30 27210 78155 / 73513

Less than 1km south of Kardamyli, the visitor comes to Kalamitsi, a place that epitomizes the notion of natural beauty. The hotel here clearly pays tribute to the architectural traditions of the Mani. Made of local stone with an impressive ceramic tiled roof, the hotel is set in an olive grove within a stone's throw of the sea.

There is a wide choice of accommodation. There are 35 rooms, 15 of which are individual bungalows (3 simple suites and 1 executive suite). All the rooms have modern amenities – satellite TV, AC, telephone with Internet connection and mini bar. The spacious verandas overlooking the sea will be a highlight of your stay. There is ample car parking in the grounds and in walking through the fragrant gardens, you may discover a quiet spot to read a book. The hotel has a residents' bar with spectacular views of the sea and sunset and a restaurant situated on an outside terrace where the mother of the family, Kyria Theano, welcomes you with a hearty breakfast of local fresh products and scrumptious homemade delicacies as well as providing an evening meal.

Kalamitsi Hotel Bungalows
PONIREA S.A.
24022 Kardamyli
Messinia, Greece
Tel: (+30) 27210 71331–3
Fax: (+30) 27210 73135
info@kalamitsi–hotel.gr
www.kalamitsi–hotel.gr

Sea view

Private beach

View over Kalamitsi

Lounge

Esperides Hotel
Kardamyli

This full service apartment hotel, with its enchanting garden, offers modern amenities in a traditional setting. Only steps away from the village centre yet an oasis of tranquillity, Esperides was designed to provide its guests with a friendly, casual atmosphere enhanced by professional and discreet service. The spacious, well-appointed studios (for 1-2 guests) and one-bedroom suites (for 2-3 guests or families) feature fully-equipped kitchenettes, en-suite bathrooms, airconditioning/heating, music, satellite TV and balconies or verandas with views of the exquisite enclosed garden or the surrounding countryside. There is also, ample parking, a bar and an optional continental breakfast may be enjoyed in the garden.

Open April-October

Esperides Hotel
24022 Kardamyli
Messinia, Greece

Tel: (+30) 27210 73173-74
Fax: (+30) 27210 73176
info@hotelesperides.gr
www.hotelesperides.gr

The garden

One-bedroom suite

Twin beds

Setting

Lithino Apartments
Stoupa

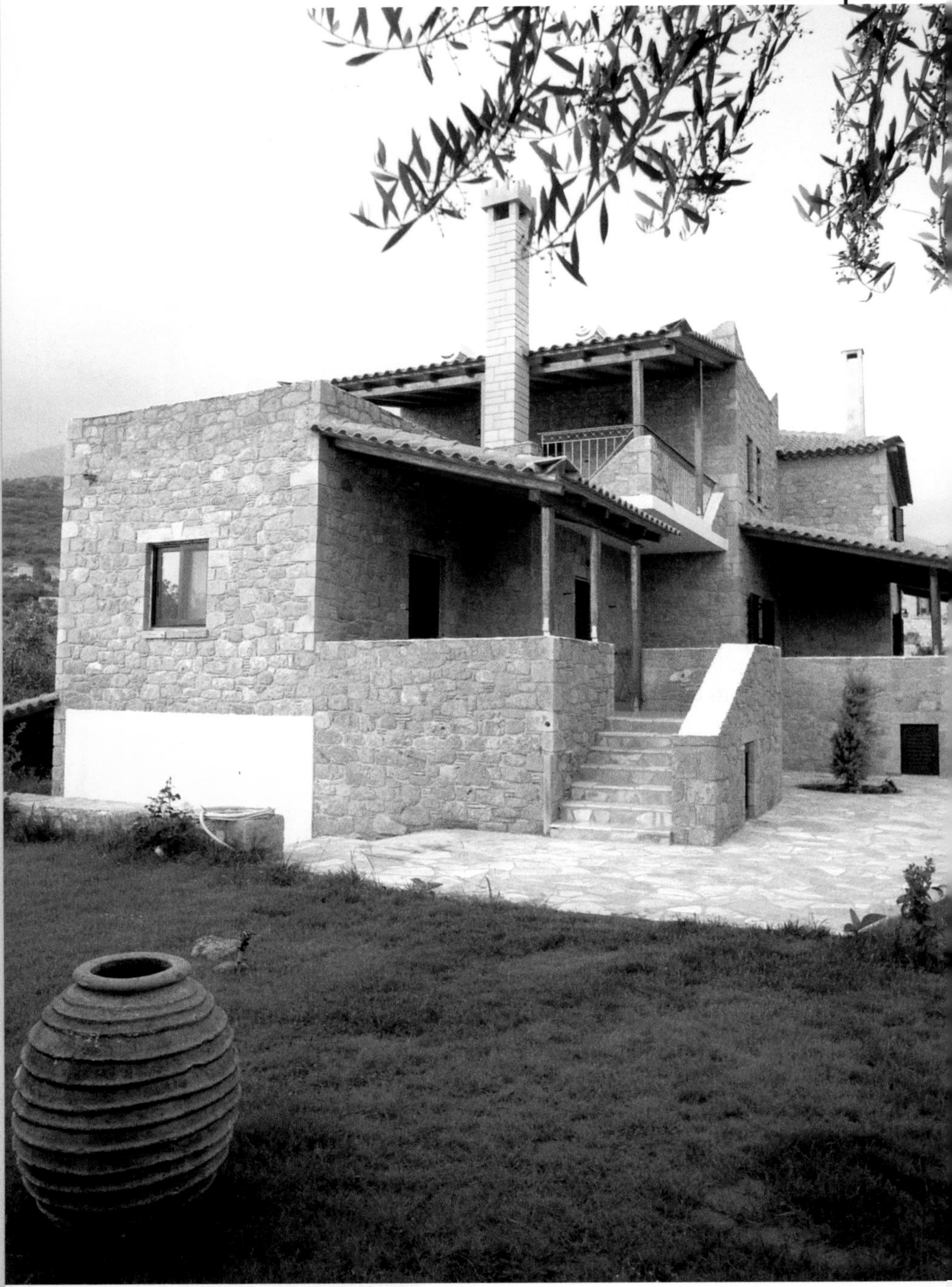

The Lithino Apartments are set back from the main road in Stoupa with enough outside space for ample parking and a lawn with tables, chairs and barbeque. Stoupa beach and its many tavernas are just a 5-minute walk away and the village bakery is right across the road. There are 5 self-catering apartments in total, all of which are air-conditioned with satellite TV and Internet connection.

Bedroom

The apartments

1. An open-plan studio with double bed, with the option of sleeping 2 children on the sofa bed.
2. A two-floored apartment with two bathrooms, 1 bedroom and again the option of sleeping 2 on a sofa bed.
3. A two-floored apartment with two double bedrooms and two bathrooms with sofa bed in the sitting room.
4. A ground floor apartment with two bedrooms and sofa bed in the sitting room.
5. A ground floor apartment with one bedroom and sofa bed in the sitting room.

All the apartments have use of a utilities room with washing machine and ironing board. Apartments 1,2 and 3 have upper balconies and open fireplaces making them also suitable for out of season renting.

Open plan sitting room/kitchen

View over Stoupa

Lithino Apartments
Stoupa, Messinia 24024
Tel: +30 27210 77801
Mob: +30 6932063083
+30 6979831142
Email: lithino@messinia.net.gr
www.lithinovillas.gr

Mani – Sonnenlink
Pyrgos/Lefktrou

MANI-SONNENLINK offers the perfect way to get away from it all and relax in a luxurious environment. Located 2km above Stoupa, between the villages of Neohori and Pyrgos, on a large plot of land with olive and other fruit trees, the SONNENHOUSE has unbeatable views down to the coast. There are three apartments available to rent throughout the year, each of which have been finished to the highest standards with vibrant colours – yellows, oranges, greens and blues give the brightness of Feng Shui culture. Externally, the house adheres to traditional Mani architecture with the local stone being complimented by terracotta terracing. Two of the apartments sleep two, while the upper accommodates up to five. Each has a fully equipped modern kitchen, large sitting room with Internet connection, bathroom and verandas looking both to the sea and back to the mountains. The larger, upper apartment also has a covered balcony, ideal for out of season occupation.

SEMINARS

The house was designed to also provide the perfect venue for hosting seminars and groups. As well as a large internal space, outside there is a Classical-Greek theatre with 150 seats, suitable for practising group work – family reconstruction, yoga, sadhanas and other therapies. There is enough equipment and meditation cushions for 60 people. Full or half board can be provided along with three bathrooms, four toilets and three kitchens. 25 people can be accommodated on site (three double rooms, mattresses and tents) and help can be given in booking other rooms on the coast.

Burgi Blauel
Pyrgos/Lefktrou, 24024, Greece
(+30) 27210 78077
mobile (+30) 6937331333
burgi@mani-sonnenlink.com
www.mani-sonnenlink.com

Stunning view to the coast

Vibrant colours–oranges,

yellows and greens

balcony with sea-view

The Spirit of Life Holistic Centre,

Near the picturesque fishing village of Agios Nikolaos is The Spirit of Life Centre. The Centre offers regular weekly yoga, qi gong and tai chi classes. It also offers week-long courses and workshops in yoga, holistic health, personal development, tai chi and dream healing. You can also take time out from the fast lane of modern life to recharge your batteries on one of their detox or healing retreats. Guest teachers from around the world also run their workshops at the Spirit of Life.

The Centre's beautiful yoga and meditation room has inspirational 360° sea and mountain views. You will also find a well-stocked library of books on holistic health and personal development.

The centre offers a variety of therapies to its guests such as shiatsu, Thai yoga massage, reiki, Bach flower, holistic life coaching and energy healing.

The food at the centre is justifiably praised by its visitors being both delicious and healthy. They use fresh vegetables and fruit from local organic growers and wild herbs from the region. The centre's chef has over 25 years experience in organic / vegetarian / holistic cooking. The Spirit of Life Centre was voted in the top 100 spa retreats in the world, by the magazine Harpers and Queen.

The Spirit of Life
www.thespiritoflife.co.uk
info@thespiritoflife.co.uk
+30 27210 78240

Accommodation

Lunch on the terrace

A morning off, visiting the local sites

Yoga

"Elixirion" Guesthouse is situated in the tiny but historically strategic hamlet of Karavostasi, beneath the ancient village of Oitylo. From here it is just a stone's throw to the Kelefa Castle and the seventeenth century monastery of Dekoulou.
The rooms have each been lovingly decorated with an individual style, and are equipped with air-conditioning, satellite TV, fridge, telephone, hi-fi system and 24 hour room service. All rooms have balconies with spectacular views across the bay to the mountain of Kouskouni.

The breakfast is a real treat: homemade specialities fresh from the oven. The welcome here is warm and genuine: the whole experience intended to be a spiritual retreat.

From June to October boat trips are available (not just to hotel guests) along the coast to remote beaches and caves inaccessible by foot. These trips reveal the rich history of piracy and conflict in the Mani and offer opportunities to swim in crystal clear waters, snorkel in the huge caves, and perhaps glimpse a turtle!

For further exploration of this wild landscape, there are opportunities to go on organized hikes with an experienced guide, go fishing, or even diving.

Hotel facade

Bedroom

View over Bay of Oitylo

Boat trip

Elixirion
Karavostasi Oitylou
Mani
Tel: 27330 59275
Mobile: 6932 233 310/1
www.mani-elixirion.gr
email: info@mani-elixirion.gr

The Kastro Maini is a traditionally built stone hotel on the outskirts of historic Areopolis. The beach at Oitylo is only 3km away and the main square of Areopolis just a few minutes on foot.

The hotel has 26 spacious rooms and 3 suites. The internal decoration and furnishings are of a very high standard and each room has AC, TV and telephone.

The back of the hotel is the perfect peaceful place for a swimming pool and bar – great views across the olives and utterly peaceful. There is also a shallow pool for children.

The hotel runs its own restaurant for breakfast and in the evening serves an imaginative cuisine. The dining room also has a large sitting area to enjoy a drink before dinner and a large fireplace sets a welcoming atmosphere for guests staying out of season as the hotel is open all year.

Tel: (+30) 27330 51302 – 51238
Fax: (+30) 27330 29514
www.kastromaini.gr

Lounge

Bedroom

Hotel facade

Pool area

Kapetanakos Tower is situated in Areopolis, capital of the Mani, 330km south east of Athens. Built in 1865, it is a perfect example of the unique stone architecture of the Mani peninsula. It has recently been restored with meticulous attention to detail, maintaining its original defensive character while instilling a little more comfort and style to the interior.

It now functions as a guest house with 7 bedrooms: 2 double rooms, 3 triple rooms and 2 five-bed rooms with an open attic area. All rooms have en suite bathrooms, air-conditioning, TV and fridge, and combine good taste with functionality.

The communal areas are designed to give a feeling of being in a "home", so breakfast is served at one big table inside the traditional vaulted dining room. The beautiful garden outside is a haven of tranquillity, the ideal place to sit and read or chat with friends.

Kapetanakos Tower
Areopolis
Mani
Tel: +30 27330 51233
Fax: +30 27330 51401

Sitting area

Shady garden

Upper terrace

Sea view

Toxotis traditional guesthouse and apartments are located in Triandafillia Pyrgou Dirou amid a huge expanse of lush olive groves, just 7km from the famous caves of Pirgos Dirou, (supposedly one of the mythical entrances to the underworld) and 7km from Areopolis (capital of the Mani). The stone building is 200 years old and has been faithfully restored in traditional style, maintaining the original vaulted ceilings, tiled roofs, cisterns and paved floors. Each apartment is unique and atmospheric, but all have kitchenette, air-conditioning, television and veranda with a sea view. Some have an open fire. There is also lovely garden and traditional cafe bar, serving home made breakfast and cakes, children's play area and ample parking. Just 100m away is a mini market, taverna and cafeteria for breakfast, lunch or dinner. This area is ideal for many outdoor activities, especially trekking, cycling and horse-riding (there is a stables just 2km from the guesthouse). In the garden, as well as tranquillity there are facilities for archery and ping pong.

From Toxotis you have easy access to not only the caves, but many fascinating Byzantine chapels, the stunning mountain of Sagias and tranquil bays for swimming in the crystal clear water of the Mani.

Open all year round. Pets most welcome!

Toxotis Traditional Guesthouse & Apartments
Triandafillia
Pirgou Dirou
Lakonia
Mani
Tel: +30 27330 51500
Mobile: 6947 522632 & 6972 081900
Email: kate.ara@vrilissia.gr

View from terrace

Apartment with fireplace

Vaulted bedroom

Mountain bikes available

Faros (Lighthouse) **Apartments** are situated in Gerolimenas, just a few miles from the southern tip of Cape Tainaron, where the Ionian meets the Aegean sea, and on the same latitude as Southern Sicily and Gibraltar. These charming stone apartments give directly onto the sea and the balconies have stunning views out over the water to the cliffs on the other side of the bay. The apartments are tastefully decorated, combining the local stone with stylish furniture and accessories. The area is quiet, and ideal for families as the beach nearby is suitable for children. Each room has air-conditioning, fridge and satellite TV.
Open all year.
Close to the Faros apartments is the traditional Epilekton Cafe, for long lazy breakfasts, an ice-cream, or a sundowner overlooking the pretty bay of Gerolimenas with its fishing boats and crystal clear water.
There is also the Epilekton Restaurant, the heart of the village, which serves unusual and excellent food (local specialities and fresh fish) accompanied by some high quality wines. In winter there is an open fire and snug atmosphere, while during summer the terrace right on the sea provides a cool respite from the heat. Friendly, impeccable service and a warm welcome ensure an unforgettable stay in Gerolimenas.

Faros Apartments
Gerolimenas
Mani
Tel/fax: +30 27330 54271,
54269 or 54227
Mobile: 6944 355 297
www.gerolimenas.net
email: gerolimenas@gerolimenas.net

Bedrrom

Reception

Epilekton taverna

Epilekton cafe

The Kyrimai Hotel in Gerolimenas has a long history. 130 years ago two traders, Michalis Katsimatis from Syros and Theodore Kyrimis from the Mani, began to develop the commercial potential of the Mani through the tiny port of Gerolimenas. The resulting warehousing has been converted into a hotel that offers guests the chance to journey into the past whilst enjoying the comfort of the present. The reception has exhibits that chart the development of trade in Greece in the 19th and 20th centuries.

There are a choice of en-suite rooms, ranging from tower rooms, charming attic rooms and luxury suites. The in-room facilities include: mini bar, TV, AC, movie channels, telephone, safe deposit box, hairdryer,
room service and in the suites only, Jacuzzi and fireplace.

Other facilities include a large pool right by the sea, a games area with a billiard table and internet connection and a restaurant. Supervision of the latter was undertaken by award winning Greek chef Yiannis Baksevanis in December 2005, ensuring the promise of many culinary delights to diners in the suitably atmospheric dining room.

Local walks, horse riding and boat trips can be arranged by the hotel.

The Kyrimai Hotel
Gerolimenas
Tel: +30 27330 54288/59327
Fax: +30 27330 59338
Email: info@kyrimai.gr
www.kyrimai.gr

Akrotiri Rooms/Restaurant
Porto Kagio

Porto Kayio, 1688

Plan of Porto Kayio castle, 1686

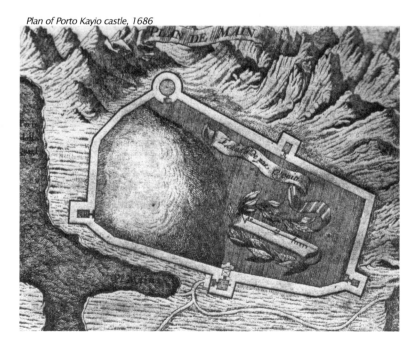

Here beneath the barren mountains at the extreme tip of the wild Mani peninsula, nestles the village of Porto Kagio, or "Bay of Quails", with its five permanent inhabitants. It is the most beautiful natural harbour, calm as a lake in contrast with the windswept seas beyond Cape Tainaron. Life slows down here and immediately the warm welcome and tranquil atmosphere of this small haven charms each and every visitor.

Simple and unpretentious, with rooms situated right on the beach, Akrotiri is the ideal place to stay for a genuine retreat. Porto Kagio is the perfect base from which to explore the many hidden coves and discover the ancient treasures scattered over the hillsides which reveal the fascinating history of this remote place. There is also the opportunity to take a private boat trip around Cape Tainaron and to visit caves and small alternative beaches accessible only by sea. The bay itself is a wonderful place for safe wind-surfing. Such a romantic setting is hard to find and draws people back year after year.

Here you will savour exceptional cuisine: accompanied by good wines or ouzo, the fish and seafood are as fresh as it gets, and the warmth and hospitality of the place is unmatched. There are 9 rooms, all with air-conditioning, fridge, phone and satellite TV. Open all summer and during the winter at weekends.

Bedroom

The"Bay of Quails"

Lunch at the Akrotiri

Vathi Bay by boat

Akrotiri Rooms/Restaurant
Porto Kagio
Mani
Tel: +30 27330 52013 & 53002
Fax: +30 27330 52010
Mobile: 6946 320 808
www.porto-kagio.com
email: akrotiri@porto-kagio.com

Kalamata

50 minutes

Kardamyli

10 minutes

Stoupa

5 minutes

Agios Nikolaos

110 minutes

Gythio

50 minutes

40 minutes

Areopolis

70 minutes

DRIVING TIMES
(approximate)

40 minutes

Alika

20 minutes

Tainaron

Index

Place names

Bibliography

Guide to Greece – Pausanias. Translation and commentary by Peter Levi. Penguin Classics. ISBN 0-14-044226-X

A Grand Tour – Letters and Journeys 1794-96 by JSB Morritt. 1985. Century Publishing. ISBN 0-7126-0993-8.

Travels in the Morea by William Martin Leake. 1830. The 4 volumes are now available from Elibron Classics. (www.elibron.com)

Reminiscences of Athens and the Morea by the Earl of Carnarvon. 1839. Out of print.

Mani – Travels in the Southern Peloponnese by Patrick Leigh Fermor. 1958. Penguin Books. ISBN 0-14-011511-0

The Flight of Ikaros by Kevin Andrews. 1959. The Riversiede Press, Cambridge. Out of print.

Mani – History and Monuments by Dora Eliopoulou Rogan. Lycabettus Press. 1973. Now out of print but gives a useful summary of churches, towers and history.

Deep into Mani by Peter Greenhalgh and Edward Eliopoulos. 1985. Faber and Faber. ISBN 0-571-13524-2. Now out of print.

The Dent Dictionary of Symbols in Christian Art by Jennifer Speake. 1994. JM Dent Ltd. ISBN 0-460-86138-7. Very helpfull in understanding certain frescoes.

Mani – Greek Traditional Architecture by Yannis Saitas. 1990. Meslissa Publishing. A detailed study of towers and buildings. In Greek, English and German.

Byzantine Frescoes in the Mesa Mani by Nikolas Drandakis. The Library of the Archaeological Society of Athens. 1995. ISBN 960-7036-40-9. Drandakis is the acknowledged authority on Byzantine churches in the Mani. He has published numerous other works and articles, all in Greek only.